The Coming End of the Age

Other Books by the Author

An Overview of the Endtime

Preparing For the Lord's Return

Greapa

The Coming of the King in Matthew 24 and 25

The Goal and Peak of Our Christian Experience
Insights into Revelation, Book 1

The Beast, His Image, and His Mark
Insights into Revelation, Book 2

Firstfruits and Harvest
Insights into Revelation, Book 3

A Place Prepared
Insights into Revelation, Book 4

Delusion and God's Salvation

A Faithful God

Booklets by the Author

The Heart of God

The Heart of God II

The Heart of God III

The Heart of God IV

The Heart of God V

Redemption and Salvation

Signs of the End

The Rapture

Urgency or Complacency

A New Creation

The Spirit

The Spirit Was Not Yet

The Lark Ascending

Visit **aplaceinthewilderness.com** for more about these books (including their introduction, table of contents, and ordering information) and booklets.

The Coming End of the Age

A Detailed Chronology of the Endtime

Paul Cozza

A Place in the Wilderness

Acknowledgments

Praise the wonderful Lord Jesus for all His dear servants who have gone before and extracted so many rich truths from the Bible concerning His second coming. Without the labors of G. H. Pember, Robert Govett, Watchman Nee, Witness Lee, and others, I could not have written this book. I am particularly thankful for Witness Lee through whose ministry I received so much help. I am also grateful to all who have helped in the preparation of this book. The Lord bless them with every child of God at His return in glory.

A Word to the Nonbeliever

It may be that you do not know the Lord Jesus, that you have never met or experienced God, and yet somehow this book has found its way into your hands. It may also be that while you have been reading this book a desire to know God has arisen in your heart. You should know that experiencing God, that being born of God, is not a difficult thing. Simply find a place away from distractions—for example, a bedroom with shut door, or a quiet spot in the forest away from people. When there, kneel and pray. Speak aloud to God. Reach out to Him. If you do not have words, then pray something like this: "Lord Jesus. Lord Jesus. You know my condition. I am a sinful person. I have committed many sins and errors. I have many problems within me. But, I believe in You. I believe that You are God become a man. I believe You died for me. I believe You rose from the dead and live now. Forgive my sins. Lord, I open my heart to receive You. Come in to me and fill me." God hears and answers the genuine prayer of a seeking heart.

Table of Contents

Note to the reader
Explanations and further details about portions of the text appear as footnotes at page bottoms. Verse references appear in the numbered **References**
list at the end of each chapter.

Preface

Most of what is in this book was written during the mid-1990s. At that point I did not feel it was the time to publish this work. It has been set aside, awaiting a time when it should be made available to God's people. Recently, I have felt some urgency from the Lord to revisit this book. The Lord's second coming draws ever closer, as evinced by current world events: the increase in the persecution of Christians, particularly by the homosexual movement and other far left movements, as well as by Islamists; the resurgence of an aggressive Russia; the increase in both population and military might in the Far East—in China and India; the increase in Islamist terrorism, which is drawing the focus of the entire earth to the Middle East; and, especially, the continuing battle between Israel and the Palestinians, centered around Jerusalem and specifically the Temple Mount, where the Jewish temple will be rebuilt. I believe at this time the Lord would release this book to His children, that they might gain a clearer understanding of the coming time, and more importantly, their responsibility before the Lord at His coming. May our God and Father bless the readers of this book with the same revelation, urgency, encouragement, hope, and love for the dear and precious Lord Jesus with which He has blessed me in the writing of it.

Amen. Come quickly, Lord Jesus!

The Author

Introduction

When will the Lord Jesus return to earth? There are those who believe that at some preordained time the Lord will simply come back to the earth. Others believe that as soon as a certain, preordained number of unbelievers are saved, then the Lord will return. But what is the Lord's view concerning His return to earth, as expressed in the Bible?

In the Gospel of Matthew the Lord Jesus uses a particular phrase to denote the time of His second coming. That is "the consummation of the age."[1] This is translated in some versions of the Bible as "the end of the world" or "the end of the age," referring to that time period during which the Lord brings all things together to accomplish His particular goal. What is the consummation of the age? In Matthew 13 the Lord tells us clearly, "the *harvest* is the consummation of the age."[2] It is not that there is some preset time for the Lord Jesus to return to the earth and end this present age. Rather, this age will close when the harvest is ripe, when the believers are mature in the spiritual, divine life. According to the Lord's word, everything concerning His second coming hinges upon the ripening of God's crop. Without a ripened harvest, the Lord could never return to earth. Without a ripened harvest, the present age could never close and the coming kingdom age could never be ushered in. It is not until the fruit is ready that the time of harvest comes.[3]

The Two Comings of Christ

And the Word became flesh, and dwelt among us (and we beheld his glory, glory as of the only begotten from the Father), full of grace and truth. (John 1:14)

And another angel came out from the temple, crying with a great voice to him that sat on the cloud, Send forth thy sickle, and reap: for the hour to reap is come; for the harvest of the earth is ripe. And he that sat on the cloud cast his sickle upon the earth; and the earth was reaped. (Revelation 14:15-16)

In order for Christ to accomplish God's eternal purpose and ultimately bring forth the New Jerusalem, it is necessary for Him to come to the earth twice. His first advent was through His incarnation to be a man. During that time, He sowed Himself as the word into man.[4] He Himself was the seed He planted in all those who believed in Him. At His second advent, He will come to reap that which He sowed in His first advent.[5] When the Lord Jesus returns to the earth, He will be the Harvester, gathering all of God's "grain" to Himself.

More than two thousand years have passed between these two comings of Christ. This has been a long period for the growth of all the believers. During this time, they were to have grown in Christ, and Christ was to have grown in them.[6] This is the Lord's understanding of the church age, as illustrated by His words in Matthew, "Let them both *grow* until the harvest."[7]

This view of the church age was also shared by the Apostle Paul. In 1 Corinthians he said, "I planted, Apollos watered, but God caused the *growth*."[8] In various other places he tells us that the building is *growing*, that we all will arrive at a full-*grown* man, that we *grow* up into Him in all things, and that the Body *grows* with the *growth* of God.[9]

Peter also realized that the believers must grow in the divine life for the Lord's return, saying "As newborn babes, long for the guileless milk of the word in order that by it you may *grow* unto salvation."[10] James likened the Lord to a husbandman waiting for his crop (i.e, the believers) to ripen.[11] Finally, the Apostle John in his Gospel, his epistles, and the book of Revelation emphasizes the growth of the believers in the divine life. In John 15 he portrays the Lord as the vine and we all as His branches, which grow and bear fruit.[12] In his first epistle, John addresses the believers as little children, young men, and fathers—a classification according to the growth in life.[13] In Revelation he speaks of the believers both as the firstfruits and the harvest, again stressing the importance of the growth in life.[14]

The Growth in Life

But as many as received him, to them gave he the right to become children of God, even to them that believe on his name: who were born, not of blood, nor of the will of the flesh, nor of the will of man, but of God. (John 1:12-13)

My little children, of whom I am again in travail until Christ be formed in you. (Galatians 4:19)

When Christ, who is our life, shall be manifested, then shall ye also with him be manifested in glory. (Colossians 3:4)

To understand the endtime adequately, we must see the matter of the believers' growth in life. Without this realization, we cannot properly apprehend the matters pertaining to the end of the age. What then is the growth in life of the believers?

At the time of our regeneration, the Triune God, embodied in Christ, enters into us, the believers.[15] This is our initial salvation. It is an instantaneous life-change in our innermost being.[16] This causes us, the believers, to be born of God in our human spirit, thus making us genuine children of God in life.[17] Through this marvelous transaction the Triune God—Father, Son, and Spirit—comes to dwell in us.[18]

After entering into the believers to be our life, Christ then lives, moves, grows, and makes His home in our heart.[19] This is what the Bible refers to when it speaks of our sanctification and transformation.[20] To be sanctified is to have Christ spread within our heart, thus making us as holy as God is.[21] To be transformed is to experience an inward change remaking us to be the same as Christ in life and nature.[22] This inward process of change and growth takes place in large part in man's soul and is life-long. It is accomplished by the subjective operation of Christ's life, which is Christ Himself in the believers.[23]

This change is not something outward, although it is accompanied by an outward manifestation of godliness in the daily living of the believers.[24] It is not accomplished by our good behavior, good works, works of power, miracles, or any such thing.[25] It is not brought about by organization, methods, or any means of self-discipline. It results solely from Christ as life, living and growing in our hearts. He accomplishes this change in us as the indwelling Spirit by the application of His death and resurrection.[26] Eventually, through this operation God brings our entire inward being into Christ Himself.[27] It was for such a change that the Apostle Paul struggled and pursued.[28] His desire was to know Christ, and the power of His resurrection, and the fellowship of His sufferings, being conformed to His death.[29] He counted everything as loss that he might gain Christ.[30] Paul did not care for anything, whether good or bad, except Christ alone.

This inward life process consummates when we, the believers, reach maturity. This is to enter into the full, divine sonship as God's children.[31] Though we believers have been born again as children of God, we must mature to become full-grown sons of God. This occurs when Christ has been fully formed in us, and when we, in turn, have been fully conformed to the image of God's Son.[32] This process culminates in the transfiguration of our bodies, which is our glorification.[33] At that time, through the operation of God's life-power within us, our bodies will be instantaneously changed that we might be fully like Christ in every way.[34]

The Requirement of the Divine Life

Let both grow together until the harvest: and in the time of the harvest I will say to the reapers, Gather up first the tares, and bind them in bundles to burn them; but gather the wheat into my barn. (Matthew 13:30)

The Lord's return is altogether dependent upon the believers' growth in the divine life. In Matthew 13, the Lord makes this requirement absolutely clear. For the harvest to be ripe, the crop must *grow* unto maturity. It is this growth in His life that the Lord is desiring and expecting to see.

It is not miracles, works of power, knowledge, or good behavior that accomplish the Lord's desire for our spiritual maturity. Growth in life is not even affected by the Spirit of God as *power* coming upon the believers outwardly, objectively. Rather, growth in life comes solely by the Spirit of life operating within man subjectively. Although in both these cases it is the same Spirit who operates, He does so in an altogether different way.

Consider, for example, the Old Testament picture of Samson. He was a man upon whom the Spirit of God came in power.[35] In human history there may not have been another person who performed such feats of physical prowess. Yet, though the Spirit of God was upon Samson, his life was particularly sinful. He repeatedly indulged himself in lust.[36] By this, we can see that the Spirit of God as *power* is not sufficient to bring forth the holy and divine sons of God. Such a transformation comes about entirely by Christ Himself growing in the believers. Such growth is fostered by the nourishment in God's Word, by watching and praying, by a constant and intimate contact with the Lord Himself, by an unreserved participation in the genuine Christian church experience, and by an ever-deepening, continual experience of Christ.[37]

The Lord desires a *ripened* harvest. How clear God's Word is that we must grow. Yet, how slowly we all have grown. Every one of us must admit and confess how short we are of Christ, how poor we are in the divine life. Instead of cooperating with the Lord to gain Him, we may continually frustrate Him. We may care more for our own things rather than for God's house.[38] We may live for our own self-satisfaction rather than for God's eternal purpose.[39] How many build up their own temporary empires, rather than labor for God's eternal kingdom?[40]

When we view the general situation today in Christianity, what is it that we see? We must be honest and genuine, and look beyond any facade or pretense. Do we see an uplifted living in Christ among the believers, or do we see the love of the world in its many different aspects and the gratification and exaltation of the self?[41] Do we see a living, Christ-filled church brightly shining as a lampstand, or do we see formalities, rituals, and doctrines? Do we see the believers exhibiting the divine oneness for which the Lord prayed in John 17, or do we rather see numerous divisions and sects?[42]

The responsibility for the condition in Christianity today rests to a great degree upon the shoulders of the leaders among the Christians. Today many leaders labor by human endeavor, natural concepts, and the flesh, about which the Apostle Paul sternly warned us all.[43] Few build with gold, silver, and precious stone (which signify the Triune God experienced and gained by the believers).[44] Rather than take the lead to experience Christ in His death and resurrection, and by such an example usher the believers into a more profound experience of Christ, many rule over the saints as overlords, caring for their own following to build up their own kingdoms.[45] There is ambition, pride, envy, and the desire for self-exaltation with the practices of rumor-mongering, surreptitious slander, sectarianism, and domination using manipulation, politics, pressuring tactics, and threats.

How sad, and even pitiful, our condition is. Such a sad condition is due totally to the shortage of the divine life. We have hindered the Lord's second coming by our lack of growth and maturity. We have failed in our responsibility. If we realized this, we would deeply repent to the Lord. Then perhaps we would begin to seek to gain only Christ and nothing else.

Despite all this, the Lord Jesus is still working to ripen His harvest. In Matthew 16 the Lord told Peter and the disciples, "I will build My church."[46] This is not something for the next age. That age will be the kingdom age, not the church age.[47] This prophecy is for today. Throughout all the past centuries, there have been some individual believers like Paul, Peter, and John who have ripened to full growth.[48] Yet, the harvest as a whole has remained immature. It is the Lord's desire to bring all the believers into the same maturity that Paul, Peter, and John shared.[49] The Lord will use every means to mature His many children into full-grown sons of God.[50] If we consider the past two thousand years, we can see that the Lord employs trials, sufferings, persecutions, and even death to accomplish what is on His heart for His many children. Only by the growth in life is God manifested and expressed.[51] Only through a church built up in the divine life is Satan put to shame.[52] The Lord will obtain that which He desires.

The Approach of the Harvest

Though the harvest has remained green (i.e., unripe), over the last two thousand years there has been a small amount of ripening. This has been accomplished despite centuries of darkness. It has been realized through a slow recovery of the truths in God's Word, which had been lost in the centuries immediately following the Lord's ascension, and had lain buried throughout the Dark Ages. This ripening has also occurred due to a gradual recovery of the experience of Christ and of the proper church living.

Because of this slow maturation, in these past years the Lord has been arranging the outward circumstances in preparation for His return. The outward situation as seen in Israel and the world corresponds to the growth and building up of the church. Yes, there are many signs of the Lord's return, but these are, more accurately, signs of at least a portion of the crop approaching maturity.

One great sign of Christ's second coming is the reformation of the nation of Israel, which occurred in 1948. For the Lord's return, Israel must exist as a nation. This was prophesied numerous times in both the Old and New Testaments.[53] Another sign of the Lord's impending return was the retaking of Jerusalem by Israel in 1967. According to prophecy, Jerusalem must have been returned to the Jews before the Lord Jesus can come back.[54] Still a third sign of the endtime is the collapse of the Soviet empire. Through this, hundreds of thousands of Jews have returned to Israel.[55] In addition, this collapse has allowed the spread of the gospel to Russia, a land darkened by 70 years of atheistic communism. The spread of the gospel to the whole earth was clearly mentioned by the Lord in the Gospels as occurring before the end would come.[56] The fulfillment of all these prophecies has much to do with the Lord's second coming.

Daily, the Lord is arranging the outward circumstances, that all the remaining Biblical prophecies might be fulfilled. However, as His believers and seekers, we should not have our heart set upon outward signs. Our heart should be fixed upon the growth in life of the believers, and the building up of the church. It is for this that we must pray and labor.[57] We must watch over the outward situation as those who have not fallen asleep, as those who have not been carried away into drunkenness with the unbelievers, and as those who do not mock the promise of our Lord's return.[58] Our hearts should be set upon the spiritual growth of the Lord's children.[59]

The time of the end will be intense for all men. On one hand, God will intervene in wisdom to arrange an environment that helps to ripen the immature believers. In addition, God will deal with the unbelieving nation of Israel, to bring her to repentance. Finally, God will step in to fully judge the nations*. On the other hand, Satan will continue in every possible way to attempt to frustrate the believers in their growth in life, the church in her building up, and the Lord in His preparation for His return. He will raise up great persecutions, and perhaps even the outright slaughter of Christians. Eventually, he will bring forth the Antichrist as his ultimate manifestation in an attempt to thwart Christ's return. Satan will do all this because he knows that his time, as the ruler of this world, nears an end.

During that final time, God's dealing with mankind will come to a pre-millennial consummation. God will, in effect, reap *everyone*! The believers will be ripened for harvest.[60] The nation of Israel, through much intense suffering, will be delivered into salvation.[61] This will also be a harvest. The Antichrist and his followers will be harvested in God's wrath.[62] The "tares"—the false, nominal Christians—will be harvested also, but for the lake of fire.[63] Even the people of the nations who survive that period of tribulation will be brought before the Lord for judgment— another harvest.[64] It is with God's great endtime harvest that this book is concerned.

References

[1] Matt. 13:39-40, 49

[2] Matt. 13:39

[3] Mr. 4:29

[4] Lu. 8:5, 11; Jn. 1:1, 14

[5] Matt. 13:30

[6] Eph. 4:15; 1 Pet. 2:2; Gal. 4:19

[7] Matt. 13:30

[8] 1 Cor. 3:6

[9] Eph. 2:21; 4:13, 15; Col. 2:19

[10] 1 Pet. 2:2

[11] Jam. 5:7

---

* The word *nations* is variously translated in the New Testament as Gentiles, nations, or peoples. It means all those who are neither Jew not Christian. Generally speaking, in this book these terms are used synonymously.

[12] Jn 15:5

[13] 1 Jn. 2:12-14

[14] Rev. 14:1-5, 14-16

[15] Col. 2:9; Jn. 1:12-13

[16] Jn. 7:38-39

[17] Jn. 3:6

[18] Eph. 4:6; Col. 1:27; Rom. 8:9-11

[19] Gal. 2:20; Eph. 3:17

[20] 1 Cor. 1:30; 1 Thes. 5:23; 2 Cor. 3:18

[21] 1 Pet. 1:16

[22] Jn. 10:10; 20:17; 2 Pet. 1:4

[23] Eph. 1:19-23; 3:20; Phil. 2:13; 2 Cor. 3:18

[24] Gal. 5:22-23

[25] Gal. 2:21

[26] Rom. 8:11, 13

[27] Phil. 3:9-10; 4:13

[28] Phil. 3:12-14

[29] Phil. 3:10

[30] Phil. 3:7-8

[31] Rom. 8:23; Eph. 4:13

[32] Gal. 4:19; Rom. 8:29

[33] Rom. 8:23; Col. 3:4

[34] Phil. 3:21; 1 Jn. 3:2

[35] Judg. 14:6, 19; 15:14

[36] Judg. 14:1-3; 16:1, 4

[37] Heb. 5:12-14; Eph. 6:18; 1 Thes. 5:17; Phil. 3:8-10; Rom. 12:1-2

[38] Rom. 14:19; 1 Cor. 14:3, 12, 26; Eph. 4:29

[39] Eph. 3:9-11

[40] Matt. 6:31-33

[41] 1 Jn. 2:15; Matt. 16:24

[42] Rev. 1:11, 20; Jn. 17:11, 21-23; 1 Cor. 1:10-13

[43] 1 Cor. 3:10-15

[44] 1 Cor. 3:12; Rev. 3:18; 21:10-11, 18-19, 21

[45] Matt. 24:45-51

[46] Matt. 16:18

[47] Lu. 20:35; Heb. 6:5; Matt. 8:11

[48] For example, 2 Tim. 4:7-8

[49] Eph. 4:13-15; Col. 1:28

[50] 1 Pet. 5:10; 2 Cor. 4:16-17; Rom. 8:18

[51] Eph. 4:13; 3:17-19

[52] Matt. 16:18

[53] Joel 2:28-32; Zech. 12:1-14:15; Matt. 24:15-22, 30; Rom. 11:25-26; Rev. 1:7; 7:4-8

[54] Matt. 24:15-22; Lu. 21:20-24; Rev. 11:1-3

[55] Perhaps Is. 60:8, 4

[56] Matt. 24:14; Mark 13:10

[57] For example, 2 Cor. 11:27-28; Col. 1:28-29; Eph. 6:18

[58] Rom. 13:11-13; 1 Thes. 5:6-7; Matt. 24:45-51; 2 Pet. 3:3-4

[59] 1 Thes. 2:7-8, 11-12

[60] Matt. 13:30; Rev. 14:14-16
[61] Zech. 13:9
[62] Rev. 14:17-20
[63] Matt. 13:30, 40-42
[64] Matt. 13:47-50; 25:31-46

CHAPTER 1

Daniel's Prophecy

As the crop of God's people ripens and the evil on earth nears a peak, the time for the salvation of Israel will come. At this juncture, God's final and consummate dealing with the nation of Israel will occur, as prophesied in Daniel 9.[1] Though this is of particular importance to the Jews, the events surrounding Israel's salvation will also have a far-reaching effect upon both the believers in Christ and the nations. One very notable event in particular will mark the end of this age.

The Seventy Weeks

Seventy weeks are decreed upon thy people and upon thy holy city, to finish transgression, and to make an end of sins, and to make reconciliation for iniquity, and to bring in everlasting righteousness, and to seal up vision and prophecy, and to anoint the most holy. Know therefore and discern, that from the going forth of the commandment to restore and to build Jerusalem unto the anointed one, the prince, shall be seven weeks, and threescore and two weeks: it shall be built again, with street and moat, even in troublous times. And after the threescore and two weeks shall the anointed one be cut off, and shall have nothing: and the people of the prince that shall come shall destroy the city and the sanctuary; and the end thereof shall be with a flood, and even unto the end shall be war; desolations are determined. And he shall make a firm covenant with many for one week: and in the midst of the week he shall cause the sacrifice and the oblation to cease; and upon the wing of abominations shall come one that maketh desolate; and even unto the full end, and that determined, shall wrath be poured out upon the desolate. (Daniel 9:24-27)

In these verses we see that there have been seventy "weeks" decreed for Israel to clear up their entire situation with respect to God: to finish transgression, to make an end of sins, to make reconciliation for iniquity, to bring in everlasting righteousness, to seal up vision and prophecy, and finally, to anoint the most holy place. It is by means of these seventy "weeks" that God brings His people, Israel, back into a holy and righteous relationship with Himself.

In this prophecy the word "week" does not refer to a period of seven days. The literal Hebrew simply means a group of seven, or a heptad. The "seventy weeks" in Daniel could properly be translated "seventy groups of seven," or "seventy heptads." From other portions of the Word, it is clear that these weeks refer not to periods of seven days, but rather to periods of seven years.[2] Consequently, these seventy weeks as a whole refer to a period of 490 years that was apportioned by God to deal with Israel.

This prophecy tells us that the seventy weeks were broken into three parts. The first consisted of seven weeks, or 49 years. The second was made up of 62 weeks, for a total of 434 years. The final part was one week, or seven years.

The first two periods, totaling 483 years, were grouped together. These marked the time from the issuing of the commandment to rebuild the wall of Jerusalem until the entry of the Lord Jesus into Jerusalem at the time of His crucifixion. The commandment to rebuild Jerusalem was issued in 445 B.C. by Artaxerxes Longimanus, as mentioned in the book of Nehemiah.[3] The Lord's entry into Jerusalem as "Messiah the Prince" was about A.D. 32. This is depicted in the various Gospels.[4] From the issuing of the commandment to rebuild Jerusalem until the time of the Lord's crucifixion was exactly 483 years.[*] The first period

---

[*] Sir Robert Anderson, in his well-researched book *The Coming Prince*, gives much detail about this interval. He provides one scenario showing how this 483-year period was fulfilled to the day. A brief outline of his calculation follows.

First, it must be noted that the Biblical or prophetic year is a period of 360 days, not our common year of 365 days. This is shown by comparing various portions of the Word that describe the last half of Daniel's seventieth week. In these portions, that last half-week is described as three and a half years ("a time, times, and half a time"), 42 months, or 1,260 days (Dan. 9:27; 7:25; 12:7; Rev. 11:2-3; 12:6, 14; 13:5). Thus these years are composed of 12 months of 30 days each, or 360 days per year. With this in hand we proceed to Dr. Anderson's computation. The 69 weeks consisted of 483 prophetic years of 360 days each, or 173,880 days. According to Dr. Anderson, the edict to rebuild Jerusalem was

of seven weeks (49 years) was the time necessary to rebuild the wall of Jerusalem. The second period of 62 weeks (434 years) refers, then, to that time remaining from the completion of the rebuilding of Jerusalem's wall until the time of Christ's crucifixion.

Between the first 69 weeks and the seventieth week there has been an indefinite period of time. This is the church age. During this period the Lord has suspended His dealing with Israel because of their rejection of Jesus as the Christ. This interval was hidden from the Old Testament prophets,[*] just as the church itself

---

issued by Artaxerxes on March 14, 445 B.C. Furthermore, Christ entered Jerusalem as her King (Matt. 21:5) on April 6, A.D. 32. The period between these two events was 476 Julian years, plus 24 days (including both March 14 and April 6). In addition, during these 476 Julian years there were exactly 116 leap years. Thus, the total number of days in this interval was 476 x 365 (or 173,740), plus 24, plus 116, or 173,880 days—exactly 483 prophetic years.

[*] This mysterious interval, though hidden, is present in Nebuchadnezzar's dream and in each of Daniel's visions concerning the world situation and Israel. In Daniel 2 Nebuchadnezzar had a dream in which he saw a giant image. Its head was of gold, its breast and arms were of silver, its stomach and thighs were of bronze, and its legs were of iron with its feet partly of iron and partly of clay. The head signified Nebuchadnezzar himself with the Babylonian empire. The breast and arms signified Medo-Persia. The stomach and thighs signified Greece. The legs signified the Roman empire. However, the feet, with their ten toes, signify the ten-nation kingdom on the earth when the Lord Jesus returns to crush all the worldly empires (vv. 44-45). Thus, there is a time gap of unspecified duration between the legs and the feet.

In chapter 7 Daniel saw a vision of four beasts rising up out of the great sea (the Mediterranean). These four beasts correspond to the four parts of the image in Nebuchadnezzar's dream. Whereas king Nebuchadnezzar saw these four kingdoms as something glorious, Daniel saw them from God's perspective—as something beastly. The fourth beast here is the Roman empire. Yet, from this empire ten kings plus the Antichrist arise (v. 24). He with his kingdom are destroyed by the Lord Jesus at His return. Thus, again there is an unmentioned time gap during the reign of the fourth beast.

In chapter 8 Daniel saw a vision that depicted the defeat of the Persian empire by Greece under Alexander the Great, and the subsequent division of the Greek empire into four parts after the death of Alexander. Yet, once again the Antichrist is mentioned as the "small horn" (v. 9). We are specifically told that this vision pertains to the "time of the end" (v. 17). Thus, once more a similar hidden interval is present.

In chapter 9 a gap is present, as discussed in the main text.

was hidden.[5] This gap can be likened to viewing two mountain peaks from a distance. From the perspective of a distant observer the peaks may seem to be situated beside each other. However, when the first peak is scaled, the observer may find that there is a long plain between the two. In like manner, to the Old Testament prophets the two peaks of Christ's two comings seemed to occur nearly simultaneously. It is only to us, the observers who are beyond the first peak of Christ's incarnation and crucifixion, that the long plain of the church age is readily apparent.

Of Daniel's seventy weeks, one week of seven years remains to be fulfilled. It is during this final seven years that God will show mercy upon Israel to bring her to repentance. This is also the interval immediately preceding the Lord's physical return to the earth in His second coming.

The World Situation Near the Endtime

After this I saw in the night-visions, and, behold, a fourth beast, terrible and powerful, and strong exceedingly; and it had great iron teeth; it devoured and brake in pieces, and stamped the residue with its feet: and it was diverse from all the beasts that were before it; and it had ten horns.... And as for the ten horns, out of this kingdom shall ten kings arise... (Daniel 7:7, 24a)

And I saw a beast coming up out of the sea, having ten horns, and seven heads, and on his horns ten diadems, and upon his heads names of blasphemy. And the beast which I saw was like unto a leopard, and his feet were as the feet of a bear, and his mouth as the mouth of a lion: and the dragon gave him his power, and his throne, and great authority. (Revelation 13:1-2)

In chapters 11-12 Daniel sees a vision that pertains to the fall of the Persian empire, the division of the Greek empire into four parts, and the subsequent conflict between two of these parts, the northern and southern kingdoms. Yet, by verse 36 the scene has changed from the ancient conflict between the Seleucid (Syrian) and Ptolemaic (Egyptian) kingdoms to the time of the end when Antichrist is reigning. We are pointedly told that this time is that of great tribulation (12:1). Once again, there is a hidden gap, which is common to all of Daniel's visions.

And the ten horns that thou sawest are ten kings, who have received no kingdom as yet; but they receive authority as kings, with the beast, for one hour. (Revelation 17:12)

To better understand the last seven years of this age, it is helpful to examine the endtime world situation in the light of the Bible. According to Scripture, at that time there will be a federation in Europe with ten kings or leaders, who presumably will be ruling over ten kingdoms or regions.[6] Whether these regions will be individual nations, groups of nations, or some other division is not yet known. These ten kings are the ten toes of the great image that King Nebuchadnezzar saw in his dream as portrayed in the book of Daniel.[7] They are also the ten horns on the beast Daniel saw in his vision. Furthermore, they are the horns of the beast the Apostle John saw. This ten-region kingdom will border the Mediterranean Sea, as depicted by its rising up out of "the great sea."[8] It will enjoy a capitalist economy.[9] In addition, it will be composed of democracies, as signified by the iron and clay in the toes of the image Nebuchadnezzar saw. There, the iron denotes the strong authoritative and dictatorial power of the Caesars of the Roman Empire. The clay signifies the weakness of a democratically elected government under which leaders are subject to the populace, and can be replaced according to the fancy or opinion of the electorate. This Mediterranean confederacy,* along with the nation of Israel, will become the center of the earth at the endtime. All the physical events happening on earth during that period will focus upon the area around the Mediterranean and Israel.†

The Rise of the Antichrist

I considered the horns, and, behold, there came up among them another horn, a little one, before which three of the first horns were plucked up by the roots: and, behold, in this horn were eyes

---

* The current movement to unite Europe will give way to the federation prophesied in the Bible. Eventually, a strong ten-part kingdom will emerge.

† This is similar, in some respects, to both World War I and World War II, when the eyes of all nations were fixed upon the events happening in Europe.

like the eyes of a man, and a mouth speaking great things. (Daniel 7:8)

Each of the ten countries of the coming kingdom will be ruled by a strong leader, as mentioned above. From the midst of these ten "kings" an exceedingly strong man will arise.[10] Though he will be opposed by three of the ten kings, he will in some way subdue them during his ascendancy to power.[11] Ultimately, both the leaders and the people of the coming kingdom will give their full allegiance to this man.[12] He will be the "Antichrist."

The Antichrist will rule over the entire ten-nation kingdom with his capital at Rome.* Thus, the kingdom will be, in effect, a revived Roman Empire. Eventually, he will extend his power throughout the whole earth.[13] It is likely that he will employ both military force and economic might to accomplish this.[14] During the great tribulation he will even be able to strictly control all buying and selling.[15]

The Bible gives us a clear and full picture of the source, appearance, character, and deeds of the Antichrist. More is prophesied concerning him than any other person except the Lord Jesus Himself.† Because the Bible is so detailed with respect to

---

* The Antichrist's capital is pictured in Revelation 18. Though it is called "Babylon the Great," we are told in the previous chapter that this Babylon is the city that sits on seven hills, i.e., Rome. The title "Babylon" refers to its source and nature. All the great worldly cities on earth today trace their origin back to the great city of Babel, which was built by that great rebel against God, Nimrod (Gen. 10:9-11). It was there at Babel that man rebelled against God to such an extent that God intervened to confound their language (Gen. 11:1-9). Babel later became Babylon, the head of which was the great king Nebuchadnezzar. It was to him that God gave the vision of the great image, whose golden head signified Nebuchadnezzar with Babylon, and whose legs and feet signified Rome with the Roman empire. Though there were many parts to this image, in God's eyes it was all just Babylon, more of the rebellious Babel founded by the evil one, Nimrod. In God's eyes the Antichrist's capital will just be the modern day Babylon, though it will be called by the name of Rome. It will share the same nature as its source, Babylon.

† There are at least eight major portions in the Word that describe the Antichrist: Dan. 7:7-27; 8:9-26; 9:27; 11:36-45; 2 Thes. 2:2--12; Rev. 13:1-18; 17:3, 7-17; 19:19-20. In addition, there are other passages, such as Rev. 11:7; 16:2, 10-11, which give further details concerning him.

the Antichrist* we are not left in darkness as to his true nature. The Antichrist will certainly arise from the Mediterranean area.† However, it is difficult to ascertain from where he will appear exactly. The various portions of the Word that refer to him seem to indicate that he will have different affiliations. It is very possible that he will arise out of Italy. It is known that his capital will be in Rome. In addition, he is depicted as the head of a revived Roman Empire.[16] Finally, in the book of Daniel the Romans are called his people. There we are told, "the people of the prince who is to come will destroy the city and the sanctuary."[17] This was literally fulfilled in A.D. 70, when the Roman armies under the leadership of Titus destroyed Jerusalem. Thus, "the prince who is to come" apparently refers to Titus. However, in the very next verse this same prince makes a pact with Israel.[18] This Titus never did. Rather, he completely demolished Israel. The one who will make this pact is the Antichrist. Therefore, the "prince" refers not only to Titus, but also to the Antichrist. Thus, the people of the Antichrist are the Roman people. According to these passages it seems that the Antichrist will arise from present-day Italy.

Yet, the Antichrist must also have very strong ties to Greece. In Daniel 8 he arises out of one of the four kingdoms into which ancient Greece was divided. These four kingdoms were, in brief, Greece-Macedonia, Asia Minor, Egypt, and northern Syria with Persia. Furthermore, we are told that the Antichrist will expand toward the east (Asia Minor), toward the south (Egypt), and toward the beautiful land (Israel and the Middle East).[19] Therefore, since he expands toward three of the ancient kingdoms of Greece, he must come from the fourth, which is Greece itself. How he can arise from both Italy and Greece is difficult to know at this point in time. It may be that his relationship to Greece is one of birth or ancestry. For example, the Lord Jesus was born in Bethlehem, yet raised in Nazareth. Consequently, he was called

---

* Only some crucial points regarding the Antichrist's initial appearance on earth are presented here. The remainder of his description is left for a later chapter.

† In Dan. 7:2-3 the prophet Daniel saw four beasts rise out of "the great sea," which is the Mediterranean Sea. These four beasts are both four kings (v. 17) and four kingdoms (v. 23). Thus, the Antichrist is synonymous with his kingdom. Both he and his kingdom arise from the Mediterranean area.

a Nazarene, though by birth He fulfilled the prophecy in Micah, which stated that He would come forth from Bethlehem.[20] The prophecies concerning the Antichrist* may come to pass in a similar manner.

No doubt the Antichrist will be extremely attractive. He will be stout, imposing, having great personal presence.[21] Eventually, the whole world will marvel after him.[22] If we, the believers, were not indwelt by Christ Himself, many of us would likely be fooled by him. The Antichrist will be *that* attractive. This is altogether unlike the Lord Jesus. Jesus was not a handsome man. Rather, he had no desirable form, nor any kind of comeliness.[23] His visage was marred above that of any man's.[24] Outwardly, the Lord Jesus was not attractive at all. Thus, in order to realize the true nature of both Christ and the Antichrist, we must exercise spiritual discernment to see through the exterior appearance of things and perceive spiritual reality. Only this kind of inward seeing will save us from the coming deception.[25]

Antichrist is said to have the "eyes of a man."[26] This indicates that he will be full of insight and knowledge. He will be a brilliant person, knowing not only politics, but perhaps science as well. He will be cunning and crafty.[27] He will be extraordinarily great in his deeds, in the art of persuasion, and in his problem-solving abilities.[28] He will be a person who understands dark sentences, riddles, enigmas, and puzzles.[29] He will astound everyone by the ease with which he is able to solve even the most complex problems.

The Final Seven Years

And he shall make a firm covenant with many for one week: and in the midst of the week he shall cause the sacrifice and the oblation to cease; and upon the wing of abominations shall come one that maketh desolate; and even unto the full end, and that determined, shall wrath be poured out upon the desolate. (Daniel 9:27)

---

* In addition, the Antichrist is also called the Assyrian (Micah 5:5-6) and the King of the North, whose kingdom included Assyria (Dan. 11:40), perhaps referring to some other status or affiliation he will have.

And one said to the man clothed in linen, who was above the waters of the river, How long shall it be to the end of these wonders? And I heard the man clothed in linen, who was above the waters of the river, when he held up his right hand and his left hand unto heaven, and sware by him that liveth for ever that it shall be for a time, times, and a half... (Daniel 12:6-7a)

And there was given to him a mouth speaking great things and blasphemies; and there was given to him authority to continue forty and two months. (Revelation 13:5)

After the Antichrist rises to power, the end—the final seven years of this age—will come quickly. It is during this time that God consummates His dealing with Israel. This period of seven years, as the last of Daniel's seventy weeks, is marked by a covenant made between the Antichrist and "the many" of Israel. The Antichrist and Israel will enter into some type of seven-year pact. That the pact is made with "the many" of Israel may indicate that a national referendum of some sort will be held in Israel to validate the pact. This covenant will allow Israel to reinstate the Old Testament method of worship. Animal sacrifices will once again be offered in Israel. This pact may also allow for the rebuilding of the temple in Jerusalem.[*]

In addition, this covenant between the Antichrist and Israel apparently guarantees Israel peace and security.[30] What Israel grants in return for the benefits it receives from this pact is not clear. Given the current world situation, however, it may be that the pact somehow resolves the seemingly intractable, inter-

---

[*] In the Bible it is clear that the temple in Jerusalem must be rebuilt before the Lord returns. The Old Testament sacrifices were to be offered only upon the altar before the temple (Deut. 12:3, 5, 11, 21; 14:23-24; 16:2, 6, 11; 26:2; 1 Kin. 5:5; 8:20, 29, 43). Since sacrifices will be offered during the period before the Lord returns (Dan. 9:27, Is. 66:3), the temple must be rebuilt by that time. In addition, the Bible tells us in numerous places that the Antichrist will defile the temple (Daniel 8:11-14, 9:27, 11:31; 12:11; Matt. 24:15; Mark 13:14; 2 Thes. 2:3-4). The Scripture, however, does not indicate the exact time when the temple will be rebuilt. It is also possible, though somewhat unlikely, that it may be reconstructed before the seven-year pact is enacted.

national problem of Jerusalem. In return, the covenant would guarantee Israel freedom of worship and security.

The final seven years are broken into two sections. During the first half of this final week, the Antichrist keeps his covenant with Israel. However, as we shall see, during the second half he breaks the pact. This second half of the final seven years of this age is also known as the "great tribulation." [*][31] This lasts exactly 3½ years, or 42 months of 30 days each, or 1,260 days.[32] This last 3½ years will be ended by the Lord's physical return to the earth to destroy the Antichrist and save Israel.[33]

---

[*] The term "great tribulation" is generally accepted to mean the trouble-filled time immediately preceding the second coming of the Lord Jesus. It is, however, somewhat of a misnomer. Specifically, it refers to the torment through which *Israel* will pass for her salvation. It does not refer to the great upheavals and supernatural judgments that occur *worldwide* during the endtime, which are called the "time of trial" (Rev. 3:10). The time of trial starts with the opening of the sixth seal (Rev. 6:12-17) and ends with the Lord's destruction of the Antichrist and his armies in the battle at Armageddon (Rev. 19:11-21). The scope of the time of trial is the whole inhabited earth (Rev. 3:10). The great tribulation starts with the setting up of the idol of the Antichrist in the temple in Jerusalem (Matt. 24:15, 21), which will occur sometime *after* the sixth seal is opened. The great tribulation will end immediately *before* the Lord Jesus returns (Matt. 24:29-30). Furthermore, the focus of the great tribulation is the nation of Israel (Matt. 24:16-21). Thus, the time of trial and the great tribulation have different durations and scopes. The great tribulation is actually a subset of the time of trial. However, in popular usage "great tribulation" typically refers to the endtime. For this reason, "great tribulation" and "time of trial" are not generally differentiated in this book.

References

[1] Dan. 9:27
[2] Dan. 7:25; 12:7; Rev. 11:2-3; 12:6, 14
[3] Neh. 2:1, 6
[4] Lu. 19:38, Matt. 21:9; Mr. 11:9-10; Jn. 12:13
[5] Eph. 3:4-6
[6] Dan. 7:23-24
[7] Dan. 2:42, 44
[8] Dan. 7:2-3
[9] Rev. 18:11-13
[10] Dan. 7:8, 24
[11] Dan. 7:8, 24
[12] Rev. 17:12-13; 13:3-4
[13] Rev. 13:7, Dan. 7:7, 19, 23
[14] Dan. 7:19, 23; Rev. 13:16-17
[15] Rev. 13:16-17
[16] Dan. 7:7, 23-24; etc.
[17] Dan. 9:26
[18] Dan. 9:27
[19] Dan. 8:9
[20] Mic. 5:2
[21] Dan. 7:20
[22] Rev. 13:3; 17:8
[23] Is. 53:2
[24] Is. 52:14
[25] Rev. 13:8
[26] Dan. 7:8, 20
[27] Dan. 8:25
[28] Dan. 8:12, 24
[29] Dan. 8:23
[30] 1 Thes. 5:3
[31] Matt. 24:15-18
[32] Dan. 7:25; 12:7; Rev. 11:2-3; 12:6, 14; 13:5
[33] Matt 24:29-30; Zech. 12:2-9; 14:2-7, 12-15

CHAPTER 2

The Beginning of the Final Week

It is crucial that we believers accurately understand the rapture and the status of the believers during the last seven years of this age.[1] Many Christians believe they will have been taken from the earth before that time. Their understanding is that the Lord simply will catch the believers away to heaven at some predetermined time. This, however, is not according to the divine revelation. Suppose a believer were in the midst of some serious sin when the time of rapture came. Would the Lord rapture such a one to His glory? Certainly not. We must see that our spiritual condition and maturity in life are absolutely related to the rapture.

Previously we saw the crucial matter of the growth in life. How does this relate to the rapture? Consider a flower seed. It is first planted. Then it sprouts. It grows over a long period of time. Finally, in its final stage, it blossoms. This process is a picture of what is happening to the believers. Every genuine believer has received Christ as the divine seed. We then experience the lifelong process of growing in the divine life.[2] During this time Christ, as the seed of life, grows and spreads within us. Eventually this divine "flower" blossoms.[3] It is at this point that the harvest is ripe. It is also at this point that we are raptured. The rapture is therefore altogether dependent upon our growth in the divine life.

The Rapture and the Last Week

For this we say unto you by the word of the Lord, that we that are alive, that are left unto the coming of the Lord, shall in no wise precede them that are fallen asleep. For the Lord himself shall descend from heaven, with a shout, with the voice of the archangel, and with the trump of God: and the dead in Christ shall rise first; then we that are alive, that are left, shall together with them be caught up in the clouds, to meet the Lord in the air: and so shall we ever be with the Lord. (1 Thessalonians 4:15-17)

Behold, I tell you a mystery: We all shall not sleep, but we shall all be changed, in a moment, in the twinkling of an eye, at the last trump: for the trumpet shall sound, and the dead shall be raised incorruptible, and we shall be changed. (1 Corinthians 15:51-52)

And I saw, and behold, a white cloud; and on the cloud I saw one sitting like unto a son of man, having on his head a golden crown, and in his hand sharp sickle. And another angel came out from the temple, crying with a great voice to him that sat on the cloud, Send forth thy sickle, and reap: for the hour to reap is come; for the harvest of the earth is ripe. And he that sat on the cloud cast his sickle upon the earth; and the earth was reaped. (Revelation 14:14-16)

And the woman fled into the wilderness, where she hath a place prepared of God, that there they may nourish her a thousand two hundred and threescore days. (Revelation 12:6)

Consider what the Bible says in these verses. In 1 Thessalonians 4, Paul tells us that all the believers who are living and who remain will be caught up at the trumpet of God. From this portion of the Word we see that the rapture of all the believers remaining on earth will occur when one of the trumpets of God sounds. But *which* trumpet is that? In 1 Corinthians 15, Paul tells us further that the believers will all be changed in a moment, in the twinkling of an eye, at the sounding of the last trumpet. Therefore, the rapture spoken of in these verses must occur at the last trumpet. According to the book of Revelation there are seven trumpets of God.[4] The final trumpet is the seventh one. It is the last of three great woes that will come upon the earth.[5] It will be preceded by the first through sixth trumpets, which bring great calamities upon man during the great tribulation.[6] When will the seventh trumpet sound? If we read Revelation carefully we will see that it occurs at the very end of the great tribulation. It is at that point that the kingdoms of the world become the kingdom of God and Christ.[7] This, of course, occurs when the Lord returns to the the earth physically to destroy the Antichrist and his armies, and to end the great tribulation.[8] Thus, from these portions of the Word it is clear that Christian believers will be on the earth during the final seven years of this age. The Lord grant us mercy to be able to receive such a word, however disconcerting it may be.

In Matthew 13 the Lord Jesus told us that He came to plant Himself as the seed of the word into mankind.[9] This seed has been growing in the believers over the past two millennia. Eventually the Lord will return to reap what He sowed.[10] When will that harvest occur? Near the end of Revelation 14, the Lord from a cloud reaps all the believers remaining on the earth. But, in this same chapter before this harvest, there is the full manifestation of the Antichrist and the accompanying persecution of the saints on the earth.[11] This persecution by the Antichrist surely occurs during the great tribulation. Once again the divine record shows that believers will be on the earth during the final seven years of this age.

Consider Revelation 12. There we see a woman clothed with the sun, standing upon the moon, and crowned with twelve stars.[12] As we will see in a later chapter,* this woman signifies the whole of God's redeemed people. While the strongest part of her, which is depicted as a manchild, is caught away to the throne of God, she herself remains on the earth for a period of $3\frac{1}{2}$ years or 1,260 days.[13] This is precisely the time of the great tribulation.† Thus, the Bible again shows us that Christians will be on the earth during the final trouble-filled period before the Lord's physical return.

Finally, in four separate instances in John 6, the Lord Himself said that He would raise up the dead believers on "the last day."[14] This must refer to the last day of this age, when the Lord is descending to the air in preparation for the battle at Armageddon. This will be the last day of the great tribulation. Since the living believers are caught up to the air with the resurrected dead believers, this also shows that Christians will be on the earth

---

* See *The Rapture of the Manchild* in Chapter 4 for a detailed discussion of the woman in Revelation 12.

† The Word tells us clearly that during this time the devil persecutes both the woman and her seed (Rev. 12:13, 17). Thus, this must be the time of the great tribulation.

during the great tribulation. With this understanding as a basis, let us go on to consider the first half of Daniel's seventieth week.

As mentioned in the previous chapter, Daniel's seventieth week is broken into two sections. The last half, which is the last 3½ years of this age, is the great tribulation.[15] It is during this time that God concludes His dealing with all men on earth—with the believers, with the Jews, with the Antichrist and his followers, with the false believers or "tares," and with the unbelievers, both good and bad. The Bible gives us great detail about the events that occur during this time.

On the other hand, the Bible tells us little about the first half of Daniel's last week. That 3½ years will be a time of preparation, a time during which the stage is set on earth for the coming great tribulation. In addition, there are some indications as to what occurs then. Let us consider each of the peoples on the earth— the believers, the nations, and the Jews—to see what the Scriptures say concerning their state of affairs during this period of time.

The Believers

And when he opened the fifth seal, I saw underneath the altar the souls of them that had been slain for the word of God, and for the testimony which they held: and they cried with a great voice, saying, How long, O Master, the holy and true, dost thou not judge and avenge our blood on them that dwell on the earth? (Revelation 6:9-10)

And a great sign was seen in heaven: a woman arrayed with the sun, and the moon under her feet, and upon her head a crown of twelve stars; and she was with child; and she crieth out, travailing in birth, and in pain to be delivered. And there was seen another sign in heaven: and behold, a great red dragon, having seven heads and ten horns, and upon his heads seven diadems. And his tail draweth the third part of the stars of heaven, and did cast them to the earth: and the dragon standeth before the woman that is about to be delivered, that when she is delivered he may devour her child. (Revelation 12:1-4)

And there were given to the woman the two wings of the great eagle, that she might fly into the wilderness unto her place, where she is nourished for a time, and times, and half a time, from the face of the serpent. (Revelation 12:14)

What will the experience of the believers be during the beginning of Daniel's seventieth week? What portions of God's Word relate to this? There are three pertinent passages in the book of Revelation. First consider Revelation 6. There the Lord Jesus opens the fifth seal.* At that time all those who have been martyred throughout the centuries cry out to God for His righteous judgment upon the murderers of God's people. What could cause them to cry out? There must be some particular event that motivates them to cry out in such a way after having remained silent for thousands of years. Some of these precious believers gave up their lives for their Lord while praying for those that martyred them.[16] Here, though, they cry out for vengeance. What happening could give rise to such an unprecedented reaction from the slain saints? It might be that a great and unparalleled persecution of the believers finally forces these dear martyrs to call out to God for vengeance.

Consider also Revelation 12. There we see a woman who represents the entire body of God's people. The devil, depicted as a great red dragon, stands before her in an attempt to devour her manchild, whom she is about to bring forth. How is it that Satan seeks to devour the woman's manchild? The answer is given in Revelation 12:11. There we are told that the overcoming believers, who compose the manchild, did not love their lives unto *death.* In other words, they had all been killed. Thus, it is by death that Satan seeks to devour the manchild. Satan seeks to devour the woman's seed through persecution and martyrdom. This is confirmed by the fact that the woman is crying out in pain.

---

* The first four seals were opened by the Lord Jesus immediately after His ascension. They refer symbolically to the spreading of the gospel (the white horse), war (the red horse), famine (the black horse), and death (the pale horse). The opening of these four seals corresponds to the Lord's prophecy in Matt. 24:6-14, where He declared what would occur from the time of His ascension until His return. The fifth seal is yet to be opened. This should occur sometime shortly before the beginning of the great tribulation (Rev. 6:11).

This cry of the living believers on the earth corresponds to the cry of the martyrs in Revelation 6.

It is true that the believers have cried out to the Lord throughout the ages. However, the painful cry of the woman depicted here in Revelation 12 is not merely something general that has been occurring for centuries. What is pictured here ultimately must be fulfilled by the intense prayer and entreaty of the saints at the end of this age. We know this to be the case because the 1,260 days of the great tribulation immediately follow the woman's cry and the delivery of her child. As the time of the end approaches, Satan's persecution of God's people will intensify greatly. At this time the living believers will pray, weep, and cry out to God in desperation. It is this situation in particular that is pictured in Revelation 12.

If these two portions of the Word are put together, a picture begins to form of what the believers will likely experience during the beginning of Daniel's seventieth week. From these two passages it appears that there will be much persecution on the earth during that time. By then, many believers will be nearing maturity, and the time for the start of the harvest will be rapidly approaching. Satan, in a vain attempt to stop the beginning of the rapture and frustrate the Lord's move to consummate the age, will instigate the violent persecution of Christians wherever possible. Many believers will be martyred. Others will begin fleeing from this persecution to a place the Bible calls "the wilderness." There the remainder of God's people, depicted by the woman in Revelation 12, will be nourished for the 1,260 days of the great tribulation, in order that they also might mature.[17]

In Revelation 12 the woman is given the two wings of the great eagle to fly into the wilderness. The wilderness denotes a place apart from culture, society, and worldly influence.[18] The great eagle refers to God Himself, and His two wings signify His heavenly bearing power in the salvation and protection of His people.[19]

However, there may also be another significance to the symbolic use of the term "great eagle" in this chapter. It is possible that God, in His foresight and wisdom, used this sign to indicate the United States, which has as its national symbol the great eagle. It may be that during this time a great number of believers will start to flee persecution arising in Asia and Europe by flying into the United States. And indeed, the United States may have become a wilderness by that time, but one for the nourishment of God's people during the great tribulation.

If the wilderness in Revelation 12 does refer to the United States, then there is a further implication in these verses. Certainly the United States, as it is today, could not be considered a wilderness in any sense of the word. Therefore, some great upheaval or disaster would have to befall the United States to change it into a kind of wilderness. This could happen in part due to great economic difficulties. By that time the Antichrist will be reigning in Europe. He will have enormous economic power. He may try to strangle the U.S. economy in some way in order to make the United States subservient to him. If, for example, there were a shortage of oil in the United States, the U.S. could face economic collapse. If the flow of oil in the United States were drastically cut, the massive highway system crisscrossing the country would lay empty for lack of gasoline. People throughout the nation would face hunger and possibly even starvation if food and other products could no longer be easily transported across the nation. This would be especially true within the large cities. Unemployment would skyrocket. Unrest and turmoil would increase. That time would become a "Greater Depression." This, coupled with the influx of a massive number of people fleeing persecution, could strain the U.S. economy to the breaking point. Furthermore, the events occurring at the beginning of the tribulation will certainly leave the U.S. greatly damaged. By the time of the last 1260 days, the U.S. will bear very little resemblance to what we see today. The result of all this could be a "wilderness," which God would use to spiritually nourish and sustain His people, even as He delivers them from the corrupting influence of the world.

Today many believers are under the mistaken concept that one day they will be taken from the earth before any of the endtime troubles occur. This erroneous teaching has lulled them into a dangerous contentment and false sense of security. Many expect the Lord to take them from the earth no matter what their spiritual condition may be. At the time of Daniel's seventieth week, a change of heart will begin to occur among Christians.

They will see the Antichrist sign a pact with Israel. Many believers may dismiss the pact, presuming they will be raptured before the endtime begins, but the light of the truth will start to dawn on at least some of the believers. They will begin to realize that they have been misled by certain teachings they have received. In addition, they will start to hear of, see, and even experience persecutions, which will only intensify as the time of the end approaches. Furthermore, many Christians will face dire economic straits at that time. Through all this, God will begin to raise up an intense seeking for Himself, which is in large part absent today among us Christians. The church as a whole will start to experience a final revival. The gospel of the kingdom will be preached as never before.[20] The tremendous difficulties men will experience in simply maintaining human life, coupled with the desperate prayers of those believers who have awakened to the real situation, will work together to soften the hardened hearts of many unbelievers, opening them to God and to the gospel. A great number of unbelievers may repent and turn to the Lord Jesus. Every Gentile* predestined by God the Father from eternity past will be saved. This will bring in what the Apostle Paul described as the "fullness of the Gentiles."[21] This will be the Lord's final gospel outreach to the nations before He turns back to Israel during the great tribulation.

The Nations

Woe, woe, the great city, Babylon, the strong city! for in one hour is thy judgment come. And the merchants of the earth weep and mourn over her, for no man buyeth their merchandise any more; merchandise of gold, and silver, and precious stone, and pearls, and fine linen, and purple, and silk, and scarlet; and all thyine wood, and every vessel of ivory, and every vessel made of most precious wood, and of brass, and iron, and marble; and cinnamon, and spice, and incense, and ointment, and frankincense, and wine, and oil, and fine flour, and wheat, and cattle, and sheep; and merchandise of horses and chariots and slaves; and souls of

---

* The word "Gentile" refers to a person who is neither a Jew nor a believer in Christ. A Gentile is one of the people of the nations.

men. And the fruits which thy soul lusted after are gone from thee, and all things that were dainty and sumptuous are perished from thee, and men shall find them no more at all. The merchants of these things, who were made rich by her, shall stand afar off for the fear of her torment, weeping and mourning; saying, Woe, woe, the great city, she that was arrayed in fine linen and purple and scarlet, and decked with gold and precious stone and pearl! for in an hour so great riches is made desolate. (Revelation 18:10b-17a)

Thus saith the Lord Jehovah: It shall come to pass in that day, that things shall come into thy mind, and thou shalt devise an evil device: and thou shalt say, I will go up to the land of unwalled villages; I will go to them that are at rest, that dwell securely, all of them dwelling without walls, and having neither bars nor gates; to take the spoil and to take the prey; to turn thy hand against the waste places that are now inhabited, and against the people that are gathered out of the nations, that have gotten cattle and goods, that dwell in the middle of the earth. (Ezekiel 38:10-12)

The world during this time will appear to be a massive paradox. On one hand, parts of the earth will be experiencing extreme prosperity. The Antichrist's empire will not only be economically sound, but probably prosperous above our imagination. For example, the description of the Antichrist's capital in Revelation 18 shows a city that is exorbitantly luxurious. During this time the Antichrist will be expanding and extending his influence, not only toward the surrounding nations of Egypt, Asia Minor, and the Middle East, but throughout the whole earth as well.[22] Through his political, diplomatic, economic, and military skills he will gain world supremacy. No one will be able to stand against his military might, or halt the expansion of his empire.

Nevertheless, it is also likely that other parts of the earth will experience desperate conditions. We have seen a possible description of the situation in the United States during this period. Other countries will also experience depression, starvation, and economic distress. For example, Ezekiel 38-39 pictures endtime Russia and its allies invading Israel and the Middle East to acquire wealth.* This indicates that the environment within Russia will degrade into a desperate condition. Otherwise, they would have no need to invade the Middle East for its wealth.

In addition, persecutions will become commonplace through-out the earth. A tide of oppression will begin to swell in the Antichrist's European confederacy. It is likely that there will be persecution in Russia and other countries such as China. During this time the 200 million horsemen,† who will come from east of the Euphrates River and who will slaughter a third of mankind during the great tribulation, may be preparing for their appear-ance.‡ These forces may very well be used by the devil to martyr many of the believers during those pre-tribulation years.

The earth will seem to be on the verge of complete madness. In one place there will be extreme prosperity, in another extreme desperation. Throughout the earth there will be persecutions of many kinds.[23] Wars will rage in many places. Men will wonder how the situation on the earth could get any worse. Yet, all this will occur before the great tribulation starts, before God's supernatural judgments ever befall the earth. These events are merely a prelude to what is about to happen.

Israel

For yourselves know perfectly that the day of the Lord so cometh as a thief in the night. When they are saying, Peace and safety, then sudden destruction cometh upon them, as travail upon a woman with child; and they shall in no wise escape. (1 Thessalonians 5:2-3)

And in their security shall he destroy many... (Daniel 8:25b)

Amazingly, Israel will be enjoying unprecedented peace and prosperity during the first half of Daniel's seventieth week. The

---

* See *The Sixth Bowl* in Chapter 7 and Chapter 9 for more detail on this invasion.

† See *The Sixth Trumpet* in Chapter 6 for more detail about the 200 million horsemen.

‡ Such a gathering could certainly not occur overnight. To gather, equip, and train such an army should take quite some time. Even the horses they ride must have been many years in breeding.

Jews will not realize that sudden destruction is about to come upon them. The temple in Jerusalem will be rebuilt, and the Levitical offerings will be reinstituted.[24] In addition, Israel will again begin to celebrate* the feasts decreed by Moses, according to the statutes of the law. Israel will once again start to gather in Jerusalem for the feasts of Passover, Pentecost, and Tabernacles.[25] Through her pact with the Antichrist, Israel will partake of enormous economic wealth, and enjoy a huge influx of expensive goods.[26] The problem of Jerusalem will have been apparently solved. Israel will be at peace with the Arabs, the Palestinians, and the Europeans. This time will seem to be the beginning of Israel's golden age. Yet, it will actually signal the coming disaster, which God will allow in order to bring Israel to salvation.[27]

An Overview

As the middle of the last seven years of this age approaches, the sufferings in many parts of the earth will intensify. The economic situation, which already seemed desperate, will worsen. The persecution of the believers will increase. The natural calamities on the earth will probably become more severe. Eventually, very near the time of the great tribulation, the Lord Jesus will open the fifth seal as portrayed in Revelation 6. All the martyrs who have died in the Lord will then cry out to God from under the earth,† asking Him to avenge their blood upon those

---

* Or, at least Israel will *plan* the celebration of these feasts. The Antichrist's breaking of his pact with Israel may prevent even the first celebration of any feast from ever occurring at the new temple.

† It is said of these martyrs that they cried out from "underneath the altar" (Rev. 6:9). The altar, as the place where they were offered to God, must refer to the earth on which they were martyred. For them to cry out from under the altar is for them to cry out from under the earth. The souls and spirits of the dead saints are not in heaven as many suppose. Rather, they are under the earth awaiting resurrection.

Hades is a place for the dead under the earth. It is a kind of temporary "way-station" for those who are awaiting resurrection. It is composed of at least two parts. It has a pleasant section for the believers and an unpleasant section for the unbelievers. This is clearly revealed in the Bible. It was into the lower parts of

who martyred them. God's answer to their cry is the great tribulation itself.[28] At this time, as the tribulation is about to begin, a large number of events occur nearly simultaneously. These events are the subject of the next two chapters.

---

the earth that the Lord Jesus went at His death (Eph. 4:9; Matt. 12:40; Rom. 10:7). He descended into Hades (Acts 2:27, 31), where He announced the defeat of Satan to the angels who were held bound in Tartarus (1 Pet. 3:19; 2 Pet. 2:4). It was to the pleasant part of Hades, called Paradise, that the thief, crucified beside Jesus, went on the day of crucifixion (Luke 23:42-43). It was to the two parts of Hades that the beggar Lazarus and the rich man went at their deaths (Luke 16:19-31). It is also from Hades that all the dead believers will resurrect. This is why the Bible says the dead will *rise* at their resurrection, not *descend* from the heavens with the Lord Jesus when He descends (1 Thes. 4:16).

Some believe that Paradise was transferred to the heavens at the Lord's ascension. This erroneous teaching is refuted by Acts 2:34, where Peter says that David, who was in Paradise, had not yet ascended to the heavens by that time, which was after the Lord's ascension. If David had not ascended, then he was still in Hades. Therefore, Paradise itself was not transferred to the heavens when the Lord ascended.

References

[1] Lu. 8:5-8, 11-15

[2] 1 Cor. 3:6; Eph. 2:21, 4:13, 15; Col. 2:19; 1 Pet. 2:2

[3] Col. 3:4

[4] Rev. 8:1; 11:15

[5] Rev. 8:13; 9:12; 11:14-15

[6] Rev. 8:1-9:21; 11:14

[7] Rev. 11:15, 19

[8] Rev. 16:12-21; 19:11-21

[9] Matt. 13:3-9, 18-23, 24-30, 36-43

[10] Rev. 14:14-16

[11] Rev. 14:9-12

[12] Rev. 12:1-2

[13] Rev. 12:6, 14

[14] Jn. 6:39, 40, 44, 54

[15] Dan. 9:27; Matt. 24:15, 21

[16] For example, Acts 7:54-60

[17] Rev. 12:6

[18] cf. Matt. 3:1, 4

[19] Ex. 19:4

[20] Matt. 24:14

[21] Rom. 11:25

[22] Dan. 8:9; Rev. 13:7

[23] For example, Matt. 25:31-40

[24] Dan. 9:27

[25] Deut. 16:16

[26] Ez. 38:8-13

[27] Zech. 13:8-9

[28] Rev. 6:9-17; 8:1-13

CHAPTER 3

Concerning the Rapture

Before continuing with our examination of the endtime events, let us consider the rapture of the believers.[*] A proper grasp of the rapture is a necessary basis for understanding the matters that will be presented in the following chapters. Throughout the years there has been much misunderstanding among Christians concerning the rapture. Due to many incorrect teachings, this matter is now perceived through a kind of spiritual fog. Some may catch glimpses of the truth in certain portions of the Bible, yet as a whole the rapture remains a mystery. Overall, the general understanding of the rapture is confused and muddled. As a result, many verses in the Bible are misapplied. Verses intended for the believers are mistakenly applied to the Jews or to the unbelievers. Other verses concerning the nations are mistakenly applied to the believers.

In such a situation it is difficult for the truths in the Bible to be properly seen and received. In order to get into the substance of the Word and see the revelation contained within it, we must let go of all our previous concepts and theories. We must come back to the pure Word of God with a sober mind, calm emotions, and an open spirit.[1] This is especially true when we address the matter of the rapture. Only then, in a pure, spiritual atmosphere and under a clear, heavenly sky, can we garner the truth God has stored for us in His Word.

Previously we have seen that the Lord's second coming and the harvest (which is the time of rapture) depend upon the growth in life of the believers. We have also seen that believers are on the earth during the last seven years of this age, even until the very last day of the tribulation, until immediately before the Lord returns to the earth physically. But not all the believers will

---

[*] This chapter presents only a preliminary discussion of the rapture. Later chapters will address the rapture more fully.

remain on earth during the great tribulation, as we will shortly see. Some will be taken before the tribulation, while the rest remain on earth to pass through the troubles of that time. In this chapter we will examine verses relating to this matter in detail, paying particular attention to what is required of us by the Lord to escape the coming time of trial.

A Word to the Young Believers

But we would not have you ignorant, brethren, concerning them that fall asleep; that ye sorrow not, even as the rest, who have no hope. For if we believe that Jesus died and rose again, even so them also that are fallen asleep in Jesus will God bring with him. For this we say unto you by the word of the Lord, that we that are alive, that are left unto the coming of the Lord, shall in no wise precede them that are fallen asleep. For the Lord himself shall descend from heaven, with a shout, with the voice of the archangel, and with the trump of God: and the dead in Christ shall rise first; then we that are alive, that are left, shall together with them be caught up in the clouds, to meet the Lord in the air: and so shall we ever be with the Lord. (1 Thessalonians 4:13-17)

Behold, I tell you a mystery: We all shall not sleep, but we shall all be changed, in a moment, in the twinkling of an eye, at the last trump: for the trumpet shall sound, and the dead shall be raised incorruptible, and we shall be changed. (1 Corinthians 15:51-52)

Let both grow together until the harvest: and in the time of the harvest I will say to the reapers, Gather up first the tares, and bind them in bundles to burn them; but gather the wheat into my barn. (Matthew 13:30)

When Paul wrote his first epistle to the Thessalonians, the church in Thessalonica had existed for perhaps only a year. The believers there were very young in the Lord, under much persecution, and extremely concerned about those who had died in the Lord.[2] When Paul wrote to the Corinthians he also treated them as spiritual children.[3] In both these instances Paul was addressing those he considered babes in Christ.[4] To this young audience the Apostle wrote words that gave a general view of the rapture, words addressed to the majority of believers. Nearly all the complex details of the rapture were omitted by Paul.* He did not want to confuse the young Thessalonians, or distract the intellectual Corinthians. In both cases he wrote a word that would minister life, calm the believers in their anxieties, and present something of the general truth concerning the Lord's second coming.

In these letters Paul is not dealing with the fine details concerning a pre-tribulation rapture of the mature believers and the subsequent rapture of the remaining believers. Rather, he presents very simple words in order to comfort the suffering Thessalonians and guide the misdirected and deceived Corinthians. He tells the Thessalonians that their dear, yet departed, brethren would be resurrected. Then they, together with them, would be caught up to be with the Lord. This was a soothing word to the young ones in Thessalonica.[5] To the Corinthians, who had been so misled as to think there was no resurrection of the dead, Paul pointed out the coming change to our bodies that will occur through resurrection and through the glorification of the living believers at the time of the Lord's coming.[6] Neither of these simple words were meant to give a complete overview of the rapture. We should not assume then that every detail concerning the rapture is revealed in them. However, as we have seen previously, these verses do indicate that many of the believers will remain on the earth until the very end of the tribulation.†

A Thief in the Night

Then shall two man be in the field; one is taken, and one is left: two women shall be grinding at the mill; one is taken, and one is left. Watch therefore: for ye know not on what day your Lord cometh. But know this, that if the master of the house had known in what watch the thief was coming, he would have watched, and would not have suffered his house to be broken through.

---

* Indeed, from Paul's writings it is not clear how much of this detail God revealed to Paul. Paul did not have the benefit of the book of Revelation, which was not set forth until about 35-40 years after 1 Thessalonians and 1 Corinthians were written.

† See *The Rapture and the Last Week* in Chapter 2.

Therefore be ye also ready; for in an hour that ye think not the Son of man cometh. (Matthew 24:40-44)

I say unto you, In that night there shall be two men on one bed; the one shall be taken, and the other shall be left. There shall be two women grinding together; the one shall be taken, and the other shall be left. There shall be two men in the field; the one shall be taken, and the other shall be left. (Luke 17:34-36)

Take ye heed, watch and pray: for ye know not when the time is. It is as when a man, sojourning in another country, having left his house, and given authority to his servants, to each one his work, commanded also the porter to watch. Watch therefore: for ye know not when the lord of the house cometh, whether at even, or at midnight, or at cockcrowing, or in the morning; lest coming suddenly he find you sleeping. And what I say unto you I say unto all, Watch. (Mark 13:33-37)

In Matthew 24 the Lord Jesus speaks concerning the rapture. He tells us that two will be in the field—one will be taken, one left. Two will be working at the mill—one will be taken, the other left. The taken ones are, of course, the raptured ones. But *when* is one taken and one left? In referring to this, the Lord Jesus tells us that this occurs "*Then.*" To understand what the Lord Jesus means by the word "then," we must look back to His previous words in Matthew 24. According to the context[*] of the Lord's speaking, "Then" must refer to that period of time immediately preceding the great tribulation, which begins about the time the Antichrist sets up the abomination of desolation in the temple.[7] Concerning the exact time of this rapture, no man knows the day or the hour.[8]

---

[*] The Lord said in Matthew 24, "When therefore ye see the abomination of desolation, which was spoken of through Daniel the prophet, standing in the holy place… for **then shall be great tribulation**… And as *were* the days of Noah, so shall be the coming of the Son of man. For **as in those days which were before the flood** they were eating and drinking, marrying and giving in marriage, until the day that Noah entered into the ark, and they knew not until the flood came, and took them all away; **so shall be the coming of the Son of man. Then** shall two man be in the field; one is taken, and one is left" (vv. 15a, 21a, 37-40). Thus, *then* refers to those days immediately preceding the "flood" of God's judgment that is the great tribulation.

But the Lord Jesus Himself has told us the approximate time—it is at the time immediately preceding the great tribulation.

Both Matthew and Luke speak of one being taken and one left. Two men are working in the field—one is taken, the other left. Two women are grinding at the mill—one is taken, the other left. Two are in one bed—one is taken, the other left. The common understanding among most Christians is that the one taken is a believer, whereas the one left is an unbeliever. However, this is absolutely not true. According to the Bible this cannot be the case. First, the Lord was not speaking to the unbelievers at that time. Rather, He was answering His *disciples'* question concerning the time of His coming. In addition, unbelievers rarely read the Bible. Thus, this word must be recorded in the Gospels for the sake of the believers, not the unbelievers.[9]

More importantly, carefully consider the Lord's words in Matthew. The Lord says, "Watch therefore, for you do not know on what day your Lord comes." He also tells us, "… be ready." If all the believers are taken, why is it necessary for us to "watch?" If all the believers are raptured, why is it necessary to "be ready?" If all the believers are automatically taken at that time, there is no need for any of us to watch or be ready. Whether we watched or not, whether we were ready or not, we would be taken. However, if we drop all our preconceived ideas, we must admit that the reason it is necessary for us to watch and be ready is that only the watchful, ready believers are taken by rapture at that time, *before* the tribulation. The other believers, those who have not watched, those who are not ready for the Lord, will be left on the earth to pass through the tribulation.

Some, in an attempt to circumvent this passage in Matthew 24, have stated that this portion of the Word is for the Jews, not the believers. Even if all of Matthew were solely for the Jews, then we must ask, "What about the Gospel of Luke?" It was written by one who was very likely a Gentile to a Gentile. It was written by Luke, probably a Gentile physician, to Theophilus, a Gentile* believer probably of some notable, official position.[10] No one can circumvent the Lord's nearly identical words in Luke. These words are for all believers. The Lord is more than emphatic

---

* Certainly a Gentile and possibly a Greek, as seen by his Greek name.

about this matter. In Mark He tells us explicitly that what He says to one, He says to *all*. Therefore, according to these verses some believers will be taken before the great tribulation while others will be left to pass through it.

In this portion of the Word, the Lord Jesus likens Himself to a thief. He is the thief coming in a hidden way during the darkest part of the night* to steal away those things that are precious to Him. This *part* of the Lord's coming is hidden.† This is not His

---

* That is, at the close of this dark and evil age.

† In the Gospel of Matthew a particular word is used to refer to the time of the Lord's second coming. In Greek the word is "parousia" (παρουσια). It appears four times in Matthew 24 (vv. 3, 27, 37, 39). It is usually translated as "coming." However, this translation sometimes leads to misunderstanding and confusion regarding the Lord's second coming. Many believers think this word refers to the Lord's physical coming to the earth. Actually, this Greek word refers to a "presence," not a "coming." This word does not refer to the Lord's physical appearing. That is the "manifestation" or "appearing" of His presence, to which the apostle Paul referred in 2 Thessalonians 2:8. Before His manifestation He is present, but in a hidden way. It is not until the Lord descends openly and physically to fight with the Antichrist that His presence is manifested.

Thus, the Lord's parousia does not refer simply to His physical coming to the earth, but to His particular presence in and with His people during the endtime. W.E. Vine, in his book *An Expository Dictionary of New Testament Words*, when commenting about the word parousia, says, "When used of the return of Christ, at the Rapture of the Church, it signifies, not merely His momentary coming for His saints, but His presence with them from that moment until His revelation and manifestation to the world." (p. 209)

The parousia begins with the rapture of the mature saints before the great tribulation (Matt. 24:39-42). At that time the Lord is present, but in a hidden way. Throughout the great tribulation the Lord's parousia continues, yet the Lord Himself remains hidden. He is only being manifested to and through His believers during their sufferings. His parousia continues through His descent to the air to meet with the saints. Yet, at that time He still remains hidden on a cloud, unseen by men on the earth (Rev. 14:14-16). Finally, after He has finished His dealing with the believers, the Lord will openly appear to the whole earth as He descends from the air to battle with the Antichrist and his armies (Rev. 19:11-16). The Lord's parousia concludes with His physical appearing, which Paul called "the manifestation of His presence." Thus, the Lord's parousia refers not to a single event but to a long period of approximately $3\frac{1}{2}$ years, during which the Lord's intensified presence is in and with the believers at the end of the age.

open, physical coming to the earth. Rather, it is His coming in secret to steal away those believers who have been watchful and who are ready for Him. No thief comes to steal away earthenware, dirty clothes, or common objects. Rather, the thief comes silently and quickly to take the precious and costly items. The Lord Jesus will come as a thief in the night to steal precious, transformed "jewels" from the earth. These "jewels" are those believers, who by watching and beholding the Lord, have been transformed into His image.[11] The transformed believers are extremely precious to God. He considers them costly stones for His building.[12]

The Lord's words in both Matthew 24, Luke 17, and Mark 13 are a strong and clear warning. These words should sober us and wake us out of any fantasy we might have concerning the rapture. We must all ask ourselves, "Am I a faithful believer watching, not only for the Lord, but also unto the Lord, readying myself for His return? Or, have I been slothful and lazy in seeking the Lord? Have I been fully transformed into something altogether precious to the Lord?[13] Or, am I still so 'muddy' and 'earthen' and made of so much 'clay'? Am I worthy to be stolen from the earth by the Lord as I am now?"

Standing Before the Son of Man

But take heed to yourselves, lest haply your hearts be overcharged with surfeiting, and drunkenness, and cares of this life, and that day come on you suddenly as a snare: for so shall it come upon all them that dwell on the face of all the earth. But watch ye at every season, making supplication, that ye may

---

It is true that the Lord is always with the believers (Matt. 28:20). However, quite often we have no sensation or realization of His presence. The disciples were frequently unaware of the Lord's presence with them after His resurrection (e.g., Lu. 24:13-31, 36). For the most part, the Lord is hidden today even to us believers. However, when the first matured saints are raptured and the tribulation starts, the Lord's presence with us will become very substantive. At that time the realization of His presence will be intense. Inwardly, the believers will burn with His presence, even as the Lord in loving care sustains them through all the desperate troubles of that time. This is the Lord's parousia.

prevail to escape all these things that shall come to pass, and to stand before the Son of man. (Luke 21:34-36)

In this portion of the Word, the Lord Jesus tells us that the great tribulation will come upon all those who dwell on the earth.* He also warns us, the believers, to be watchful and beseeching, that we might escape that time. If all the believers escape the tribulation by being raptured, then what need is there to be watchful and beseeching? What need is there to have a life in which we are constantly looking to the Lord in prayer? Many believers ignore these verses and assume that all Christians will escape the great tribulation. Consequently, many become preoccupied and even slothful. They rarely, if ever, look to the Lord to watch and behold Him, and are extremely short of prayer. However, according to these verses not all believers escape the tribulation—only those who are watchful, only those who are praying to prevail and overcome, will escape. In order to prevail to stand before the Son of Man and escape the tribulation, we must have a prayerful life through which every hindrance, obstacle, and blockage between us and the Lord is removed.

In our daily lives we are surrounded by evil things such as the world, the flesh, sin, self, and Satan. We certainly must overcome these to be qualified to stand before the Son of Man. But we are also surrounded by many good things such as moral causes, religious endeavors, spiritual seeking,† and even past, genuine experiences of Christ. We also must forget all these, and every positive or good thing‡ other than Christ Himself.[14] The believer who prevails leaves everything behind, whether good or bad, to seek Christ, behold Christ, and gain Christ.[15] Again we must ask ourselves, "Am I a watchful believer, constantly looking to the Lord? Am I one who is beseeching the Lord that I might

---

* In Luke 21:35 the word "it" refers back to the day (v. 34) of the Lord's judgment during the great tribulation (vv. 20-27).

† That is, seeking after spiritual things and matters other than Christ, things such as spirituality, spiritual knowledge, spiritual success, spiritual position, and the like.

‡ Even good things can distract us and keep us from Christ. It was for this reason that the apostle Paul said that he counted *all* things loss, even those that were gain to him, that he might gain Christ (Phil. 3:7-8).

prevail to stand before Him in that day? Or, am I one who lives a life with little prayer, a life of sloth, a life full of self and the world? Or, am I one who has cared about spiritual goals and spiritual attainments, but has not cared for the Lord Himself?" Once again the Lord's stern warning to us should sober us concerning the rapture. Not every Christian escapes that time of tribulation. Many are left to pass through it.

The Church in Philadelphia

Because thou didst keep the word of my patience, I also will keep thee from the hour of trial, that hour which is to come upon the whole world, to try them that dwell upon the earth. I come quickly: hold fast that which thou hast, that no one take thy crown. He that overcometh, I will make him a pillar in the temple of my God, and he shall go out thence no more: and I will write upon him the name of my God, and the name of the city of my God, the new Jerusalem, which cometh down out of heaven from my God, and mine own new name. (Revelation 3:10-12)

In chapters 2 and 3 of the book of Revelation, seven epistles are written to seven of the churches that were in Asia Minor at the time the Apostle John received this revelation.[16] It is clear, then, that these epistles were written to the believers, as the church is composed only of believers.[17] Those who are not the genuine, born-again children of God are not members of the church.* Furthermore, what was written in these chapters to each of the churches was written to *all* the churches. What was written to one church was written to all the believers in all the churches throughout all the ages. This is stated emphatically by the Lord

---

* Some say that the tares in Matthew 13, who are false believers, are part of the church. However, according to the Lord's own word, the field in which the tares were sown is the *world* (Matt. 13:24-25, 38). The false, nominal Christians are sown in the world, not in the church. The church is composed only of genuine believers in Christ.

seven times in these epistles by the words, *"He* who has an ear, let him hear what the Spirit says to the *churches."* [*] [18]

To the church in Philadelphia the Lord gives a particular promise: He will keep her out of the hour of trial coming upon the whole earth. No doubt the "hour of trial" refers to the last $3\frac{1}{2}$ years of this age. To be kept out of the hour of trial means to be kept, not from the trial itself, but from the *time* of trial. Therefore, those in whom this promise is fulfilled must be taken from the earth before the time of trial. Thus, these words indicate a pre-tribulation rapture for some of the believers.

Nevertheless, even to the church in Philadelphia there is a requirement. Not every believer in Philadelphia receives this reward. The Lord tells those of the church in Philadelphia, *"Hold fast* what you have that no one take your crown." It is possible to believe, yet lose the crown. It is possible to believe, yet not receive the reward. Not every believer shares the reward of a pre-tribulation rapture. Only those who have the ears to hear what the Spirit is saying to the churches hold fast their crown. Only these are taken from the hour of trial. The remaining ones are left to pass through the great tribulation.

What is it that the Lord appraises so highly in the Philadelphian church? For one thing, she had a little power.[19] The church in Philadelphia was not renowned for great works, miracles, or might. Rather, she had a *little* power. Do we have a little power? In much of Christianity today, great works are very highly regarded. Large numbers in meetings are greatly prized. Notoriety and success are avidly sought after. But the Lord *loves* the church that has only a *little* power! He treasures what is genuine and hidden. He appraises highly those who have, keep, and profitably use the little power He has given them, and who are not seduced by the enticement of greatness prevalent in today's religious world.

The church in Philadelphia also keeps the Lord's word, a word of endurance. Throughout all the trials, discouragements, problems, opposition, and seeming delay in the Lord's return, the

---

* There were not just seven churches in Asia Minor at that time. The seven were chosen by the Lord as representatives for *all* the churches. So the Lord says, "… what the Spirit says to the *churches.*" However, only some of the believers in the churches will hear the Lord's word, so He also says, *"He* who has an ear…"

church in Philadelphia keeps the Lord's word. This does not mean that these believers memorize the word. Neither does it mean that they simply obey the Lord's words as New Testament commandments. Rather, this refers to a change of nature in the heart of the believers through the living and indwelling word of God.[20] These believers are constantly fed by the word and thus become rich in it.[21] They treasure God's Word as they treasure the Lord Himself.[22] They do not put the words of any man on a pedestal. Rather, they are filled with the living word of God.

The church in Philadelphia also does not deny the Lord's name. These believers love the name of Jesus. They love the Person of Jesus. They love His presence. They love His shining. They love His inflowing and filling. They love to commune and fellowship with their dear Lord.[23] To them the most precious name, even the most precious word, in all the universe is "Jesus."[24] "Jesus" is on their tongues and in their hearts. They keep His name, not in a ritualistic, outward way, but practically in their daily life. They continually seek Him; they seek His Person. In particular they love Him in their midst. Their times together are times with Christ. Are we such ones, loving and keeping the Lord's Person, whether we are alone, with other believers, or in the world? Or do we put Him aside, even ignore Him? Perhaps to us He is on the outside, knocking on the door to get in (as He is to the church in Laodicea[25]), having been pushed out of our lives and gatherings by spiritual pride or Christless religious practices and endeavors.

One final, extremely important aspect of the church in Philadelphia is seen in her name. Philadelphia means "brotherly love."* The church in Philadelphia is the church of brotherly love. The believers who live in the divine reality live out the divine love toward the other believers.[26] They love the brothers and sisters even as Christ loves them.[27] We must ask ourselves, "Do I love the brothers and sisters even as God does? Or am I divided from others and sectarian? Am I closed to many Christians because of practices or doctrinal beliefs? Have I separated myself

---

* Philadelphia comes from the two Greek words "philos," meaning fond, and "adelphos," meaning brother. Thus it means "fond of the brethren" or "love of the brothers."

from others because of my personal preferences?" If we pray over all these matters, I believe the Lord will begin to enlighten us in our shortcomings and needs, and reveal our true spiritual condition that we might repent and come back to the Lord Himself and to what is in His heart.

The Firstfruits

And I saw, and behold, the Lamb standing on the mount Zion, and with him a hundred and forty and four thousand, having his name, and the name of his Father, written on their foreheads. And I heard a voice from heaven, as the voice of many waters, and as the voice of a great thunder: and the voice which I heard was as the voice of harpers harping with their harps: and they sing as it were a new song before the throne, and before the four living creatures and the elders: and no man could learn the song save the hundred and forty and four thousand, even they that had been purchased out of the earth. These are they that were not defiled with women; for they are virgins. These are they that follow the Lamb whithersoever he goeth. These were purchased from among men, to be the firstfruits unto God and unto the Lamb. And in their mouth was found no lie: they are without blemish. (Revelation 14:1-5)

And I saw, and behold, a white cloud; and on the cloud I saw one sitting like unto a son of man, having on his head a golden crown, and in his hand sharp sickle. And another angel came out from the temple, crying with a great voice to him that sat on the cloud, Send forth thy sickle, and reap: for the hour to reap is come; for the harvest of the earth is ripe. And he that sat on the cloud cast his sickle upon the earth; and the earth was reaped. (Revelation 14:14-16)

The 144,000 believers* depicted in Revelation 14:1-5 have been redeemed from the earth as firstfruits to God. These are ones

---

* Many Bible students and expositors confuse this group with the 144,000 mentioned in Revelation 7:1-8. In order to understand Revelation 14 properly we must see clearly that these are two separate groups of God's redeemed. Those mentioned in Revelation 7 are of Israel. Twelve thousand are sealed from

who are the first ripe among the harvest of the believers. They, through a lifelong process of growing in Christ, seeking and gaining Him, and living as a testimony to mankind, have ripened earlier than the majority of God's crop. These are the ones who are the closest to Christ's heart, who have come to know Him in the deepest and most intimate way. They follow Him wherever He may go, and through whatever experience He may lead them. Their heart is set solely on Him. Therefore, they are raptured to the heavenly Mount Zion to stand with the Lamb before the throne of God.

In Revelation 14 there is also another group of believers, referred to as the "harvest." This passage is a reference to Matthew 13. There the Lord Himself told us that the wheat of God's harvest were the sons of the kingdom growing on the earth until the time of the consummation of the age.[28] The very harvest of which the Lord Jesus spoke in Matthew 13 is shown here being reaped (that is, raptured) by the Lord.

In Revelation 14, between these two parts of the rapture, we see the Antichrist's persecution during the great tribulation. From the placement of the verses in Revelation 14, it is apparent that the firstfruits are taken before the persecution, suffering, and martyrdom that occur during the tribulation, while the harvest— the majority of the believers—is reaped at the very end of the tribulation.

---

each of the twelve tribes of Israel. They are on earth, as they receive the seal of the living God to protect them from harm during the great tribulation (Rev. 7:3; 9:4). Thus, this group of 144,000 refers to Jews who have been sealed by God prior to the great tribulation. They remain on earth during the last $3\frac{1}{2}$ years of this age as a testimony to the nation of Israel (Matt. 10:17-23).

The 144,000 in Revelation 14 are not Jews, but believers, since they follow the *Lamb* wherever He goes. They are not on earth, as they have been purchased *from* the earth. They are not from one country, Israel, but rather from the whole *earth*. They are not in Israel or anywhere else on earth. Rather, they are with the Lamb on the *heavenly* Mount Zion, before the throne of God. This is a completely different group of 144,000. One group is of Israel, the other is of the nations; one is on earth, the other is in the heavens; one is sealed to protect them during the great tribulation, the other is kept in the heavens from any kind of tribulation; one is a testimony to Israel in the endtime, the other has been brought to the heavens for the Father's satisfaction. These are two completely distinct and separate groups of 144,000.

This rapture of the believers is pictured in the Old Testament. There, the firstfruits of Israel's crop were brought to God in His house for His satisfaction before the time of the harvest.[29] The full harvest was reaped later, and was not brought into God's house. Similarly, the firstfruits in Revelation 14 are raptured to the heavens for the Father's satisfaction. However, the majority of the believers are not raptured to the heavens, but to the air. Christ, as the Son of Man, will descend *from* the heavens to the air near the end of the great tribulation.[30] At that point all the remaining believers will be caught up to the air to meet with Him.[31]

Both the firstfruits and the harvest are of the same crop. They share the same divine life and same divine nature of God.[32] Both are God's grain for God's satisfaction. However, one of the major differences between the two is that the firstfruits ripen earlier than the rest of the harvest. Because of this, the firstfruits are raptured to God's house in the third heavens before the tribulation, whereas the main harvest is caught up to God's "barn" in the air at the end of the tribulation.[33] Both the firstfruits and the harvest are raptured. However, they are not raptured at the same time, nor are they raptured to the same place.

Knowing these things, we all must examine ourselves in God's light by asking: "Am I properly growing in the Lord? Is He maturing in me? Is He maturing in me quickly enough? Am I one who follows the Lamb and nothing else? Am I living a life that affords the Lord all the opportunity He needs to purify my heart from so many other things?" May the Lord speak to us, that we might see the real meaning of our Christian life.

Two Categories

It is evident from so many passages in the Bible—some of which we have examined in this chapter—that the rapture is of two categories. The Lord stresses this matter again and again in the Word, in order that we might not be left under any kind of misconception. The first category consists of those believers who mature properly and overcome. Day by day they seek and pursue Christ to enjoy Him, gain Him, and possess Him. They stand against and overcome Satan, the world, and even their own selves, that God's kingdom might be brought to earth.[34] Consequently, they mature earlier than the majority of God's crop. As a reward to them for their lifelong seeking, diligence, faithfulness, and love they are raptured before the great tribulation. These dear ones, these *overcomers*, will be caught up to the heavens to be with Christ and to satisfy the Father. They will be saved from that time of trouble that is coming upon the whole earth.[35] There in the heavens, they will enjoy God and Christ for 3½ years in a particular, precious way.

The majority of believers fall into a second category. Rather than seek the Lord wholly, and lay down everything in order that they might gain Him, they pursue something other than Christ. They may pursue something humanly good, such as success in a job, earthly fame, or a pleasant family life, all of which are not necessarily sinful. They may even seek spiritual success, spiritual attainments, or religious fulfillment. But they do not seek Christ first.[36] They love something more than the dear Lord Jesus.[37] They seek something other than God. Some thing, some matter, or some person is more important to them than God and God's kingdom. Thus, these are defeated in their daily life. They are overcome and subdued by sin, the world, the flesh, the self, or some other item or situation in their daily lives, whether good or bad. Consequently, these dear and genuine believers in Christ will not be fully ripened by the time the great tribulation begins. When the mature saints are caught away to the heavens, the immature Christians will be left behind to pass through the great tribulation. This will be a time of great suffering, arranged by a wise God to help His dear children grow.

Revelation 14:14-16 speaks concerning the harvest of the majority of the believers. There it says that the harvest has become "ripe." The word "ripe" literally means "dry." It refers to the drying out of a green crop by the sun, that it might be ripened for the harvest. Just as the sun dries out the wheat in the field, so the heat of persecution and suffering during the great tribulation will dry out all the believers from the "water" of worldly pursuits. Everything of the world—whether a job, education, sports, amusements, family life, social life, or religious matters—will be "dried out" of the believers during that time. God will dry up *everything* during those years. The believers left on the earth to pass through that time of suffering will be left with Christ and Christ alone. By this, they will grow to maturity. At the end of the tribulation they, with the resurrected dead believers, will be raptured to the air to meet with Christ. There all the believers will stand before the judgment seat of Christ to give answer to Him for what they did during their Christian lives.* [38]

A Spirit of Sobermindedness

The rapture is not a simple matter. We all must be delivered from today's wrong teachings. There are many candy-coated doctrines designed to soothe the ears, yet they leave the hearers spiritually deadened and unmotivated to seek the Lord. Doctrines saying that once we believe in the Lord there is no further need to go on, to grow and mature in Christ, are misleading and deceiving. The rapture is a very serious and sobering matter. It is not an automatic trip away from the tribulation into some kind of golden mansion in heaven. In fact, the endtime will be a time of intense suffering to many genuine Christian believers. God's own children—those who have been genuinely born of Him—may indeed pass through the great suffering of the tribulation. The Bible tells us this clearly and emphatically. The Lord in His mercy makes these things known to us, that we might seek Him. His words should move us to repent from loving the world and so many other things. We all must repent to love the Lord Jesus alone. Eventually, by such a genuine seeking and sincere repentance, His words will issue in our seeking Him, resulting in the proper growth in life—growth of which we all are short. May the Lord grant us the ears to hear what the Spirit says in the holy Word.

---

* The matter of the judgment seat of Christ will be given more consideration in Chapter 8.

References

[1] Matt. 5:3

[2] 1 Thes. 4:13

[3] 1 Cor. 3:1

[4] 1 Thes. 2:7

[5] 1 Thes. 4:18

[6] 1 Cor. 15:35-54

[7] Matt. 24:15-22

[8] Matt. 24:36,42

[9] 1 Cor. 10:11

[10] Col. 4:11, 14; Acts 16:6-17; Lu. 1:3; cf. Acts 24:3; 26:25

[11] 2 Cor. 3:18

[12] 1 Pet. 2:5

[13] Rom. 12:2

[14] Phil. 3:7-15

[15] Phil. 3:8; 2 Cor. 3:18

[16] Rev. 1:4, 11

[17] 1 Cor. 1:2

[18] Rev. 2:7, 11, 17, 29; 3:6, 13, 22

[19] Rev. 3:8

[20] Jn. 5:38

[21] Col. 3:16

[22] Jn. 1:1

[23] 1 Cor. 1:9; 1 Jn. 1:3

[24] Phil. 2:9

[25] Rev. 3:20

[26] Jn. 13:35; 1 Jn. 4:7-8, 12

[27] 1 Jn. 4:9-11, 19

[28] Matt. 13:38

[29] Ex. 23:19

[30] 1 Thes. 4:16; Rev. 14:14

[31] 1 Thes. 4:17

[32] Jn. 3:16; 1:12-13; 2 Pet. 1:4

[33] Matt. 13:30; 1 Thes. 4:17

[34] Eph. 6:11; 1 Jn. 2:15; Lu. 14:26

[35] Matt. 24:40-41; Rev. 3:10

[36] Matt. 6:23; 10:37-39

[37] Rev. 2:4

[38] 2 Cor. 5:10

CHAPTER 4

The Change of the Age

The present age is the age of grace. The coming age is the age of the kingdom. In between these two ages is the 3½ year transitional period of the great tribulation. This transition is similar to the time when the Lord Jesus ministered on earth. Before His coming forth there was the age of law. After His resurrection, the dispensation had changed to the age of grace. Between these two ages were the 3½ transitional years of the Lord's ministry. By that 3½ years the Lord changed the age from the age of law to the age of grace. By the coming 3½ years of the great tribulation He will change the age from the age of grace to the age of the kingdom..

In addition, the present time is called the "day* of man."[1] It is man's day, the time in which man judges. God, in a very real sense, has given man a free hand to do as he wills on the earth. Though there are currently many natural calamities, tribulations, trials, and sufferings, these are not generally God's direct supernatural intervention. God has allowed man to do as he pleases, even to the point where the earth has become unspeakably sinful and violent. God has allowed rampant homosexuality, runaway violence, abuses of all kinds, inhuman cruelties, and an abounding indulgence in lust. Television and the present-day movie industry produce nearly nothing except that which glorifies sin—sin in violence, sin in lust, sin in all of its aspects. Yet, God remains silent and hidden. Even as the unbelievers declare "There is no God," God continues to work in a hidden way, desiring that all men might be saved and come to the full knowledge of the truth.[2]

---

* The word "day" in this context refers not to a physical 24-hour period, but rather to the current time in a general sense. For example, we may speak of the "fashions of the day," referring to the fashions of this current age or period of time.

When the great tribulation begins, the day of man will be over.[3] At that time God will intervene with supernatural judgments* to deal with sinful, evil mankind. It will no longer be man's day, but the "day of the Lord." At that time God will take His rightful position as Lord of all things, and judge all men on earth—the genuine believers, the false believers, the Jews, Christ's open opposers, and the unbelievers.† The coming of this great day has been prophesied repeatedly in both the Old and New Testaments.

The Proximity of Events

The beginning of this momentous change of age is marked by the occurrence of many great and awesome events. Sometimes these events occur simultaneously. Other times they follow one upon another, like dominoes falling in sequence. One striking thing about all these phenomenal happenings is that they occur within an extremely short period of time. It may be that all the events we are about to describe happen in one, two, or three days. This is both remarkable and sobering.

Joel 2:28-31 is a prophecy concerning the events immediately preceding the beginning of the great tribulation. If we compare this portion of the Word with Revelation 6:12-9:2, which details the beginning of the great tribulation, we will find some important similarities. Joel mentions blood, fire, and pillars of smoke, followed by the sun being darkened and the moon being turned to blood. The blood mentioned in Joel is similar to the blood of the first and second trumpets in Revelation.[4] The fire spoken of

---

* That these judgments will be supernatural does not mean that there will be no natural cause for them. Many, and perhaps even all, of the physical events during the tribulation may be traceable to natural occurrences. However, these judgments will be supernatural due to the time at which they occur and their precise duration, location, and extent. Thus, the great earthquake of the sixth seal may have a definable physical source. Yet, it is supernatural in that it happens exactly when it does, where it does, and to the extent that it does.

† At the end of the day of the Lord, which will occur immediately after the Millennium (2 Pet. 3:8-10), God will judge even the angels, the demons, the dead unbelievers, the nations on earth during the Millennium, death, Hades, and the whole universe as well (Rev. 20:9-21:1). Thus, the day of the Lord lasts a little more than one thousand years.

in Joel is similar to the fire of the first, second, and third trumpets in Revelation.[5] The pillars of smoke mentioned in Joel include part of the fifth trumpet in Revelation.[6] In Joel the sun is darkened and the moon is turned to blood.[7] These are aspects of the opening of the sixth seal in Revelation.[8] However, the happenings mentioned in Joel occur *before* the day of the Lord,[9] whereas the trumpets occur *during* the day of the Lord.[10] What Joel mentions should refer to the happenings at the time of the opening of the sixth seal, which is the precursor to and warning of the impending judgment of the day of the Lord. But the striking similarities of the events in Joel and Revelation are a strong indication that the sixth seal and the first five trumpets occur within a very short period of time.

A further indication of the proximity of events during this time is seen with the sealing of the 144,000 of Israel in Revelation 7.[11] This occurs immediately after the sixth seal is opened.[12] At that time, four angels are seen restraining the four winds of the earth. The Lord Jesus, shown as "another Angel,"[*] commands the angels not to harm the earth, the sea, or the trees until the 144,000 are sealed. The harm spoken of here is that which occurs in the first two trumpets. This indicates that the first and second trumpets occur shortly after the 144,000 are sealed. In addition, when the fifth trumpet sounds, an army of "locusts" will ascend from the abyss.[13] They will be able to hurt all men except those who do not have the seal of the living God—that is, except the sealed Jews. Thus, the first five trumpets must occur very shortly after the sealing of the 144,000 and the opening of the sixth seal.

In Matthew 24 and Luke 17 the Lord Jesus told us that the days prior to the great tribulation will be like the days of Noah and the days of Lot.[14] He says that shortly after Noah entered the ark, the flood of God's judgment came. On the very day that Lot came out of Sodom, the fire of God's judgment fell. The Lord likens these events to the rapture of the overcoming saints. The Lord says, in effect, that shortly after the rapture of the matured saints, the great tribulation as the flood of God's judgment will strike the earth. This shows us that the rapture of the matured

---

[*] Christ is called "another Angel" four times in the book of Revelation, in 7:2, 8:3, 10:1, and 18:1.

believers must occur somewhat prior to the beginning of the great tribulation.

Furthermore, in Revelation 12, the manchild[*] is raptured to God's throne.[15] Immediately after the rapture of the manchild, the woman flees to the wilderness for the 3½ years of the tribulation. In addition, at that time Satan with all of his evil angels are cast out of heaven.[16] However, at the sounding of the fifth trumpet this same Satan, having just fallen to earth, is seen opening the abyss to loose the army of "locusts."[17] This indicates that the rapture of the manchild is also prior to the sounding of the fifth trumpet and near the beginning of the great tribulation.

When all of these passages are taken together, we see that this short period will be a complex time in which many events occur to produce a change of age. Since many of these happen virtually simultaneously, it is not possible to give a precise, time-wise linear description of the beginning of the great tribulation. However, by presenting all the pieces of this "puzzle" it is possible to paint an accurate picture of what those days will be like.

The Fifth Seal

And when He opened the fifth seal, I saw underneath the altar the souls of them that had been slain for the word of God and for the testimony which they held. And they cried with a great voice, saying, How long, O Master, the holy and true, dost thou not judge and avenge our blood on them that dwell on the earth? And there was given to them to each one a white robe; and it was said unto them, that they should rest yet for a little time, until their fellow-servants also and their brethren, who should be killed even as they were, should have fulfilled their course. (Revelation 6:9-11)

As we saw in Chapter 2, the fifth seal occurs near the end of this age. When the Lord Jesus opens that seal, the souls of the martyred saints, who are being kept in the pleasant section of Hades until the time of their resurrection, cry out to God for

---

[*] This manchild refers to some of the dead overcoming saints. This is discussed in detail below.

vengeance. They are told to wait a little time until their number should be completed. God will answer their prayer for vengeance when the number of martyrs has been fulfilled. The answer to this prayer will be the great tribulation ending with the Lord's physical return to the earth to slaughter the Antichrist and all of his armies. Since the time from their cry until the Lord's return is said to be a "little while," this indicates that the fifth seal is opened sometime near the great tribulation. It is not possible to say exactly when this seal is opened; it may occur near the end of the first half of the final seven years of this age.

The Rapture of the Living Overcoming Saints

Then shall two men be in the field; one is taken and one is left: two women shall be grinding at the mill; one is taken and one is left. Watch therefore: for ye know not on what day your Lord cometh. (Matthew 24:40-42)

In that day, he that shall be on the housetop, and his goods in the house, let him not go down to take them away: and let him that is in the field likewise not return back. Remember Lot's wife. Whosoever shall seek to gain his life shall lose it: but whosoever shall lose his life shall preserve it. I say unto you, In that night there shall be two men on one bed; the one shall be taken, and the other shall be left. There shall be two women grinding together; the one shall be taken, and the other shall be left. There shall be two men in the field; the one shall be taken, and the other shall be left. (Luke 17:31-36)

But watch ye at every season, making supplication, that ye may prevail to escape all these things that shall come to pass, and to stand before the Son of man. (Luke 21:36)

Because thou didst keep the word of my patience, I also will keep thee from the hour of trial, that hour which is to come upon the whole world, to try them that dwell upon the earth. I come quickly: hold fast that which thou hast, that no one take thy crown. (Revelation 3:10-11)

And I saw, and behold, the Lamb standing on the mount Zion, and with him a hundred and forty and four thousand, having his

*name, and the name of his Father, written on their foreheads. ...
These are they that follow the Lamb whithersoever he goeth.
These were purchased from among men, to be the firstfruits unto
God and unto the Lamb. (Revelation 14:1, 4)*

It is possible that sometime near the opening of the fifth seal,
the rapture of the living matured saints occurs.* It is not possible
to ascertain exactly when this happens. The Lord Jesus Himself
told us that no man knows the day or the hour.[18] But it is clear
from many portions in the Word that this rapture occurs prior to
the great tribulation. It is also apparent from Matthew 24 and
Luke 17 that the great tribulation follows, if not immediately,
then very closely after this rapture.[19] Therefore, the living overcomers may be taken to the heavens close to the beginning of the
final 3½ years of this age. Remember: the Lord told us emphatically that the day Lot left Sodom the judgment by fire upon
Sodom occurred. Similarly, shortly after the living and overcoming saints are raptured, the judgment of the great tribulation
will begin.

This rapture should precede the opening of the sixth seal. The
sixth seal is the warning from God to those who dwell on the earth
that the great tribulation is about to begin. It could be considered
the initiation of the great tribulation. It certainly will be a time of
great suffering to mankind.† Since the Lord promised the overcomers in the church in Philadelphia that He would keep them
out of the time of trial that will come upon the whole inhabited
earth, it would seem that their rapture must occur before the sixth
seal.

In addition, as we have seen, the ones taken by the Lord at
this time have already fully ripened. Of what purpose would it
serve the Lord to leave them on the earth for the suffering of the
calamities of the sixth seal? Our God is in no way cruel. He only
assigns us what we need for our growth and maturity in life.
Furthermore, the sixth seal will be an event that shakes both the
heavens and the earth.[20] Every Christian passing through that time

---

* It is also possible that the rapture of those who have fully matured in Christ will
occur not only before the opening of the fifth seal, but even before the seven
year pact begins, for *no man knows the day or the hour!*

† See the section on the opening of the sixth seal below.

will know the great tribulation is starting. All Christians will certainly be desperate to seek the Lord by that time. Most saints will become diligent to watch for the Lord. Therefore, the rapture of the living overcomers, which catches many believers unawares, should precede the sixth seal. Furthermore, the fact that the saints are pictured* in the heavens immediately following the sixth seal seems to indicate that the rapture has already begun. Accordingly, it is our understanding that the Lord will take the living overcoming saints before the sixth seal is opened.

It is important to pay attention to the Lord's description of those days. He tells us that as it was in the days of Noah, so shall it be in the days of the coming of the Son of Man. They were eating, drinking, marrying, and giving in marriage until Noah entered the ark and the flood swept them away.[21] The Lord's words indicate that even by the time the great tribulation is about to begin, most of the people on the earth will not realize what is about to happen. They will continue to go about their human lives as if nothing were wrong. No doubt these people must include some believers. The one believer left in the field, the one left grinding at the mill, and the one left in the bed certainly had little, if any, realization and concern that the rapture was about to occur. Otherwise, they also would have been watching and ready. Therefore, in spite of the hardships and persecutions that occur during the first half of Daniel's seventieth week, many believers will still not be ready for the Lord's secret coming.

At that time the Lord will call all His dear saints to Himself. Some may be working; some may be sleeping; others may be involved in various matters. Whatever our situation might be, the Lord will call us to Himself. But who will respond to the Lord's call? Perhaps some will be watching television when the Lord Jesus calls. In their amusement they may not even recognize His beckoning word. Perhaps some will be at a sports event cheering

---

* The vision of the raptured saints in Revelation 7:9-17 is not an indication that *all* the believers are raptured at that time. We are expressly told at the opening of the seventh seal that saints still remain on the earth, praying (Rev. 8:1-4). Therefore, what this vision depicts is God's faithfulness to all of His children throughout their daily trials and during that future time of great tribulation. Their eternal state is fixed, no matter what they may pass through in their present life. However, it may also indicate that the rapture has already begun.

for their favorite team. Will they hear the Lord's gentle voice above the roar of the crowd? Perhaps a husband and a wife, both believers, will be arguing with each other. Could they perceive the Lord's word above their anger and animosity? Could they respond even if they heard? Perhaps some will be so engrossed with their job or some other matter that they simply do not care for the Lord's call. Instead, they might tell Him they do not have time for Him, that He should come back later. Perhaps some will be engaged in sinful activities. The Lord's word will certainly pass by many unheard.

The Lord strongly, urgently warns us about that time. He tells us to remember Lot's wife. At that time, if anyone of us would turn back to look at the world or our human involvements, it will be too late. We will be left to pass through the tribulation. If anyone of us would neglect the Lord's call for any reason, it will be too late. We will be left to endure the sufferings of the great tribulation. We will become a kind of "pillar of salt," as Lot's wife did. We will become a shame for not having been ready. One look away* from the Lord at that time will bring $3\frac{1}{2}$ years of enormous suffering.

Who will answer the Lord's call? No doubt it will be those who are always watching the Lord, looking away to Him, beholding and reflecting Him.[22] It will be those who are constantly in prayer, constantly beseeching to overcome in this age.[23] It will be those who—through a life of constantly contacting the Lord—know, hear, and respond to His voice. When the Lord says "Come," they simply come. All disobedience, rebellion, doubt, and condemnation will have been purged from them through the operation of God's divine life within them, in their constant experience of Christ throughout their lives. When He tells them to come, they—as His reflection—simply come.

In Revelation 14 the firstfruits are mentioned as being before the throne of God and before the Lamb on the heavenly Mount Zion. Yet, interestingly, there is no indication as to how they got there. There is no mention of their rapture. When the manchild is mentioned, his rapture is clearly indicated. But, in Revelation 14

---

* This looking away is an indication that this distracted believer is in need of further growth in life to reach maturity.

the firstfruits are simply there in the heavens with Christ. How did they get there? Why is their rapture not mentioned? It must be that these firstfruits live a life of such constant, intimate contact with Christ that they are every day already in the heavens with Him. The spiritual reality of their position in the heavenlies in Christ is their practical reality day by day.[24] In their experience they have, in the words of the Apostle, "entered within the veil."[25] They live a heavenly life on earth. Their rapture will come as no surprise to them. It will be merely a change in the position of their physical body. In experience, their inward being is already in the heavens with Christ. When the Lord calls these ones, their answer is an immediate and faithful, "Amen, Lord."

When the rapture of the living overcomers occurs, it should include at least some of the firstfruits in Revelation 14,[*] the overcoming saints in the church in Philadelphia, any overcoming saints in the church in Thyatira who are alive at the time of the Lord's coming, the ones taken in Matthew 24 and Luke 17, as well as those prevailing and accounted worthy to stand before the Son of Man in Luke 21. All the overcoming saints on earth will be transfigured and caught away. There likely will be some brief manifestation of glory as this event occurs.[26] This will greatly amaze not only the unbelievers, but also those believers who are left on the earth.

The Rapture of the Manchild

And a great sign was seen in heaven: a woman arrayed with the sun, and the moon under her feet, and upon her head a crown of twelve stars; and she was with child; and she crieth out, travailing in birth, and in pain to be delivered. And there was seen another sign in heaven: and behold, a great red dragon, having seven heads and ten horns, and upon his heads seven diadems. And his tail draweth the third part of the stars of heaven, and did

---

[*] From the first five verses in Revelation 14 it would seem that the firstfruits here are those who have made themselves eunuchs for the sake of the kingdom of the heavens (Matt. 19:12), and by living a life entirely focused upon the Lord, have matured early and fully to satisfy God. They are remarkable, and there is much to be gleaned from these verses. These firstfruits should be all those throughout the ages who have lived such a life.

cast them to the earth: and the dragon standeth before the woman that is about to be delivered, that when she is delivered he may devour her child. And she was delivered of a son, a man child, who is to rule all the nations with a rod of iron: and her child was caught up unto God, and unto his throne. (Revelation 12:1-5)

And I heard a great voice in heaven, saying, Now is come the salvation, and the power, and the kingdom of our God, and the authority of his Christ: for the accuser of our brethren is cast down, who accuseth them before our God day and night. And they overcame him because of the blood of the Lamb, and because of the word of their testimony; and they loved not their life even unto death. (Revelation 12:10-11)

In Revelation 12 we see a woman clothed with the sun, standing upon the moon, and having a crown of twelve stars. She brings forth a son who is to rule all nations with a rod of iron. Her manchild is caught up to God and God's throne. Who is this woman and who is her son?* This woman represents all of God's

---

* Over the past centuries there have been various views regarding the identity of the woman and manchild in Revelation 12. Some have held that the woman is Mary and that the child is Jesus. However, such an interpretation presents insurmountable difficulties. When was Mary ever clothed with the sun, or standing upon the moon, or crowned with stars? In addition, Jesus did not ascend to the heavens immediately after His birth, as depicted here. Furthermore, after Jesus ascended there is no record that Mary fled into the wilderness for 3½ years (cf. Rev. 12:6, 14). Consequently, this woman and child cannot be Mary and Jesus.

Another view is that the woman refers to Israel, and that the child then is also Jesus. However, this interpretation also presents great difficulties. After Jesus ascended to the heavens, Israel did not flee into the wilderness to be nourished for 3½ years. Neither was she kept from the face of the serpent (Rev. 12:14). In fact, about 38 years after the Lord's ascension Israel was utterly destroyed by Titus with his Roman armies. Therefore, this woman cannot refer to Israel.

Other expositors say that the woman refers to the earthly city of Jerusalem in Israel. This interpretation must also be discounted. In the book of Revelation Jerusalem has already been referred to as Sodom, Egypt, and the place where the Lord was crucified (Rev. 11:8). How could it be pictured so gloriously here?

A fourth view is that this woman is the church. While I would agree that the woman certainly includes the church, it cannot be that it solely consists of New Testament believers. As mentioned above, this woman's seed is said to consist

redeemed throughout all the ages. The New Testament saints are signified by the woman being clothed in the sun. In the New Testament Christ came as the light of life and the dayspring, the rising sun.[27] He is the true sun of righteousness.[28] We, the New Testament saints, enjoy this Christ as our covering, our robe by which we are justified before God.[29] Thus, as the woman is clothed with the sun, she includes all the New Testament believers.

The Old Testament saints are signified by the woman standing on the moon. In the Old Testament the law was given.[30] This law was not the reality, but rather a picture of the reality. The law was not God, but rather a picture of God, depicting God's nature. The law was a shadow of Christ, the reality Who was to come.[31] Similarly, the moon upon which the woman stands does not have any light of its own. Rather, it merely reflects the light of the sun.

---

of those who not only have the testimony of Jesus, but also keep the commandments of God. "Those who keep the commandments of God" does not refer to the members of the church, nor can it. In the Old Testament God's seeking saints were charged to keep the commandments. But in the New Testament Christ is the end of the law to all those that believe (Rom. 10:4). Today, the righteous live by faith, not by keeping the commandments (Rom. 1:17; Gal. 3:11; Heb. 10:38). The righteous requirement of the law is fulfilled, not by those who, through the flesh, attempt to keep the law, but rather by those who walk according to Spirit (Rom. 8:4). In the New Testament age the believers have something much higher, much greater than keeping the law. We express God Himself by walking according to the Spirit. Thus, we live Christ (Phil. 1:21). In our lives Christ is expressed and magnified (Phil. 1:20). Through such a living God is manifested in the church (1 Tim. 3:15-16). Since the law came from God and was according to God's nature, those who magnify Christ to express God by walking according to the Spirit not only fulfill the law spontaneously, but also live a life in which God Himself is seen. This is much higher than the living of the Old Testament saints. Such a life is depicted in Matthew 5-7 and was manifested by the Lord Jesus and the apostle Paul. Since the woman includes those who keep the commandments, she cannot be solely the church.

To understand this great sign, we must look back to the Old Testament. There, in Genesis 37, Joseph, the son of Jacob, had a dream. In it he saw the sun, moon, and eleven stars bowing down to do him homage. The sun signified Jacob; the moon signified Leah, Jacob's wife (Rachel, Jacob's second wife, had died by that time); the eleven stars signified Joseph's brothers. Together, these composed the totality of God's called-out people. In the same principle, the woman in Revelation 12 should also signify the totality of God's people. This woman must be the body of all God's redeemed, including both Old Testament and New Testament saints.

The woman standing on the moon,[*] then, indicates that she includes the Old Testament saints.

The patriarchs, who were God's people living before the law was given, are signified by the woman being crowned with twelve stars.[†] Before the moon rises, it is the stars that give light to the earth. Similarly, before the law was given, it was the patriarchs who illuminated the world. Thus the stars crowning the woman signify that the woman includes God's people in the time of the patriarchs.

If the woman in Revelation 12 signifies all of God's redeemed people throughout the ages, who then does her son signify? Since the woman is corporate, composed of many people, the manchild to whom she gives birth must also be corporate, composed of many people. The manchild does not signify an individual person. Rather, he signifies a particular, stronger part of the woman. The manchild is composed of certain overcoming saints within the body of all God's redeemed, who own a particular function in the Body of Christ.

The reference to a *man* born of a woman indicates that this corporate entity must be a stronger part of the woman. Not all of God's people are strong. There are many examples in the Bible showing that some of God's people are weak. In the New Testament consider the Corinthians. Paul called them fleshly, carnal.[32] Were they weak or strong? Surely we must deem them extremely weak. Consider the babes to whom Paul referred in Ephesians 4.[33] These were tossed by every wind of teaching. Were they weak or strong? Since they were being tossed, they certainly were weak. As a third example, consider those in Asia Minor who left the Apostle Paul's ministry.[34] These were deceived and seduced to turn away from the suffering Apostle. Surely these also were weak in the faith. However, only the strongest part of God's people are part of the manchild.

---

[*] Here, in this sign, the woman *stands* on the moon, signifying that God's people are justified before God by the righteous requirement of the law being fulfilled (which was accomplished by Christ's death on the cross).

[†] The twelve stars should be a reference to the twelve sons of Israel who represent all the patriarchs.

That the believers who constitute the manchild are overcomers is made clear by Revelation 12:11. There the manchild is referred to as "they" who "overcame." They overcame the devil with all his wiles, all his temptations, all his attacks, and all his frustrations. They overcame by the blood of the Lamb. They know the power of the blood of Christ for forgiveness before God and for protection against their enemy's accusation. They also overcame the evil one by the word of their testimony. They did not keep silent, nor use their mouth for vain talking or foolish jesting. Their voice was used to testify Christ, minister Christ to others, and speak the living word of God.

These overcoming saints also did not love their life* even unto death. The mention of the word "death" here indicates that those who are part of this manchild have died physically. It also indicates that their soul-life was daily on the cross with Christ. They did not live for their own pleasure or gratification; they did not care for themselves or their own exaltation. Rather, they allowed the cross of Christ, as conveyed by and experienced through His Spirit, to touch them, operate within them, and put them fully to death.[35] By such an experience, Christ Himself lived in them, and was expressed and magnified through them.[36]

Finally, these overcomers have a particular function. When God first created man, He gave man dominion over all the earth.[37] However, man was seduced by the serpent and fell.[38] By this fall, man gave up his dominion to the evil one, Satan.[39] However, God still requires a man through which he can administrate the earth— and He requires not an individual man, but a race of men, a corporate man.[40] Jesus in resurrection was the first of this new race, this "second" man who replaces the fallen first man, the Adamic race.[41] The overcoming saints in Revelation 12 are also part of this second man, and are called the manchild just as Christ was.[42] This manchild has a particular function, to meet a particular need for God. Through the particular portion of Christ they enjoyed in their life on earth and in their human experiences, the overcomers of the manchild were constituted in a certain way to serve as the core of Christ's administration, to carry out God's will

---

* "Life" here refers to the life of the human soul, as opposed to the life of the physical body.

and purpose on the earth. As such, they should form the very heart of Christ's army and take the lead to defeat God's enemy, Satan.

Shortly after the rapture of the living overcomers, the manchild will be resurrected* and raptured to the throne in the heavens. In 1 Thessalonians 4 we are told that the resurrected believers are caught up to the *air* to meet with the Lord.[43] Since the manchild is raptured to the throne of God†, this shows that those in the manchild are not part of the majority of the believers referred to in 1 Thessalonians. Furthermore, since the woman in Revelation 12 flees into the wilderness to be nourished there for the 3½ years of the tribulation *after* the rapture of the manchild, the manchild must be resurrected and taken immediately before the tribulation, near in time to the rapture of the living overcomers.

The manchild, then, is composed of believers who were faithful to the Lord unto death. Not only were they faithful unto their own physical death, but they were faithful to allow the Lord to put their souls to death in their daily lives. By such an operation of Christ within them, they matured during their time on earth. Thus, they will be rewarded with an early, special resurrection and rapture to be with the Lord in the heavens. How many of us would be counted by the Lord to be in this category today? How many of us experience the cross of Christ throughout our daily lives? How many of us allow the cross to touch all of our being, including our deepest and most hidden parts?

---

* Resurrection is indicated here by the woman giving birth. Resurrection is a kind of birth. The Lord Jesus, before He died, referred to His resurrection as a birth (Jn. 16:21). Furthermore, in Acts 13:33 Peter said that the day of resurrection was the day on which Christ was begotten. It was then that God told Jesus, "You are My son. Today I have begotten You." (Heb. 1:5) Resurrection, as a kind of birth, is another indication that the manchild consists of believers who have died.

† This manchild is caught up to the throne of God from where he will rule all the nations. In Revelation 2-3 the Lord promised the overcomers in the churches, particularly the overcomers of the church in Thyatira, that they will sit with Him on His throne and rule all nations with a rod of iron (Rev. 2:26-27). During the Millennium all the overcoming saints will share Christ's throne and reign with Him as a reward to them for their overcoming life (Rev. 20:4). Thus, these other portions in Revelation corroborate that the manchild is indeed composed of overcoming believers.

Satan Cast out of Heaven

And she was delivered of a son, a man child, who is to rule all the nations with a rod of iron: and her child was caught up unto God, and unto his throne. And there was war in heaven: Michael and his angels going forth to war with the dragon; and the dragon warred and his angels; And they prevailed not, neither was their place found any more in heaven. And the great dragon was cast down, the old serpent, he that is called the Devil and Satan, the deceiver of the whole world; he was cast down to the earth, and his angels were cast down with him. (Revelation 12:5, 7-9)

The overcoming saints, depicted by the manchild, loved the Lord unto death. In addition, they also have been constituted fighters for Christ's army. These overcomers not only love Christ to the uttermost, but also hate Satan to the uttermost. They do not countenance his doings, his speakings, his frustrations, or his interference. They overcame *the accuser*. By and during their daily lives they were constituted in a certain way. Thus God resurrects and raptures *these* believers for a particular purpose. When these overcoming saints are raptured to the heavens they will see the real situation there. They will see that Satan still has access to God.* When they see Satan in the heavens they will not tolerate it. As those who share the Lord's own authority and position (as indicted by their being caught up to God's *throne*) they will command Satan to be cast out of the heavens. It is just this command from His corporate body that the Lord has awaited these past two thousand years.

---

* It is evident from a number of passages in the Bible that Satan has direct access to God, even though he has openly rebelled against Him. In Job 1:6-12; 2:1-7 and Zechariah 3:1-2 God and Satan converse directly. In Luke 10:18 the Lord Jesus told His disciples, after He sent them out to preach the gospel, that He was watching Satan fall from heaven. Though some amount of God's judgment upon the rebellious Satan was carried out at that time through the 70 disciples, Satan still has had access to God throughout the New Testament age, as indicated in Revelation 12 where he is shown accusing the Christian brothers before God day and night (v. 10). It is not until the beginning of the great tribulation that Satan is cast fully from heaven and denied access to God forever. During the millennial kingdom he will be bound with a chain in the abyss (Rev. 20:1-3). After the Millennium he will be cast into the lake of fire for eternity (Rev. 20:7-10). Hallelujah!

At that time a great war will occur in the heavens. Michael and the other faithful angels will follow the command to cast Satan out. Satan, with that third of the angels who followed him in his rebellion, will fight to maintain his position in the heavens. But there will be no place found for him. Satan will be cast with his followers to the earth, where his sphere of activity will be greatly limited. Woe to the earth at that time because of the great wrath of the evil one, Satan, who will know that he has but a short time before he is chained and bound in the abyss for the Millennium.[44]

The Opening of the Sixth Seal

And I saw when he opened the sixth seal, and there was a great earthquake; and the sun became black as sackcloth of hair, and the whole moon became as blood; and the stars of the heaven fell unto the earth, as a fig tree casteth her unripe figs when she is shaken of a great wind. And the heaven was removed as a scroll when it is rolled up; and every mountain and island were moved out of their places. And the kings of the earth, and the princes, and the chief captains, and the rich, and the strong, and every bondman and freeman, hid themselves in the caves and in the rocks of the mountains; and they say to the mountains and to the rocks, Fall on us, and hide us from the face of him that sitteth on the throne, and from the wrath of the Lamb: for the great day of their wrath is come; and who is able to stand? (Revelation 6:12-17)

And I will show wonders in the heavens and in the earth: blood, and fire, and pillars of smoke. The sun shall be turned into darkness, and the moon into blood, before the great and terrible day of Jehovah cometh. (Joel 2:30-31)

At the time that Satan is being cast to the earth, the Lord Jesus in the heavens will open the sixth seal. This seal will mark the beginning of the supernatural calamities that are to strike the earth during the endtime. As the start of God's judgment upon the sinful, evil mankind, the sixth seal will announce the impending great tribulation. It will be a warning to mankind that the great tribulation is about to begin.

The opening of the sixth seal will be signaled by two major events—one on the earth, the other in the heavens. The first will be a great earthquake, one that is unprecedented in human history. The second will be accompanying signs in the heavens. Concerning the great earthquake that will strike the earth at this time, the Word of God tells us that every mountain and island will be moved out of their places. We cannot begin to imagine the enormity of such a quake. To date, every temblor experienced by man has produced localized damage. Even the largest of earthquakes in human history have struck but an extremely small percentage[*] of the earth's surface. The earthquake recorded in Revelation 6 will shake the *whole* earth. Such a quake is beyond human experience, and unfathomable to us at this time.

When some readers of the Bible come to this portion of the Word, they gloss over the description of the sixth seal, assuming that the event described here will simply be another big earthquake. They may not realize that it will be something supernatural, the result of the Lord's direct intervention for His judgment upon mankind. This earthquake should not be compared to any others that men have experienced. It will be in another class altogether. This temblor will be so enormous, so great, that it may very well outrange scientists' seismometers. It could measure 11 or even more on the Richter scale.[†]

By experience we know that a large earthquake may last a minute or so. Thus, the duration of most earthquakes is relatively short. However, the duration of the great earthquake of the sixth seal will very likely be quite long. It may last for a number of hours. It may cascade around the earth, as one initial, immense upheaval gives rise to a rapid succession of violent convulsions across the face of the earth, spreading in a kind of chain reaction. The massive forces released as earth's huge tectonic plates suddenly shift will trigger a worldwide cataclysm, as the whole of the earth's crust experiences this tumultuous shaking. No part

---

[*] Perhaps somewhere in the neighborhood of one or two ten-thousandths of the earth's surface.

[†] On the Richter scale, 11 is about 300 times stronger than the largest recorded earthquake to strike North America, which occurred in Alaska in 1964, and about 10,000 times stronger than the earthquake that rocked San Francisco and the Bay Area in 1989.

of the earth will be left untouched. This quake should also be accompanied by numerous huge and brutal aftershocks. According to the book of Revelation, the earth's surface will tremble again and again until the Lord's return at the end of the tribulation.

An earthquake of this magnitude will unquestionably give rise to great cracks in the earth's crust. Even relatively small quakes create fissures in the earth's surface. With this supernatural judgment, the earth's surface will no doubt split open in countless places. It is extremely likely that volcanoes in many areas will become active, erupting in seething fury.

In addition, great tsunamis from the upheavals taking place under the sea could devastate shorelands. The eruption of Krakatoa in 1883, with the accompanying collapse of its volcanic dome, created a tsunami with waves that were felt world-wide. How much *more* will the great earthquake of the sixth seal generate immensely destructive tsunamis.

The damage from this earthquake will be both immense and global. The destruction will be incalculable monetarily. The deaths and injuries from such a massive temblor may be nearly innumerable. Perhaps tens millions of people or more will die in this judgment. In the Pacific rim alone the losses will be staggering. This area is called the Ring of Fire* by seismologists, because more than half of the earth's approximately 500 active volcanoes are located here. In addition, most of the epicenters of the world's earthquakes are located along this rim. Coincidentally, a large number of the earth's great population centers are also found along this ring. Santiago, Lima, Caracas, Mexico City, San Diego, Los Angeles, San Francisco, Seattle, Tokyo, Osaka, Seoul, Taipei, Manila, Hong Kong, Bangkok, Singapore, Jakarta, and many other great metropolitan areas lie within this danger zone. The population of these areas alone is over 100 million. The total population in the areas along this Ring of Fire may approach one billion. The losses suffered there will probably be unimaginable. The densely populated regions near the great

---

* The Ring of Fire runs through the Andean arc from Chile to central Mexico, up the west coast of North America and through the Cascades, across to Japan and the islands off the eastern coast of Asia, through Southeast Asia including Malaysia and Indonesia, then on down to New Zealand.

fault lines running through central Asia, the Middle East, and southern Europe should also experience enormous upheaval resulting in untold death, injury, and damage. It is difficult to describe the magnitude of the catastrophe that will strike the earth at that time.

This massive earthquake will be accompanied by four spectacular signs in the heavens—the sun will be darkened, becoming as black as sackcloth; the moon will turn red like blood; the earth will be struck by a great meteor shower; and finally, the sky will be removed like a scroll being rolled up. How is it possible for the sun to be darkened, and yet the moon give light? Since the moon simply reflects the sun, this must indicate that the sun itself will not be damaged during the sixth seal. Rather, it must be that the earth's atmosphere will be harmed in some way. It is probable that the sky will be completely blanketed by the soot and ash spewing forth into the atmosphere from the great earthquake and accompanying volcanic eruptions.* The many pillars of smoke mentioned in Joel 2 also indicate this. The sky will be blackened by the great upheavals happening on the earth.

At the same time, the moon will be turned to blood. While the sun is darkened, the moon will still give some light. Thus, the moon at that time should be on the horizon, while the sun should be opposing it on the other horizon. The smoke billowing forth from the earth and spreading throughout the atmosphere will not yet have covered the entire sky. The horizon, though not fully blanketed, will have been damaged enough to cause the moon to turn blood-red in color. Both these signs (along with the pillars of smoke) will be visible in the sky over the nation of Israel, as indicated by the context† of their description in Joel 2.

At the same time, a massive meteor shower will strike the earth. Stars will fall in the sky from every direction. A great storm of rocks will pummel the earth. The earth's sky will be aglow with shooting stars. It is possible, indeed likely, that some of these will strike the earth with enormous force, causing still further destruction and damage beyond that of the great earth-

---

* See the Appendix for further detail about this event.

† The context of these signs in Joel 2 is the outpouring of the Spirit upon the Jews in Israel.

quake.* Furthermore, as these meteors ablate in the atmosphere they will add to the ash blanketing the sky.

In addition, the heavens, or sky, will be rolled up like a scroll. This should be the result of the soot and smoke spreading in the atmosphere. As the cloud of ash rapidly expands across the sky, the heavens will appear to be rolled up like a scroll.

An asteroid or comet could cause the type of events recorded in the sixth seal.† The collision of a small heavenly body like an asteroid or comet with the earth would trigger enormous earthquakes worldwide. In addition, huge amounts of debris would be expelled upward. This debris would then reenter the atmosphere causing an enormous shower of "stars." The end result would be the sky appearing to be rolled up by the soot and ash enveloping at least a section of the earth.

Revelation also records the reaction of men to God's supernatural intervention to judge the earth. All people—whether the stately kings, the proud great men, the powerful generals, the high-class rich, the brave, the strong, the lowly, or the commoner, no matter what kind of person—all will be terrified and flee into the caves‡ and rocks, seeking some kind of protection and security. Every person on the face of the earth will be humbled, brought low, and terrified by the beginning of God's judgment. They will cry out to the mountains and to the rocks to fall upon and kill them, that they might be hidden from God's face and Christ's wrath.§ They will begin to realize that the time of God's judgment has come.

---

* It may be that the impact from one or more of these meteors precipitates the great earthquake of the sixth seal.

† See the Appendix for more detail about this possibility.

‡ It is interesting that caves, especially those located in bedrock, are a much safer haven than man-made structures during an earthquake.

§ It is probably at this point that the angel preaching the eternal gospel, as recorded in Revelation 14:6-7, will tell men to fear God, for the hour of His judgment has come. Men will therefore attribute the coming destruction to God's judgment. However, here the Word records the people of the earth saying that the wrath of the *Lamb* has come. How is it that the earth's populace will attribute the judgment of the sixth seal to God *and* Jesus? Most people are unbelieving—denying Christ, His redemptive death, and His death-overcoming

The Sealing of the 144,000 from Israel

After this I saw four angels standing at the four corners of the earth, holding the four winds of the earth, that no wind should blow on the earth, or on the sea, or upon any tree. And I saw another angel ascend from the sunrising, having the seal of the living God: and he cried with a great voice to the four angels to whom it was given to hurt the earth and the sea, saying, Hurt not the earth, neither the sea, nor the trees, till we shall have sealed the servants of our God on their foreheads. And I heard the number of them that were sealed, a hundred and forty and four thousand, sealed out of every tribe of the children of Israel: (Revelation 7:1-4)

And it shall come to pass afterward, that I will pour out my Spirit upon all flesh; and your sons and your daughters shall prophesy, your old men shall dream dreams, your young men shall see visions: and also upon the servants and upon the handmaids in those days will I pour out my Spirit. (Joel 2:28-29)

On the day of Pentecost, Peter and the other apostles stood to announce the gospel to the people of Jerusalem.[45] He declared that what the people were seeing and hearing was what was spoken of by Joel the prophet, quoting Joel 2:28-32. He told the men assembled there that the Spirit about which Joel spoke was being poured out on that day. However, Peter did not say that Joel's prophesy was fulfilled. In fact, all the signs mentioned in Joel did not occur on the day of Pentecost. There were no signs in the heavens and the earth—no blood, fire, or vapor of smoke. The complete fulfillment of these verses awaits a coming day. Indeed, Joel tells us specifically that the outpouring of which he spoke and the signs about which he prophesied would occur immediately prior to the great and terrible day of the Lord. The day of Pentecost was a partial, incomplete fulfillment of this

---

resurrection. It may be that during the beginning of Daniel's seventieth week the strong among God's people trumpet the coming judgment of God during the great tribulation and, in particular, the earthshaking events of the sixth seal. Therefore, when this earthquake happens, it will come as a fulfillment to the prophesying of many of the Lord's servants. They will predict this event as the beginning of Christ's dealing with the evil world. When it comes to pass, the people on the earth will therefore attribute it to God and to Christ.

prophecy, a small foretaste of what will happen before the day of the Lord.

The Bible records two great outpourings upon Israel in the last days. The first of these, recorded in Joel 2, will come immediately before the great tribulation. It is called the "former rain"—the rain that falls at the beginning of the agricultural year.[46] The second outpouring is recorded in Zechariah 12.[47] This will come at the very end of the great tribulation. It is called the "latter rain"—the rain that falls immediately before the harvest. It is through these two outpourings that the Lord Jesus will bring all Israel to salvation, fulfilling the Apostle Paul's word in Romans, "And thus all Israel will be saved."[48]

Immediately before the great tribulation, the Holy Spirit* will be outpoured upon many within the Jewish nation. Some will see

---

* How crucial this Spirit is to God's move on the earth. Without the Spirit, God could not have accomplished any of what He has accomplished. This Spirit, as the Spirit of God, brooded over the waters of the pre-adamic earth during God's preparation for the creation of man. (Gen. 1:2) This Spirit, as the Spirit of Jehovah, came upon many of the Old Testament saints in God's move to prepare the nation of Israel for His incarnation. (Judg. 3:10, 6:34, 11:29, etc.) This Spirit was present in the speaking of the Old Testament prophets, who foretold both the sufferings and glory of the coming Christ. (1 Pet. 1:11) This Spirit, as the Holy Spirit, acted to beget Christ through the incarnation, and was within Christ throughout His life and upon Him during His ministry. (Luk. 1:35, 4:18-21) This Spirit, as the eternal Spirit, was in and with Christ during His sufferings and crucifixion. It was through such a Spirit that Christ offered Himself to God. (Heb. 9:14) This Spirit was within Christ during His death, enlivening Him and becoming resurrection to Him. (1 Pet. 3:18) It was this Spirit that Christ Himself became in His resurrection, that He might give life to all of those who believe into Him. (1 Cor. 15:45; 2 Cor. 3:17) This Spirit, who in the New Testament is the Spirit of the incarnated, crucified, resurrected, and ascended Christ, has been breathed into Christ's believers to be their life, and poured out upon them to be their power. (Jn. 19:22; Luk. 24:49; Acts 1:8, 2:2-4) As the sanctifying Spirit He separates the unbelievers from the world, their environment, and even themselves, that they might believe into Christ. (1 Pet. 1:2) This begetting Spirit regenerates everyone who receives Him that they might be born of God to become God's children. (Jn. 3:5-6) This Spirit, as the Lord Himself, joins Himself to the believers spirit that the two might become one spirit. (1 Cor. 6:17) As the Spirit of Christ He indwells the believers, imparting Himself as life and resurrection into them. (Rom. 8:11) To them He is the renewing, sanctifying, and transforming Spirit, that all their inward being might be made like the Lord Himself. (1 Cor. 3:18) He is the Spirit of Jesus Christ to be the

visions; others will dream dreams. At that time Joel's prophecy will be completely fulfilled. Many of the Jews in Israel will open to experience the outpoured Spirit. They will be convicted concerning their sinfulness in their rejection of Jesus, and, repenting, they will call upon His name for salvation.[49] In all, 144,000 Jews will be sealed.

The Spirit will operate in an intensified way to prepare these 144,000 for the impending day of the Lord. The great signs in the heavens and the earth recorded in Joel will accompany this outpouring, as depicted in the sixth seal and the first five trumpets of God's judgment upon the earth. It may be that the great shaking of the earth during the sixth seal will in some way help to bring these 144,000 Jews to the Lord.

Who are these sealed from among the tribes of Israel? We should not think that they will be great gospel preachers sent out into all the earth to save the Gentiles before the Lord's return. This is a wrong understanding. Paul told us clearly that hardness in part had come upon Israel *until the fullness of the Gentiles comes in.*[50] Over the ages, Israel as a whole has remained hardened, and will continue to be until all the predestinated Gentiles are saved. At that time the fullness of the Gentiles will have come in, and God will turn from the Gentiles back to Israel. This return to Israel will be marked by the sealing of the 144,000. At that time, God's dealing to bring the unbelieving Gentiles to salvation will be over.

Who then are these redeemed from Israel? It is these who will remain on the earth during the time of the great tribulation, as a

---

bountiful supply to the believers during the trials of their daily life. (Phil. 1:19) In the book of Revelation He has become the seven Spirits—the seven-fold intensified/amplified Spirit—to enable the believers to overcome the degradation of the church during this age. (Rev. 1:4) It is this Spirit who is the essence of the Body of Christ, and the One in whom we are all baptized. (Eph. 4:4; 2 Cor. 12:13) This Spirit, called "the Spirit," becomes in the believers rivers of living water flowing out of their innermost being, and who with the bride calls whosoever will to come and freely drink! (Jn. 7:37-39; Rev. 22:17) Eventually, it is this Spirit who conforms the believers to the image of the Firstborn Son of God, even transfiguring their mortal body into a body like His own. (Rom. 8:23-29) It is such a wonderful, marvelous, mysterious, complete, and bountifully rich Spirit, who has passed through so many processes, who is everything to God's move on the earth to accomplish His eternal purpose according to His heart's desire.

testimony to the whole nation of Israel. They will pass throughout the whole country, city by city, announcing to the Jews who are still in unbelief Christ's incarnation, life on the earth, vicarious death, regenerative resurrection, transcendent ascension, presence with them as the Spirit, and impending physical return to the earth* to usher in the kingdom of the Messiah.†[51] That tribulation will be a time of great suffering to Israel in particular, during which two thirds of the Jews will die.[52] Yet Christ will bring the remaining third through the fire to salvation at the time of His return.[53] The 144,000 will prepare the hearts of these Jews to receive their Lord.

Given the extraordinary hardness of heart among most Jews, and their extreme animosity toward Christ, it is hard to believe that even 100 Jews could be saved in Israel at any one time. Indeed, the extremely religious, yet Christ-denying orthodox Jews do all that is in their power to keep the gospel from the Israeli people. This is as it was in the Lord's time on the earth, when the extremely religious Pharisees sought to silence Christ in every way possible. How then could 144,000 Jews be saved in Israel? This is not yet known, but our God has a way. What He has spoken will be fulfilled.

During the 3½ years preceding the great tribulation, Israel will once again begin to worship God according to the Levitical law. The sacrifices and offerings will have begun.[54] The yearly festal celebrations—the feasts of Passover, Pentecost, and Tabernacles—will await the completion of the rebuilding of the temple, which should occur immediately before the beginning of the great tribulation. It may be that around the time one of these feasts is to first be celebrated, perhaps the Passover, the sixth seal will be opened while numerous Jews are in Jerusalem. Many among them—old ones, young ones, men and women—will have been prepared for this time through the Spirit's operation in visions and dreams. The signs spoken of by Joel will occur before their

---

* These are, of course, the great and important points of the gospel. It was of these the apostles spoke, as shown in Acts 2:14-36 and in their epistles.

† The kingdom of the Messiah (2 Sam. 7:13; Acts 1:6) will be the earthly part of the millennial kingdom, which will be the kingdom of God during the one thousand-year reign of Christ in which He will restore the earth to its proper state.

eyes, astounding them, perhaps confirming the visions and dreams. In some way the Spirit will gather them to hear the gospel, as He did in the apostles' day.[55] At that time the 144,000 will be convicted, and, repenting, they will be saved and sealed for the time of the end.

This event marks a great change of age. When the Lord was on the earth He told the Jews that *their* house was left to them desolate.[56] God had left the nation of Israel. From that time forward, the testimony of Jesus was given to the church. It was the church that was to bear Christ's expression and manifest Him to the earth. Furthermore, this church would be primarily composed of non-Jews. Indeed, Paul said, "From henceforth I go to the Gentiles."[57] But at the very point in time when the 144,000 Jews are sealed, the age changes. The testimony of Jesus passes from the church back to the Jews. Once again the responsibility for bearing the expression of all God is to the world will rest with Israel.

The Death and Rising Again of the Antichrist

And I saw one of his heads as though it had been smitten unto death; and his death-stroke was healed: and the whole earth wondered after the beast... and there was given to him a mouth speaking great things and blasphemies; and there was given to him authority to continue forty and two months. (Revelation 13:3, 5)

And he deceiveth them that dwell on the earth by reason of the signs which it was given him to do in the sight of the beast; saying to them that dwell on the earth, that they should make an image to the beast who hath the stroke of the sword and lived. And it was given unto him to give breath to it, even to the image to the breast, that the image of the beast should both speak, and cause that as many as should not worship the image of the beast should be killed. (Revelation 13:14-15)

When therefore ye see the abomination of desolation, which was spoken of through Daniel the prophet, standing in the holy place (let him that readeth understand)... for then shall be great trib-

ulation, such as hath not been from the beginning of the world until now, no, nor ever shall be. (Matthew 24:15, 21)

At some point prior to the beginning of the great tribulation, the Antichrist will be slain by the sword. Nevertheless, he will be revived. His resuscitation will cause the whole world to marvel after him and admire him. This will be the devil's imitation of Christ's resurrection. The Antichrist's coming will be according to Satan's operation, with all the power and signs and wonders of a lie.[58] The beginning of these signs and wonders is the Antichrist's resuscitation. After reviving, the Antichrist will continue forty-two months, precisely the time of the great tribulation. Therefore, his death should precede the great tribulation by some short period of time, while his rising from death should occur at its very beginning.

Shortly after he is revived, the Antichrist, through the hand of the "false prophet," will erect an image of himself* in the temple, thus profaning it.[†] [59] This will be the abomination of desolation spoken of by Daniel the prophet.[60] This event will mark the beginning of the tribulation to the Jews.[61]

The Eternal Gospel

And I saw another angel flying in mid heaven, having eternal good tidings to proclaim unto them that dwell on the earth, and unto every nation and tribe and tongue and people; and he saith with a great voice, Fear God, and give him glory; for the hour of his judgment is come: and worship him that made the heaven and the earth and sea and fountains of waters. (Revelation 14:6-7)

According to Revelation 14:7, about this time God will send an angel to preach the eternal gospel from mid-heaven[‡] to every man and woman upon the earth—to every nation, tribe, tongue, and people. The angel will tell men to fear God and give Him

---

* This image will be far more than a statue. See the book *The Beast, His Image, and His Mark* for more about this image.

† This, with some other verses (e.g., 2 Thes. 2:3-4; Rev. 12:18-13:1), may indicate that the Antichrist will be slain and revived in Israel.

‡ That is, from the earth's sky.

glory because the hour of His judgment has come. The hour of His judgment, of course, refers to the last 3½ years of this age. In addition, this angel also tells people to worship the Creator who made the heaven, the earth, the sea, and the springs of waters. On the one hand, this is a reminder to the earth's people that the Creator's judgment upon His creation is about to begin.[62] On the other hand, this is a warning to men not to worship the Antichrist during the great tribulation, but rather to worship the true God, the true Creator.[63] Thus, these facts indicate that the eternal gospel will be preached near the start of the tribulation.* It may be that about the time of the opening of the seventh seal (see below) God will send this angel to preach the eternal gospel to man.

The preaching of the eternal gospel should not be confused with the preaching that takes place by the believers during the church age. During the church age the gospel is the gospel of grace.[64] Its basic contents are a repentance from sins to God and belief in the Lord Jesus Christ.[65] Through this, men can receive Christ and be born of God to become children of God.[66] The gospel of grace brings men into a life relationship with God Himself. It is preached by men to men.

The eternal gospel is completely different. Its contents do not include a believing in the Lord Jesus Christ for forgiveness of sins and rebirth, but rather a fearing of the Creator. The result of believing the eternal gospel is not a life relationship with God, but rather an entering into the millennial kingdom as one of the people who will be ruled by Christ and His believers.[67] Furthermore, it is preached by an angel to men. Therefore, these two gospels are both distinct and separate.

The preaching of the eternal gospel at that time is very significant. It shows that a change of age has occurred, that the age of grace to the Gentiles is over. Before that time, the gospel preached to the unbelieving nations was the gospel of grace. But, at the beginning of the great tribulation it will become the eternal gospel. This indicates that the fullness of the Gentiles will have been brought to salvation by that time, and that God will have turned back to the Jews to bring them to repentance.[68]

---

* There is no indication as to how long this angel preaches the eternal gospel. We are only told that this gospel is preached to everyone upon the whole earth.

Those unbelieving people on the earth who hear and believe the eternal gospel will fear God and act accordingly. During that time they will treat God's people with kindness, compassion, and mercy. Out of fear for God they will take care of His people—feeding them, tending to their wounds and injuries, and even visiting them in prison during their persecutions.[69] This kindness will be repaid to them by the Lord at His return.[70]

The Opening of the Seventh Seal

And when he opened the seventh seal, there followed a silence in heaven about the space of half an hour. And I saw the seven angels that stand before God; and there were given unto them seven trumpets. And another angel came and stood over the altar, having a golden censer; and there was given unto him much incense, that he should add it unto the prayers of all the saints upon the golden altar which was before the throne. And the smoke of the incense, with the prayers of the saints, went up before God out of the angel's hand. And the angel taketh the censer; and he filled it with the fire of the altar, and cast it upon the earth: and there followed thunders, and voices, and lightnings, and an earthquake. (Revelation 8:1-5)

When the seventh seal is opened, there will be silence in heaven for about half an hour. This event is so grave and so solemn that the heavens will be quiet. The age is changing. God's judgment upon the heavens, the earth, and especially man is about to begin. The tumult and upheaval of the sixth seal were merely a warning. The real judgment is about to take place. This seal should mark the beginning of the day of the Lord.

When the seventh seal is opened, seven angels with seven trumpets appear. The seventh seal is actually composed of these seven trumpets. Therefore, it will continue from the beginning of the great tribulation until the end of the seventh trumpet.

At that time another Angel, signifying Christ, will stand at the heavenly altar to offer up incense to God. The incense He offers is not the prayers of the saints, but rather He Himself in His sweet and acceptable fragrance to God. He adds Himself to the prayers of the saints to make these prayers acceptable to God.

It is Christ in the prayers of the saints that moves God to begin His judgment of the earth.

Here we see that when the seventh seal is opened, there will be many saints—genuine believers, born-again Christians—on the earth, praying. The seventh seal marks the beginning of the great tribulation. Yet, at that time there will be Christians on the earth. This is another strong proof that many believers will be left on the earth to pass through the great tribulation.

Most of the believers will be crying out to God desperately in prayer. They will be aware of the rapture of the overcoming saints and realize that they must suffer through the final $3\frac{1}{2}$ trouble-filled years of this age on the earth, in particular the judgments of the first four trumpets. They will have experienced the great calamity of the sixth seal. They may have heard, or even observed, the sealing of the 144,000 in Israel. It is also probable that by this time the Antichrist will have been slain and resuscitated. In addition, the persecution of the believers will be coming to a climax. All these factors will pressure the saints on the earth to cry out to the Lord in desperation—desperation for His intervention, desperation for His preservation, desperation for His judgment, desperation for His return.

The Lord Jesus will mix Himself as the sweet incense to the fervent prayers of the saints. Those prayers will be answered by God. He will respond by judging the earth through Christ. The Lord will cast fire from the heavenly altar to the earth, bringing about thunders, voices, lightnings, and yet another earthquake. This earthquake will be another enormous shaking. The earth will tremble again under the supernatural judging hand of God.

The First Four Trumpets

And the seven angels that had the seven trumpets prepared themselves to sound. And the first sounded, and there followed hail and fire, mingled with blood, and they were cast upon the earth: and the third part of the earth was burnt up, and the third part of the trees was burnt up, and all green grass was burnt up. And the second angel sounded, and as it were a great mountain burning with fire was cast into the sea: and the third part of the sea became blood; and there died the third part of the creatures which were in the sea, even they that had life; and the third part of the ships was destroyed. And the third angel sounded, and there fell from heaven a great star, burning as a torch, and it fell upon the third part of the rivers, and upon the fountains of the waters; and the name of the star is called Wormwood: and the third part of the waters became wormwood; and many men died of the waters, because they were made bitter. And the fourth angel sounded, and the third part of the sun was smitten, and the third part of the moon, and the third part of the stars; that the third part of them should be darkened, and the day should not shine for the third part of it, and the night in like manner. (Revelation 8:6-12)

And I saw another angel ascend from the sunrising, having the seal of the living God: and he cried with a great voice to the four angels to whom it was given to hurt the earth and the sea, saying, Hurt not the earth, neither the sea, nor the trees, till we shall have sealed the servants of our God on their foreheads. (Revelation 7:2-3)

And there shall be signs in sun and moon and stars; and upon the earth distress of nations, in perplexity for the roaring of the sea and the billows; (Luke 21:25)

The earthquake of the sixth seal will be general, striking the entire earth. The pestilences of the first four trumpets will be more specific. They are targeted toward certain parts of the environment and toward a certain area on the earth. The wonderful Creator has blessed us with a marvelous, enjoyable environment in which to live. The first four trumpets will destroy this pleasant environment. This will make it unsuitable and difficult for man to live. Man's habitat will become unbearable and barely survivable. With these first four trumpets God will take away the excellent things on the earth and in the heavens, things to which man has so frequently turned even as he ignored God, the Creator of them all. Thus, God's initial judgments during the great tribulation put an end to man's enjoyable surroundings.

During each of the first four trumpets *the* third part will be judged—*the* third part of the earth, *the* third part of the trees, *the* third part of the sea, and so forth. This is not *a* third part, but *the* third part. It is not that a random third of the earth or the heavens will be damaged, but rather a specific, contiguous third, which should be the most evil part of the earth. During these first four trumpets God will judge that particular, evil third—the part He considers the most sinful and rebellious.

In addition, these four trumpets, though mentioned in Revelation successively, will probably be experienced nearly simultaneously. It is not that one trumpet will start and finish, and then be followed by another. Rather, these four trumpets are intertwined. While one judgment will touch the earth, another will strike the sea, and the third will fall upon the rivers and springs of waters. Together these will bring about the judgment of the fourth trumpet upon the heavenly bodies. The earth at that time will be in great upheaval and convulsion as judgment upon judgment strike with no respite.

When the first angel sounds, hail and fire mingled with blood will be cast to the earth. The third part of the earth will be burned up, and with it the third of the trees and all the green grass. The hail of this trumpet should not refer to frozen water. It is, after all, mingled with fire. The Greek word translated "hail" literally means "something let go." Hence, it is that which falls from the sky. The hail in this case should not be ice, but rather a hail of fiery debris and meteors. The blood mentioned here should refer to the crimson color with which this judgment will light the sky. The sky will glow from the red-hot burning rock as a meteor storm enters the atmosphere. It will turn blood-red. The hail and fire will affect the third part of the earth's surface, burning it, scorching it, searing it. Violent winds will cause uncontrollable, rampaging firestorms, which will engulf everything in their path. The angels who previously held back the winds while the 144,000 were sealed will release them, causing an enormous, unfathomable wildfire on earth. The trees in that third part of the earth will be completely destroyed. Globally the green grass will be burned up. Who can imagine the immensity of this catastrophe?

When the second trumpet sounds, a great mountain burning with fire will crash to the sea. The third part of the sea will become blood and the creatures and ships in that portion of the ocean will be destroyed. An enormous asteroid will strike the ocean. The third part of the oceans, with the creatures and ships in them, will be judged. That third part will become blood—that is, it will turn deep red in color, probably due to its reflection of a sky burning red hot from both the asteroid itself as it passes through the atmosphere, and the reentry into the atmosphere of the debris spewed forth from the collision.* The concussive force radiating outward from the collision of the burning mountain with the sea will kill the creatures in the third part of the earth's oceans. Great super-hurricane-force gales, probably well in excess of 200† miles per hour, will strike vessel after vessel. These winds, combined with the superheated atmosphere and the intense concussive force, will destroy these vessels, leaving none intact. Huge and unparalleled waves, generated by the impact of the fiery mountain striking the water, will unmercifully lash and devastate the ocean shores. No doubt the winds will also play a major role in this destruction.

When the third trumpet sounds, a great star burning like a torch will fall upon the rivers and springs, turning them bitter. Material from the falling heavenly body itself, debris spewed forth when this "star" slams into the earth, or acids formed in the atmosphere from this asteroid strike, will contaminate all the sources of water on the third part of the planet. This bitterness will not simply make the drinking water unpalatable—it will cause death. The judgment of the third trumpet will turn the drinking water in the third part of the earth poisonous. While men are fleeing from the wild, raging fires, and seeking water to ease their suffering, the water itself will be judged and become a source of death. Many men will die. It may be that many millions will perish from this alone.

When the fourth trumpet sounds, the third part of the heavenly bodies will be judged. It is not that two-thirds of the sun will remain shining; it is not that one-third of the stars in the sky will be blotted out. Rather, the sun, the moon, and the stars will not shine over the third part of the earth, for we are specifically told that the day and the night would not appear for the third part of them. In other words, over one-third of the earth all the heavenly

---

* The color of the water is due mostly to the color of the sky. A sky aflame with burning debris and blood-red in color would turn the sea to "blood."

† The wind speed in certain areas may exceed 1000 mph.

bodies will not be seen. This should refer to that particular evil third of the earth that will be the focus of the judgments of the first three trumpets. The smoke, debris, soot, ash, and fire, together with volcanic eruptions and pillars of smoke, will completely blot out the sky over a third of the earth. Men will not know whether it is day or night. This darkness will increase the terrible torment to those people still left alive on the earth.

The first four trumpets may all be different aspects of the same great event. In 1994 the comet Shoemaker-Levy 9, broken into 21 fragments from a previous encounter with Jupiter, plunged into the Jovian atmosphere. The largest fragments, estimated to be about 2.5 miles in diameter, struck Jupiter with an explosive force equivalent to several *million* megatons of TNT!* In spite of the violent Jovian winds,† the atmospheric damage from these impacts lasted for months. From the description of the first four trumpets recorded in Revelation 8, it is very likely that the earth will experience a similar assault at the beginning of the great tribulation. The fire raining from the heavens, the burning mountain falling into the sea, and the great star striking the rivers and fountains of waters during the first three trumpets may all be due to the successive impacts of asteroids or pieces of a comet, as was observed with Shoemaker-Levy 9. The disaster of the fourth trumpet may simply be the result in the atmosphere of these collisions.

Blow after blow will strike the earth. First, the land will be smitten with fire from heaven. Next, a great flaming mountain will plunge into the sea. Finally, a great burning star will strike the rivers and fountains. We cannot begin to imagine the kind of upheaval these supernatural judgments will cause upon the earth. The third part of the earth and sea will suffer an intense bombardment of fire from the heavens, virtually destroying it. The rest of the earth will be severely shocked and convulsed by the far-reaching side effects of this barrage. The whole world will be turned upside down. Nothing will be left untouched.

---

* The largest nuclear bomb ever exploded on earth was a "mere" 50 megatons in comparison.

† Storm winds on Jupiter exceed one thousand miles per hour.

The Opening of the Abyss

And the fifth angel sounded, and I saw a star from heaven fallen unto the earth: and there was given to him the key of the pit of the abyss. And he opened the pit of the abyss; and there went up a smoke out of the pit, as the smoke of a great furnace; and the sun and the air were darkened by reason of the smoke of the pit. And out of the smoke came forth locusts upon the earth; and power was given them, as the scorpions of the earth have power. ... They have over them as king the angel of the abyss: his name in Hebrew is Abaddon, and in the Greek tongue he hath the name Apollyon. (Rev. 9:1-3, 11)

When the fifth trumpet sounds, a plague of supernatural locusts will break forth upon the earth. As mentioned previously, the opening of the pit of the abyss also occurs at the beginning of the tribulation. However, this particular judgment will extend into the great tribulation itself, and last for a period of five months. Consequently, it will be discussed in detail in a later chapter. What is pertinent here is the origin of the locusts. The locusts themselves, as the judgment of the fifth trumpet, will swarm the earth following the first four trumpets. However, Revelation 9:1-3 depicts the source from which these locusts come. Since these verses give the background for the locust plague of the fifth trumpet, what is portrayed here may occur before this trumpet sounds. These verses reveal Satan's actions after he has been cast out of heaven. He is seen opening the pit of the abyss* to release not only the locusts, but also their king. That king, as we will see shortly, is the Antichrist. Though he will be a man born on earth, he also, in a very mysterious way, will come up out of the abyss.[71] Since the Antichrist will be slain and resuscitated at the very beginning of the tribulation, what is depicted at the beginning of Revelation 9 must happen prior to

---

* The abyss is the dwelling place where the demons and, evidently, certain other spirits dwell (Luke 8:31).

the plague of locusts, which is the actual judgment of the fifth trumpet.*

It is possible, from the perspective of Satan's actions at the beginning of the tribulation, that the following sequence of events will occur. The living mature believers and the manchild will be raptured to the heavens. A great war will break out resulting in Satan with his angels being cast to earth. This evil one will have been given the key to the abyss. He will have the power to open the dwelling place of the demonic spirits. When he does, smoke will billow forth from the earth blanketing the sky and darkening the sun and the air. It seems likely that the opening of the abyss, with its accompanying pillar of smoke and darkening of the sun and air, will take place at the time of the judgment of the sixth seal, though it is documented in the record of the fifth trumpet.[72] From God's perspective, the shaking of the earth during the sixth seal will be His judgment. Nevertheless, Satan may use this for his own ends. Locusts will arise from the abyss along with their king, Abaddon, who will take part in the resuscitation of the Antichrist. All this should occur about the time the Lord opens the seventh seal and the judgments of the first four trumpets smite the earth.

The Two Witnesses

And I will give unto my two witnesses, and they shall prophesy a thousand two hundred and threescore days, clothed in sackcloth. These are the two olive trees and the two candlesticks, standing before the Lord of the earth. And if any man desireth to hurt them, fire proceedeth out of their mouth and devoureth their enemies; and if any man shall desire to hurt them, in this manner must he be killed. These have the power to shut the heaven, that it rain not during the days of their prophecy: and they have power over the waters to turn them into blood, and to smite the earth with every plague, as often as they shall desire. (Rev. 11:3-6)

---

* In other words, when the fifth trumpet sounds, the five-month torment of the locusts begins. The events by which these locusts came to be on earth, as depicted in Rev. 9:1-3, occur some time before the actual five-month plague begins.

And his disciples asked him, saying, Why then say the scribes that Elijah must first come? And he answered and said, Elijah indeed cometh, and shall restore all things: (Matthew 17:10-11)

Behold, I will send you Elijah the prophet before the great and terrible day of Jehovah come. (Malachi 4:5)

And after six days Jesus taketh with him Peter, and James, and John his brother, and bringeth them up into a high mountain apart: and he was transfigured before them; and his face did shine as the sun, and his garments became white as the light. And behold, there appeared unto them Moses and Elijah talking with him. (Matthew 17:1-3)

At this very same time, still another mysterious event will occur. God will send His two witnesses to testify to the nation of Israel. They will prophesy for 1,260 days, including the entire time of Israel's suffering during the great tribulation. Who are these two witnesses? It is clear from a number of verses in the Bible that one of these witnesses is Elijah. He was caught away from the earth and preserved, that he could return to prophesy to Israel during those 3½ years.[73]

There has been some debate concerning the second witness. Some have thought that he must be Enoch, because only he and Elijah were taken from the earth without tasting death. Those who hold this concept quote Hebrews to say that since it is reserved for men to die once, and after this comes judgment, Elijah and Enoch must return to experience that one death.[74] However, this is not logical. Consider Lazarus, the widow's son, and the ones whom Peter and Elisha raised.[75] Did they not die more than once? Consider also the believers who are living at the time of the Lord's second coming. Will they have tasted death at all? Clearly the word in Hebrews is not a legal statement that every man must die precisely one time. Therefore, this verse cannot be used to say that Enoch must be the second witness.

If we consider the plagues that these two witnesses will bring upon the earth, it is clear who they must be. They have the power to shut up the heaven, that no rain fall during the days of their prophecy. Elijah did this very thing when he was on the earth.[76] This confirms the understanding that one of the witnesses is Elijah. They also have the authority to turn the waters into blood and to smite the earth with every plague as often as they desire. Moses, when he was on the earth, turned the waters into blood.[77] He also repeatedly struck Egypt with plagues.[78] Therefore, the two witnesses should be Moses* and Elijah.

Moses and Elijah represent the entire Old Testament. Moses gave the law, while Elijah was the foremost of the prophets. Together they represent the Law and the Prophets, which comprise the Old Testament.[79] The Law and the Prophets testified of Christ. They pointed toward the coming One. As Moses and Elijah testified of Christ to Israel during the Old Testament times, so they will do again before the Lord's second coming. They bore witness to Him on the mount of transfiguration. They will also bear witness to Him during the coming great tribulation.

An Earth in Upheaval

In a very short time, perhaps as little as one day, God will turn the whole earth upside down. Once the mature believers and manchild are raptured, God will intervene to judge mankind as He did in the days of Noah and again in the days of Lot. In the space of a few hours He will unsettle and throw into chaos everything upon the face of the earth.

The Lord will rapture some of the believers and leave the rest on earth to pass through the great tribulation. This will be both terrifying and immensely disconcerting to the remaining believers. The nation of Israel, which was formerly hardened in unbelief, will experience 144,000 believing and Christ-testifying Jews preaching the gospel throughout the tribulation. They will be confirmed and emboldened by Moses and Elijah, who will also testify strongly during those evil days concerning Christ, His salvation, and His second coming. In but a moment the land of Israel will be transformed from a place of great prosperity into an area of intense suffering, the likes of which has never been seen before in history.[80] For the unbelieving Gentiles the age will change from believing in Christ to be saved by His grace, to fearing God and hoping in the eternal gospel. Unbelieving

---

* It may be for this reason that Michael disputed with Satan over the body of Moses, God wanting to preserve it for the coming time (Jude 9).

mankind will see the door of regeneration shut forever. The Antichrist will be transformed through his death and resuscitation into someone more vile, evil, and diabolical than any man who has ever lived on the face of the earth. Finally, the earth itself as a whole will be changed nearly instantaneously from a pleasant and enjoyable place, which had experienced but occasional natural and local calamities, into a barely survivable, unbearable land of confusion and tumult, filled with the supernatural judgments of a righteous and wrathful God. All this will come as a great shock to those who are on the earth at that time.

References

[1] 1 Cor. 4:3 (Greek)

[2] 1 Tim. 2:4

[3] Joe. 2:1, 30-31

[4] Joe. 2:30; Rev. 8:7-8

[5] Rev. 8:7-8, 10

[6] Rev. 9:2

[7] Joe. 2:31

[8] Rev. 6:12

[9] Joe. 2:31

[10] 1 Thes. 5:2

[11] Rev. 7:1-8

[12] Rev. 6:12-17; 7:1-4

[13] Rev. 9:1-2

[14] Matt. 24:37-39; Lu. 17:26-30

[15] Rev. 12:5

[16] Rev. 12:9

[17] Rev. 9:1-2

[18] Matt. 25:13

[19] Matt. 24:38-39; Lu. 17:26-30

[20] Rev. 6:12-14; Heb. 12:26

[21] Matt. 24:38

[22] 2 Cor. 3:18

[23] Luk. 21:36

[24] Eph. 2:6

[25] Heb. 6:19; 10:19-20

[26] Col. 3:4

[27] Jn. 1:4; Luk. 1:78

[28] Mal. 4:2

[29] 1 Cor 1:30; Gal. 3:27

[30] Jn. 1:17

[31] Col. 2:16-17
[32] 1 Cor. 3:1, 3
[33] Eph. 4:14
[34] 2 Tim. 1:15
[35] Rom. 8:13
[36] Phil. 1:20
[37] Gen. 1:26, 28
[38] Gen. 3:4-6
[39] Luk. 4:5-6
[40] Eph. 2:15; Col. 3:10
[41] 1 Cor. 15:47
[42] Jn. 16:21; Rev. 12:5
[43] 1 Thes. 4:17
[44] Rev. 20:1-3
[45] Act. 2:1-36
[46] Joe. 2:23, 28-29
[47] Zech. 12:10-13:1
[48] Rom. 11:26
[49] Rom. 10:13
[50] Rom. 11:25
[51] Matt. 10:16-23
[52] Zech 13:8
[53] Zech. 13:9
[54] Dan. 9:2
[55] Act. 2:2-6
[56] Matt. 23:38
[57] Act. 18:6
[58] 2 Thes. 2:9
[59] Matt. 24:15; Rev. 13:14
[60] Dan. 9:27; 12:11
[61] Matt. 24:21
[62] Rev. 8:3-12
[63] Rev. 14:9-11
[64] Act. 20:24
[65] Act. 5:31; 20:21
[66] Jn. 1:12
[67] Luk. 19:17, 19
[68] Rom. 11:25-26
[69] Matt. 25:35-40
[70] Matt. 25:34
[71] Rev. 9:11; 11:7; 17:8
[72] Rev. 9:1-2
[73] 2 Ki. 2:11
[74] Heb. 9:27
[75] Jn. 11:1-44; Lu. 7:11-17; Act. 9:36-42; 2 Ki. 4:18-37
[76] 1 Ki. 17:1
[77] Ex. 7:20
[78] Ex. 7:20-11:10

[79] Lu. 24:27
[80] Matt. 24:21

CHAPTER 5

The Antichrist and the False Prophet

The Antichrist is a mystery. Very few people have a clear understanding of this man. And understandably so, for mystery is associated with him. However, the Bible, when interpreted properly, discloses everything of importance concerning him so that we would not be left in darkness with regard to his appearing, nature, and actions.

The Mystery of Lawlessness

Now we beseech you, brethren, touching the coming of our Lord Jesus Christ, and our gathering together unto him; to the end that ye be not quickly shaken from your mind, nor yet be troubled, either by spirit, or by word, or by epistle as from us, as that the day of the Lord is just at hand; let no man beguile you in any wise: for it will not be, except the falling away come first, and the man of sin be revealed, the son of perdition, he that opposeth and exalteth himself against all that is called God or that is worshipped; so that he sitteth in the temple of God, setting himself forth as God. ... For the mystery of lawlessness doth already work: only there is one that restraineth now, until he be taken out of the way. And then shall be revealed the lawless one, whom the Lord Jesus shall slay with the breath of his mouth, and bring to nought by the manifestation of his coming; even he, whose coming is according to the working of Satan with all power and signs and lying wonders, and with all deceit of unrighteousness for them that perish; because they received not the love of the truth, that they might be saved. (2 Thessalonians 2:1-4, 7-10)

... the spirit that now worketh in the sons of disobedience (Ephesians 2:2)

Second Thessalonians reveals that Satan's rebellious operation to overthrow all that is of God—the mystery of lawlessness—is working even today. This is the spirit that is now operating in the sons of disobedience. When we observe the world and the things in the world through the eyes of the Spirit, what do we see? Nothing but lawlessness. Today there are strong movements for abortion rights, homosexual rights, transgender rights, and other similar liberal crusades. What are all these? Lawlessness. They are a blatant disregard for and rebellion against the divine order in God's creation. If we were to sum up Hollywood, what would the result be? Lawlessness. The promotion and glorification of all kinds of sin. In the academic community, where God is mocked and denied, and evolution, atheism, and fanciful theory is worshipped, what do we see? Hardly anything but lawlessness. In corporate America, what do we see? Lawlessness. In the educational system? On television? In the amusement places? Everywhere, there is lawlessness. Throughout the world, this spirit of lawlessness is working in a hidden and mysterious way. Few realize its presence. Many are completely deceived by it. So many, including dear Christian brothers and sisters, are influenced by it. It is that strong.

However, there has been some power* restraining this mystery of lawlessness, preventing its full manifestation. As this power is removed, the world is becoming one in total rebellion against God. It is becoming unlivable. Sin and sins—murder, theft, adultery, fornication, homosexuality, violence—are beginning to reign. These are rampant today. Lawlessness is growing as the end of the age approaches and the restraining power is removed.

By the time of the great tribulation, this restraining power will be completely removed. That will be a time of great darkness—full of evil, full of Satan's operation. Then Satan's power will be manifested to its fullest. He will be given the freedom to do as he pleases—to damage, to persecute, to torment, to torture, and to destroy the earth. It is only then that the lawless one, the Antichrist, will be revealed.† He will be the full manifestation of

---

* This restraining one should be the Holy Spirit, *in His restraining power*. The Holy Spirit is always with us, but His restraining power is being removed.

† In 2 Thessalonians the apostle Paul tells us that our gathering together to the Lord, that is, the rapture of the saints as revealed in 1 Thessalonians 4 and 1

Satan. His coming will be with great power, full of signs and wonders of a lie, and in all deceit. With him there will be nothing but rebellion against God. He will be lawless and sinful in every respect. He will rejoice and exult in evil. He will promote every kind of wickedness, and seek to do away with everything that is of or for God. In his days, lawlessness will reign on earth.

The Antichrist's coming is in a mystery. There is much about him that is seemingly paradoxical. For example, the Bible tells us that he is born a man, that he comes from the Gentile world.[1] Yet, in some mysterious way he rises from the abyss.[2] In addition, when the Antichrist first appears he is simply an ordinary man— a man with very special capabilities, but nonetheless, an ordinary man. Yet, the Bible also tells us that his appearing is according to Satan's operation with wonders and signs.[3] Furthermore, in Daniel 9 the Antichrist signs a pact with Israel for seven years.[4] Thus, he is known to the world for some time longer than those seven years. Nevertheless, the Bible also tells us that he continues only forty-two months, or $3\frac{1}{2}$ years.[5] Finally, the Antichrist signs a peace pact with Israel, guaranteeing her security and prosperity.[6] Yet, this very same person persecutes Israel almost to extinction.[7] How can these seeming contradictions be resolved? To understand the Antichrist we must paint layer upon layer until a complete and accurate picture is portrayed. Like a jigsaw puzzle, all the Biblical "pieces" concerning him must be assembled properly. Only then can the mystery of the Antichrist be known.

The Beast – the Roman Empire

After this I saw in the night-visions, and, behold, a fourth beast, terrible and powerful, and strong exceedingly; and it had great

---

Corinthians 15, will not come until the Antichrist is manifested. This is another strong proof that the rapture of all the saints does not occur before the seven-year pact, nor before the great tribulation. Rather, this word states emphatically that the rapture of all the saints occurs only after the Antichrist is manifested as the lawless one with his great signs and wonders in power, as depicted, for example, in Revelation 13. This will occur during the time of great tribulation. It is not until after that time that the rapture of the saints will occur. The Bible is clear, emphatic, and consistent that many saints will *not* escape the great tribulation.

iron teeth; it devoured and brake in pieces, and stamped the residue with its feet: and it was diverse from all the beasts that were before it; and it had ten horns. ...The fourth beast shall be a fourth kingdom upon earth, which shall be diverse from all the kingdoms, and shall devour the whole earth, and shall tread it down, and break it in pieces. (Daniel 7:7, 23)

And I saw a beast coming up out of the sea, having ten horns, and seven heads, and on his horns ten diadems, and upon his heads names of blasphemy. ... And I saw one of his heads as though it had been smitten unto death; and his death-stroke was healed: and the whole earth wondered after the beast. (Revelation 13:1, 3)

Here is the mind that hath wisdom. The seven heads are seven mountains, on which the woman sitteth: and they are seven kings; the five are fallen, the one is, the other is not yet come; and when he cometh, he must continue a little while. (Revelation 17:9-10)

The beast described in Revelation 13 is the Roman Empire. It is the same as the fourth beast Daniel saw in the vision recorded in the seventh chapter of his book. That dreadful and terrible beast was the fourth kingdom that would come upon and reign over the earth. The first three, according to the book of Daniel, were Babylon, Medo-Persia, and Greece.[8] The fourth, according to history, was the Roman Empire, which was in power at the time John wrote the book of Revelation. John also reveals that this beast is the Roman Empire by stating that the seven heads of the beast are seven mountains upon which the woman, Babylon the Great, sits. This, of course, is an obvious reference to Rome, which is situated upon seven hills. Thus, the beast must be Rome. In addition, the seven heads are seven kings, one of whom was reigning at John's time. This reference to the Roman emperor confirms the fact that the beast alludes to Rome.

Revelation says that the seven heads of the beast are seven kings. These are seven prominent, noteworthy, and powerful leaders of the Roman Empire. These are not the only emperors who have reigned over Rome. Rather, they have been singled out as particular and notable. On them were names of blasphemy. That is, they called themselves gods, requiring their subjects to worship them. Furthermore, the first five had *fallen* by the time

John wrote the book of Revelation. This means that they had died unnaturally. According to history, these five must be the Caesars Julius, Tiberius, Caligula, Claudius, and Nero. All these claimed to be divine. All these were either murdered or committed suicide. They died unnatural deaths.

At the time John was writing, one of the seven heads still was. This was Domitian, who was reigning when John was exiled to Patmos, the place where he received the book of Revelation.[9] Domitian was also particularly evil, and claimed divine status. In A.D. 96, a short while after Revelation was written, he too was murdered.

The holy Word also tells us that one of the seven heads was slain to death, and that the death stroke was healed. According to history, no Caesar of the Roman Empire has ever been revived from death. Therefore, this must refer to a coming *seventh head,* or Caesar, who had not yet appeared by John's time, and has yet to appear. This will be the coming Antichrist *before* his death. He will be the head over a revived Roman Empire. When he comes he will continue only a short while, somewhat more than 3½ years. Then he will be slain, immediately *prior* to the beginning of the great tribulation.

The Beast – the Antichrist

These great beasts, which are four, are four kings, that shall arise out of the earth. (Daniel 7:17)

The beast that thou sawest was, and is not; and is about to come up out of the abyss, and to go into perdition. And they that dwell on the earth shall wonder, they whose name hath not been written in the book of life from the foundation of the world, when they behold the beast, how that he was, and is not, and shall come. Here is the mind that hath wisdom. The seven heads are ... seven kings; the five are fallen, the one is, the other is not yet come; and when he cometh, he must continue a little while. And the beast that was, and is not, is himself also an eighth, and is of the seven; and he goeth into perdition. (Revelation 17:8-11)

The beast described in Revelation 13 is not only a kingdom, but also a king. Revelation 17 says that the beast himself is an eighth head, and that he was, is not, and is about to come up out of the abyss. At the time John wrote this book the Roman Empire still existed. Yet, the beast as the eighth head *was not* at John's time. Therefore, the beast must refer not only to the Roman Empire as a kingdom, but also to a particular king of that empire. This corresponds to Daniel 7 where we are told that the four beasts were not only four kingdoms, but also four kings. These kings are the most prominent leaders of each of those kingdoms, and thus represent and wield all the authority of those kingdoms. In like manner, the gold head of the image depicted in Daniel 2 was not only the kingdom of Babylon, but also Nebuchadnezzar as its most notable emperor.[10] Thus, this beast is both the Roman kingdom and the most noted king of that kingdom, who has yet to appear. The beast, as the *eighth head*, will be the Antichrist *after* his death and resuscitation. Thus, in some way the seventh head will undergo a mysterious metamorphosis to become the eighth head.

In addition, the eighth head had already existed by John's time. John said the beast himself is the eighth, the one *who was*, who had ceased to be, and who would come up out of the abyss. How puzzling! He had already been, but was no more. Yet, he will come again. Truly, the Antichrist is a mystery.

The beast, as the eight head, is said to be *of* the seven other heads. That is, he will be a composition of some of the previous seven Caesars. Certainly for his body he will have the body of the coming seventh Caesar, who will be slain and resuscitated. However, what of the revived Antichrist's spirit? After his death and resuscitation he has the body of the seventh Caesar, but whose spirit does he have?

The Number of the Beast

and that no man should be able to buy or to sell, save he that hath the mark, even the name of the beast or the number of his name. Here is wisdom. He that hath understanding, let him count the number of the beast; for it is the number of a man: and his number is Six hundred and sixty and six. (Revelation 13:17-18)

The beast that thou sawest was, and is not; and is about to come up out of the abyss, and to go into perdition. (Revelation 17:8)

The Bible does not leave us in the dark with respect to this crucial matter. It gives us another clue to decipher this puzzle. We are told that the beast has a number, that the number is the number of his name, and that the name is the name of a man. Therefore, the number is a number of some particular man—not of some organization, nor of some empire, but of a particular person.

Furthermore, John said that the one with wisdom could understand to whom this number referred. Therefore, even in John's day the name of the beast, as depicted by the number 666, could be known. John knew of whom he was speaking. Although it required wisdom to know who this man was, it was knowable 1900 years ago. John and those in his day who had wisdom knew whom the number 666 represented. Thus this number cannot refer to a name like "Fox," or any other present-day designation. It refers to someone of whom John knew.

The name spoken of here must be the name of one of the five fallen Caesars referred to in Revelation 17.[11] For, first we are told that this number is the number of the beast. Next, we are told that the beast lived before John's time, but had ceased living by the time John wrote this book. Furthermore, we are told that the beast is out of the seven, composed of some of the seven Caesars. Therefore, the number 666 must in some way refer to one of the previous five Caesars, one of the five heads who had died by the time John wrote this book. We can now readily identify to whom John was referring. The one spoken of here is Caesar Nero,[*] the fifth head of the beast.

It is very revealing to see that Caesar Nero's name adds up to 666 in Hebrew. Both the Hebrew and Greek alphabets were used to designate numbers. Each letter corresponded to a particular number. According to the Hebrew representation of the name Caesar Nero, the numbers corresponding to the letters of his name add up to 666 as follows:

---

[*] This explains why John wrote Nero's name in a cryptic way, by the number 666. It was because Rome was still in power at that time.

English		Greek		Hebrew		Number
Ne	→	Νε	→	נ	→	50
r	→	ρ	→	ר	→	200
o	→	ο	→	ו	→	6
n	→	ν	→	נ	→	50
Kai	→	Και	→	ק	→	100
sa	→	σα	→	ס	→	60
r	→	ρ	→	ר	→	200
				Total	=	666

Thus the beast's name is Caesar Nero. It is no wonder that the world will marvel after him!

The number 666 has a particularly evil significance. Six is the number of man, because man was created on the sixth day.[12] However, it is not the number of man in his original pure state. Rather, it refers to man after the fall. Six denotes fallen, sinful man. The Antichrist whose name is represented by the number 666, is a man of triple sin, of complete sinfulness, a man who is fully evil, a man who is altogether one with the source of sin, Satan himself. The number 666 is particularly suited to the vile person of the Antichrist.* Caesar Nero was exceptionally evil. He was extremely sinful personally, perhaps beyond those who had come before him. He was also the first to persecute the Christians. He burned them at stakes, using them to illuminate his garden. How cruel, vile, malicious, and wicked he was. According to church history the Apostle Paul, and perhaps Peter as well, were slain by him. Furthermore, it was he who initiated the war that resulted in the destruction of Jerusalem in A.D. 70. The spirit of

---

* Interestingly, the name "Jesus" adds up to 888 in Greek. The eighth day is the first day of a new week. It was on the eighth day that Jesus was resurrected (Luke 24:1-6). Thus, the number eight refers to resurrection. The number three refers both to the Triune God and to resurrection, since Jesus was raised on the third day after His death (Matt. 16:21). Thus, the number 888 signifies that Jesus is the Triune God in resurrection.

this Nero, as perhaps the most evil, base, and satanic person of all time, will resuscitate the slain Antichrist.

With this as a background the mystery of the Antichrist can now be revealed. At the same time that the coming seventh Caesar of the revived Roman Empire is slain, Satan will be cast from the heavens to the earth.[13] He will then open the abyss, from which the spirit of Nero will rise to enter into the body of the slain seventh Caesar, thus resuscitating him. The resuscitated Antichrist will have the body of the seventh Caesar plus the spirit of the fifth. He is, therefore, a composition of the seven, being partly the fifth and partly the seventh.[14] He also was, had ceased to be, and will come out of the abyss.[15] He was, as Caesar Nero. He was not at John's time, because Caesar Nero had died. His spirit is currently being kept in the abyss until the endtime. He will then come up from the abyss to inhabit the body of the slain seventh Caesar.

The seeming paradoxes surrounding the Antichrist can now be easily resolved. He will be born a man as the seventh Caesar, but he, as the spirit of Nero, comes up out of the abyss to become the eighth Caesar. He is an ordinary man as the seventh head of the beast, but his coming is according to the power of Satan, with all signs and wonders of a lie, as the eighth head. He signs a pact of peace with Israel for seven years as the seventh Caesar. He continues forty-two months, persecuting Israel to the uttermost, as the eighth.

The Antichrist will appear shortly before the seven-year pact with Israel is enacted. He will be powerful, extremely intelligent, and have amazing capabilities. He will rise to power quickly. At that time he will be admired by many. Yet, his true evil nature and person will not yet be revealed by then. His desires for global domination and the destruction of all religion will be hidden. Who he really is and what he will do will not be manifested by that time. At his initial appearing he will seem to be one who can solve all the earth's problems. He will make a pact with Israel for seven years and keep it for the first $3\frac{1}{2}$ years. Israel will prosper. Peace will seem to reign. All will be according to the covenant between Israel and himself. Yet, at the very middle of that time, he will be slain. Satan will be cast to earth and open the abyss. The spirit of Caesar Nero will ascend to enter into the body of the slain Antichrist causing him to be revived. He will then become the beast as the eighth head of the Roman Empire.

The Great Transformation

... and the dragon gave him his power, and his throne, and great authority. And I saw one of his heads as though it had been smitten unto death; and his death-stroke was healed: and the whole earth wondered after the beast; and they worshipped the dragon, because he gave his authority unto the beast; and they worshipped the beast, saying, Who is like unto the beast? And who is able to war with him? and there was given to him a mouth speaking great things and blasphemies; and there was given to him authority to continue forty and two months. ... and there was given to him authority over every tribe and people and tongue and nation. And all that dwell on the earth shall worship him, every one whose name hath not been written from the foundation of the world in the book of life of the Lamb that hath been slain. (Revelation 13:2-5, 7-8)

... a king of fierce countenance, and understanding dark sentences, shall stand up. And his power shall be mighty, but not by his own power ... And through his policy he shall cause craft to prosper in his hand ... (Daniel 8:23-25)

It is crucial to see that the Antichrist passes through an extraordinary transformation. This transformation will come about through his death and resuscitation. Before that he will be powerful and exceptional. After that he will become super-powerful and full of signs and wonders. After he is revived, the Antichrist will become very different in character. He will be completely evil. He will have within him the evil and vile spirit of Caesar Nero. He will be one with Satan to the uttermost, being Satan's full embodiment and expression. Satan's person will be his person. He will enjoy Satan's power, throne, and authority.

He will become supernatural, having Satan's power, full of signs and wonders. He will, no doubt, do many deceptive and incredible miracles, misleading those who do not have a love for the truth.[16] He will be the greatest deceiver of all deceivers, even as Satan himself. Yet, in all his supernatural doings he will neither give life, nor bring men closer to God. Rather, he will only promote himself.

He will be skilled in ambiguities. No one will know how to interpret what he is saying. By this, he will both flatter and deceive everyone. All of Satan's evil intents, desires, and wiles will be his. He will outwit and outmaneuver everybody.

After his resuscitation the whole world will marvel after him. Before then many will admire him. After that the whole world will follow after him. He will be given authority over the whole earth. As we will see shortly, this authority will probably be exercised through economic means, at least in part. He will also be great militarily. No one will be able to stand against him, and even the saints will be given into his hands. For that 3½ years he will do as he pleases. Indeed, the Lord warns us not to fight against him, because all authority over the earth will have been given to him.[17]

Destroying in an Extraordinary Manner

And the beast which I saw was like unto a leopard, and his feet were as the feet of a bear, and his mouth as the mouth of a lion: and the dragon gave him his power, and his throne, and great authority. (Revelation 13:2)

After this I saw in the night-visions, and, behold, a fourth beast, terrible and powerful, and strong exceedingly; and it had great iron teeth; it devoured and brake in pieces, and stamped the residue with its feet ... (Daniel 7:7)

... a king of fierce countenance, and understanding dark sentences, shall stand up. ... and he shall destroy wonderfully, and shall prosper and do his pleasure; and he shall destroy the mighty ones and the holy people. (Daniel 8:23-24)

They have over them as king the angel of the abyss: his name in Hebrew is Abaddon, and in the Greek tongue he hath the name Apollyon. (Revelation 9:11)

The Antichrist will be in appearance like a leopard, have feet like a bear, and a mouth like a lion. In the book of Daniel, Nebuchadnezzar, the king of Babylon, was described as a lion.

He devoured the world like a lion. Darius the Mede was portrayed as a bear. The Medes and Persians, with him as their head, stomped the world like a bear. Alexander the Great was described as a leopard. He conquered the world in an incredibly short time, and with but few men.* When the Antichrist appears he will be the totality of these three men. He will devour ravenously like Nebuchadnezzar. He will crush brutally like Darius. He will consume fiercely and quickly like Alexander.

The Antichrist will be dreadful, frightful, and exceedingly strong. He will be of fierce countenance. He will terrify everyone. His teeth will be like iron, with which he will viciously tear the world to pieces. He will be full of devouring, crushing, and trampling. He will truly be like a great, wild beast, rampaging through the earth, attacking and killing whatever he finds. He will be without reason or logic, destroying for destruction's sake.[18] He will be motivated by the hateful, enraged, and crazed Satan who will know that he has but a short time.[19]

The Antichrist will smash, tear down, and demolish anything and everything in his way. He will destroy in an extraordinary manner. He is even called "Destruction" (Abaddon) and "Destroyer" (Apollyon). No one will be able to stand against him. He will destroy militarily, economically, politically, and religiously. He will seek to eradicate everything on the earth, and redo it in his image. His destroying might, power, and authority will mesmerize the whole world into following him.

Hating All Religion

... and there was given to him a mouth speaking great things and blasphemies; and there was given to him authority to continue forty and two months. And he opened his mouth for blasphemies against God, to blaspheme his name, and his tabernacle, even them that dwell in the heaven. And it was given unto him to make war with the saints, and to overcome them... (Revelation 13:5-7)

---

* For example, he defeated the Persian emperor, Darius Codomannus, who had an army of perhaps 1,000,000 infantrymen with battle elephants and scythed chariots, with about 40,000 infantry and 7,000 cavalry.

I beheld, and the same horn made war with the saints, and prevailed against them... And he shall speak words against the Most High, and shall wear out the saints of the Most High; and he shall think to change the times and the law; and they shall be given into his hand until a time and times and half a time. (Daniel 7:21, 25)

And it waxed great, even to the host of heaven; and some of the host and of the stars it cast down to the ground, and trampled upon them. Yea, it magnified itself, even to the prince of the host; and it took away from him the continual burnt-offering, and the place of his sanctuary was cast down. (Daniel 8:10-11)

... and he shall magnify himself in his heart, and in their security shall he destroy many: he shall also stand up against the prince of princes; but he shall be broken without hand. (Daniel 8:25)

And the king shall do according to his will; and he shall exalt himself, and magnify himself above every god, and shall speak marvellous things against the God of gods; and he shall prosper till the indignation be accomplished; for that which is determined shall be done. Neither shall he regard the gods of his fathers, nor the desire of women, nor regard any god; for he shall magnify himself above all. (Daniel 11:36-37)

The Antichrist will blaspheme God and God's tabernacle in the heavens. This devilish person will mock Jesus and revile God. He will speak extraordinary things, great things. He will berate the Hebrew and Christian God, and magnify himself above everything. He will declare his own greatness and praise his own remarkable power. He will probably explain away the rapture of the overcoming saints with some fantastic and marvelously constructed story that will be believed by his followers. He may use science and science fiction to account for the disappearance of all the raptured believers. He will explain away the great quakes and God's other judgments upon the earth, perhaps even taking credit for them himself. He may say that these were signs centered around his death and resuscitation.* No one will be able to withstand his words.

The Antichrist will declare himself to be God.[20] He will stop the temple worship in Israel, including the sacrifices and the oblations.[21] He will put an end to the reinstituted Levitical service. He will seek to change the Mosaic law and the times of the Jewish festivals. He will sit in the temple saying that he himself is God, and have an image of himself erected in the holy place of the temple. He will persecute people, forcing them to worship him and his image.[22] This satanically empowered madman will oppress all religions. He will hate every kind of religion. He will particularly and especially persecute Israel. He will make war with the believers and wear them out. Eventually, he will defeat all the believers on the earth, even including Moses and Elijah.[23] It will seem as if the Antichrist has more power than God. This will be a time of great trial, especially for the Jews.

The False Prophet

And I saw another beast coming up out of the earth; and he had two horns like unto lamb, and he spake as a dragon. And he exerciseth all the authority of the first beast in his sight. And he maketh the earth and them dwell therein to worship the first beast, whose death-stroke was healed. And he doeth great signs, that he should even make fire to come down out of heaven upon the earth in the sight of men. And he deceiveth them that dwell on the earth by reason of the signs which it was given him to do in the sight of the beast; saying to them that dwell on the earth, that they should make an image to the beast who hath the stroke of the sword and lived. And it was given unto him to give breath to it, even to the image to the breast, that the image of the beast should both speak, and cause that as many as should not worship the image of the beast should be killed. And he causeth all, the small and the great, and the rich and the poor, and the free and the bond, that there be given them a mark on their right hand, or upon their forehead; and that no man should be able to buy or to

---

* This may again be in imitation of Christ's death and resurrection, when there were great earthquakes (Matt. 27:51, 54; 28:2).

sell, save he that hath the mark, even the name of the beast or the number of his name. (Revelation 13:11-17)

And the beast was taken, and with him the false prophet that wrought the signs in his sight, wherewith he deceived them that had received the mark of the beast and them that worshipped his image... (Revelation 19:20)

Then if any man shall say unto you, Lo, here is the Christ, or, Here; believe it not. For there shall arise false Christs, and false prophets, and shall show great signs and wonders; so as to lead astray, if possible, even the elect. (Matthew 24:23-24)

... whosoever acknowledgeth him he will increase with glory; and he shall cause them to rule over many, and shall divide the land for a price. (Daniel 11:39)

At the end of this age, another evil person will also appear. The Bible calls him the false prophet. He is said to come up out of the earth. The Antichrist will rise up out of the sea.[24] The sea signifies the Gentiles.[25] This indicates that he will come forth from the nations. On the other hand, the land signifies Israel. Thus, the false prophet will come out of Israel, and therefore be a Jew.

Some have thought that this false prophet must be Judas Iscariot. In the Old Testament when men died they were said to be gathered to their people.[26] But this was not true of Judas Iscariot. When he died he went "to his own place."[27] It may be that he has been kept in that special place for the coming time. Furthermore, what could have caused Judas to betray Christ, the Son of God? It may be that Satan offered to make him the king of the Jews at some future time. Perhaps Judas betrayed Christ in exchange for Christ's rightful position as King of Israel. This certainly would be in character for Judas. It is therefore not unreasonable to think that the false prophet may be Judas Iscariot. About the time the spirit of Caesar Nero ascends out of the abyss, Judas himself will also be released to become the false prophet.

The false prophet will appear to be a lamb. Only Christ is a real lamb. He is truly meek, even to the point of being slaughtered for our sins. This coming false prophet will only give the *impression* of meekness and gentleness. He will be altogether deceptive. Yet, he will be known by his deeds. His deeds will show him to be a serpent.

The Antichrist will install the false prophet as his deputy authority. Therefore, he will exercise all the authority of the Antichrist in his sight. He will even be able to call fire down out of heaven, something Elijah did in the Old Testament.[28] By his signs he will deceive the whole earth, causing everyone to worship the Antichrist.

Both the Antichrist and the false prophet will be absolutely one with the devil, Satan. They will be evil to the uttermost. There will be nothing of the truth in them. These two—the most evil one from among the Gentiles and the most evil one from among the Jews—together with the devil will form a satanic trinity. Satan will be the counterfeit of the Father, the Antichrist will be the counterfeit of Christ, and Judas will be the counterfeit of the Spirit.

What a terrible time that will be. Satan himself, with all his fallen angels, will be on the earth. The Antichrist, inhabited by the spirit of the devilish Caesar Nero, will have authority over the entire earth. All of Antichrist's followers will share in his power, exercising his control over the whole world. His chief cohort Judas Iscariot, as the false prophet, will promote him with miracles and great signs, forcing people to bow and worship both the Antichrist and his image. These three together—Satan, Antichrist, and the false prophet—will wear out and put down the power of all God's people on the earth. No one will be able to stand against them. What a dreadful time this will be. It will indeed seem that Satan is victorious, and that God has been utterly and totally defeated. It is not without reason that the Bible tells us that here is the endurance and patience of the saints.[29] Those left on earth will have to endure 3½ years during which the evil one will do as he pleases. Woe to the earth and those on the earth during that time.[30]

References

[1] Dan. 11:37; Rev. 13:1

[2] Rev. 9:1-2, 11; 11:7; 17:8

[3] Dan. 8:24

[4] Dan. 9:27

[5] Rev. 13:5

[6] Dan. 9:27

[7] Rev. 13:7, 12, 15

[8] Dan. 2:38-40; 8:20-21

[9] Rev. 1:1, 9

[10] Dan. 2:38-39

[11] Rev. 17:10

[12] Gen. 1:26-31

[13] Rev. 12:9

[14] Rev. 17:11

[15] Rev. 17:8

[16] 2 Thes. 2:9-10

[17] Rev. 13:10

[18] Rev. 11:8

[19] Rev. 12:12

[20] 2 Thes. 2:4

[21] Dan. 9:27

[22] Rev. 13:7, 14-15

[23] Rev. 11:7

[24] Rev. 13:1

[25] Rev. 17:15; Is. 57:20

[26] Gen. 25:17; 35:29; 49:29; Num. 20:26, etc.

[27] Acts 1:25

[28] 1 Ki. 18:17-39

[29] Rev. 14:12

[30] Rev. 12:12

CHAPTER 6

The Great Tribulation

The judgments of the sixth seal and first four trumpets will bring great worldwide disaster. The injuries and deaths from these calamities will be innumerable. There will be so many men wounded that the doctors will be unable to care for them all. Hospitals will overflow with the injured. The earth will be full of the dead—dead men, dead animals, dead fish. Corpses will be rotting everywhere. The third of the creatures in the sea will have died. The stench from their rotting carcasses will be unbearable, should there be any men left nearby to smell them. Many dead men will remain unburied because emergency personnel will not be able to handle this enormous catastrophe. Much of the coastal region around the world will have been utterly destroyed by the great tsunamis that accompany these judgments. Many cities will be devastated. The destruction will be worldwide.

In addition, soot and ash from the pillars of smoke and great fires sweeping over the third of the earth will gradually spread over a large part of the world. This ash will remain in the atmosphere for a long time, causing severe cold throughout much of the earth. In 1815 there was a great eruption of a volcano in Sumbawa. The year following that eruption became known as "the year there was no summer." It actually snowed in July in parts of the northern hemisphere. If the eruption of one volcano could cause such a dramatic change in climate, how much more will the eruptions and fires on the earth at the beginning of the tribulation adversely affect the weather? This will cause the suffering of men to intensify further.

There will be great power outages throughout the earth. Very little will be left running. Fuel oil and gasoline will be difficult, even impossible, to obtain. Natural gas and oil lines will rupture in many places. Drilling facilities and refineries will be damaged throughout the earth. By all this the energy production and distribution needed to maintain today's society will be totally disrupted.

This will be a very difficult time. The severe cold will cause great food shortages. Power outages and lack of fuel will exacerbate the suffering of those days. Many people will be without clean water, electricity, and heat. It is hard to imagine how terrible the world will be. In addition, there will be total economic disaster in nearly all countries.*

Through the judgments of the sixth seal and first four trumpets God will completely disrupt the environment on the entire earth. Today many people spend their time in luxuries, entertainments, amusements, frivolity, and other godless occupations. God will intervene to end all these diversions. By His judgments at the beginning of the tribulation, all amusements will be over.

At that time Hollywood will be completely destroyed. All the sinful and wicked movies—movies that propagate nothing but sin, rebellion, and godlessness—will be ended. Television will probably be limited to emergency broadcasts, if that. All the nonsensical talk on today's radio will be terminated. The great and only topic of discussion will be "Is this the time of God's judgment?"

All the sports events that enthrall people today will be ended. There will be no more professional or college football, no more golf, no more tennis, no more Olympics, no more world championships, no more sports of any kind. All of this will have been terminated.

The vacations, of which so many people worldwide are fond, will be over. There will no longer be any place pleasant on the earth in which to vacation. There will be no more sea cruises, for the oceans will be a churning turmoil of great billowing waves. All the beautiful parks and garden spots on the earth will be damaged and inaccessible.

All of today's hobbies will be realized as vanity. Stamp collecting, coin collecting, baseball card collecting—all kinds of collecting—will become things of the past. No one will want or care for them. All the distracting crafts and pleasures will be put

---

* This will pave the way for the Antichrist to control the world.

aside. People will be fully occupied with gathering sustenance to live.

The computer revolution will be abruptly cut short. Most of the personal computer manufacturing will come to an end. The financial world will be in complete chaos. Many great institutions will simply cease to exist. Stock exchanges will be shut. Bond markets, mutual funds, and other financial entities will be obliterated.

Because of the extreme and dire circumstances facing man, a state of emergency will be declared almost everywhere. Political activity will be halted indefinitely. Many governments will collapse into anarchy. In the United States it is very possible that our constitutional freedoms, including the Bill of Rights, will be suspended during this dark time.

The worlds of education, business, sports, science, and the military will all be in complete upheaval. From that time, nothing will be "as usual." In one day, God will overthrow everything. He will overthrow all that man has strived for, all that man has constructed. Yet, God will not make a complete end. He will still leave enough intact that man could live during the great tribulation, in order that he could be given the opportunity to repent.

Only the Beginning

When therefore ye see the abomination of desolation, which was spoken of through Daniel the prophet, standing in the holy place (let him that readeth understand)... for then shall be great tribulation, such as hath not been from the beginning of the world until now, no, nor ever shall be. And except those days had been shortened, no flesh would have been saved: but for the elect's sake those days shall be shortened. (Matthew 24:15, 21-22)

For those days shall be tribulation, such as there hath not been the like from the beginning of the creation which God created until now, and never shall be. (Mark 13:19)

... and there shall be great earthquakes, and in divers places famines and pestilences; and there shall be terrors and great signs from heaven. ... And there shall be signs in sun and moon and stars; and upon the earth distress of nations, in perplexity for

the roaring of the sea and the billows; men fainting for fear, and for expectation of the things which are coming on the world: for the powers of the heavens shall be shaken. (Luke 21:11, 25-26)

Therefore rejoice, O heavens, and ye that dwell in them. Woe for the earth and for the sea: because the devil is gone down unto you, having great wrath, knowing that he hath but a short time. (Revelation 12:12)

Yet, as bad as this is, it will merely be the beginning of sufferings. The great tribulation will have only started. Those last 3½ years will be the most tumultuous time on earth since man was created. Indeed, they will be the worst since the beginning of the creation itself. There will never again be a period of tribulation like that. Not many men will survive that time. If those days were not cut short, no flesh would survive. They will be that bad. The three greatest calamities—the woes of the fifth, sixth, and seventh trumpets—will strike the earth during those years. These woes will be the main components of the great tribulation.

The judgments and trials of that time will come from three directions. God will judge the earth and man with supernatural calamities. Satan, having been cast down to the earth with his angels, will do all in his power to destroy the believers, the Jews, and all of mankind as well. The Antichrist and his followers will cooperate with the evil one, Satan, to inflict torment and suffering upon men. This tribulation will make the earth unbearable.

This suffering will come upon three kinds of people. First, it will fall upon those saints who are still on the earth. God will not destroy His children during that time. He will even preserve them in what the Bible terms a "wilderness." Yet, Satan and the Antichrist will do what they can to annihilate them. Furthermore, the shortage of many necessities and God's judgment upon all the worldly pasttimes will also cause much suffering to the saints during that time.

The tribulation will come upon the Jews in particular. God will intervene through all these judgments to bring the nation of Israel to repentance. The Jews are the children of Abraham according to the flesh. Because of His promise to Abraham God will intervene to turn the godless nation of Israel back to Himself.

Finally, the great tribulation will come upon the nations. The unbelievers are too sinful, too evil, too damaged. They live in the vanity of their mind and the lust of their flesh. They live without God, not caring for God, and even despising, hating, and reviling God. God will bring the tribulation upon the unbelievers to save them, if possible, from the enslavement of the evil one, Satan, and eternal perdition in the lake of fire. He will intervene to bring them back to the proper relationship between the creature and the Creator. Through all the trials and sufferings of that time the Lord will bring the earth and mankind back to the proper God-ordained order.

The Antichrist's Authority Over the Earth

And the beast which I saw was like unto a leopard, and his feet were as the feet of a bear, and his mouth as the mouth of a lion: and the dragon gave him his power, and his throne, and great authority. ... and there was given to him a mouth speaking great things and blasphemies; and there was given to him authority to continue forty and two months. ... And it was given unto him to make war with the saints, and to overcome them: and there was given to him authority over every tribe and people and tongue and nation. ... And it was given unto him to give breath to it, even to the image to the breast, that the image of the beast should both speak, and cause that as many as should not worship the image of the beast should be killed. And he causeth all, the small and the great, and the rich and the poor, and the free and the bond, that there be given them a mark on their right hand, or upon their forehead; and that no man should be able to buy or to sell, save he that hath the mark, even the name of the beast or the number of his name. (Revelation 13:2, 5, 7, 15-17)

And out of one of them came forth a little horn, which waxed exceeding great, toward the south, and toward the east, and toward the glorious land. And it waxed great, even to the host of heaven; and some of the host and of the stars it cast down to the ground, and trampled upon them. (Daniel 8:9-10)

And at the time of the end shall the king of the south contend with him; and the king of the north shall come against him like a whirlwind, with chariots, and with horsemen, and with many ships; and he shall enter into the countries, and shall overflow and pass through. He shall enter also into the glorious land, and many countries shall be overthrown; but these shall be delivered out of his hand: Edom, and Moab, and the chief of the children of Ammon. He shall stretch forth his hand also upon the countries; and the land of Egypt shall not escape. But he shall have power over the treasures of gold and of silver, and over all the precious things of Egypt; and the Libyans and the Ethiopians shall be at his steps. (Daniel 11:40-43)

The Antichrist will be a person of enormous energy. He will be empowered by Satan himself. During the last 3½ years of this age the Antichrist will exhibit supernatural strength. He will accomplish an incredible amount in an extremely short time. He will destroy everywhere. He will control everything and everyone. He will remake all the institutions on the earth. He will coerce the whole world to worship him. He will have authority over the entire inhabited earth. Nobody will be able to withstand him, resist him, or depose him.

Much of the Antichrist's control over the earth will be gained through military conquest. He will expand through Eastern Europe, Asia Minor, the Middle East, and North Africa. Throughout the whole Mideast there will be war and destruction. Whenever any nation or group of people rise up against him, the Antichrist will swiftly destroy them. No one will be safe from his hand.

The Antichrist will be a military genius, swift in his movements, full of the cunning and wiles of the devil. No one will be able to stand against him militarily. He will stomp upon and trample down all the nations around the Mediterranean. He will swiftly seize control of these countries and bring them under his influence. His military victories will be extraordinary and remarkable. He will combine the military talents of all the outstanding leaders that have gone before him—Nebuchadnezzar, Darius the Mede, Alexander the Great, and the Roman Caesars. He will outshine all who have preceded him in his brilliant military victories.

The Antichrist will not fight with every country on the face of the earth. He will not need to. Those countries that he does not defeat by his military prowess he will control through economic means. He may use the economic chaos brought about by the sixth seal and first four trumpets to seize control in what remains of the financial markets and institutions throughout the world. Today many countries are in massive debt. When the judgments at the beginning of the tribulation strike the earth, the economies of countries worldwide will be devastated. The Antichrist will somehow manipulate all of this to his advantage. He will, no doubt, have extraordinary economic resources. He may use his conquests in the Middle East and North Africa to control much of the world's oil supply. By these and other means He will reign over the earth's finances.

The Antichrist may also have top level access to what remains of the world's computer systems. Even today the whole earth's finances are dependent upon computers and computer networks. The one who controls these controls the world. The Antichrist will probably have this power. He will be able to shut down whatever financial entity he pleases through his control of computers. He will be able to bankrupt, and thereby destroy, any institution or company. He will be able to shut off the flow of capital and resources to whomever he wills. By these he will control the whole inhabited earth.

The Antichrist's economic power is revealed in Revelation 13. There, through the false prophet, he even limits buying and selling. Only those who have the mark of the beast, the Antichrist's name or number, upon their wrist or forehead will be able to buy or sell anything.* This mark may include a connection to a vast computer network and artificial intelligence.† Only through

---

* This shows the evil of today's commerce. The Lord Jesus calls money the "mammon of unrighteousness" (Luke 16:9). It is unrighteous by its very nature. One day money will fail. Thus, in the coming kingdom age there will be neither money nor commerce.

The evil hidden in commerce will be exposed in the last days. At that time, in order to carry out Satan's evil system of trade, the mark of the beast, the Antichrist, will be needed. This will be the satanic approval to participate in the satanic system.

† See the book, *The Beast, His Image, and His Mark,* for more about the mark of the beast.

such a connection would the purchase of goods be allowed.* It may be that all transactions will be directed by an artificial intelligence under the control of the Antichrist.

The Antichrist's manipulation of finances will result in enormous suffering throughout the earth. Many people will refuse to accept the mark of the beast. Certainly Christians will reject it. Many Jews and unbelievers also will. Those who do not receive this mark will be designated for persecution. They will have extreme difficulty living. Food, clothing, lodging, medical assistance—everything needed to sustain life—will be very difficult to procure. Many will have to rely on the mercy of others for food, clothing, and other assistance. A large number of unbelievers will have compassion on God's people. Heeding the eternal gospel[†] they will fear God and accordingly treat God's people with kindness—feeding them, clothing them, tending to their wounds, and visiting them in prison. Without this care from the unbelievers many more of God's people would die. The Lord will repay these God-fearing people at His return for their kind treatment of His brothers.[1‡]

The Desolation of the Temple

Yea, it magnified itself, even to the prince of the host; and it took away from him the continual burnt- offering, and the place of his sanctuary was cast down. And the host was given over to it together with the continual burnt-offering through transgression; and it cast down truth to the ground, and it did its pleasure and prospered. (Daniel 8:11-12)

And he will make a firm covenant with the many for one week, but in the middle of the week he will put a stop to sacrifice and grain offering; and on the wing of abominations will come one who makes desolate, even until a complete destruction, one that

---

* If true, this would imply that a cashless society will exist at that time.

† See *The Eternal Gospel* in Chapter 4.

‡ See *Judging the Nations* in Chapter 10

*is decreed, is poured out upon the one who makes desolate.** *(Daniel 9:27)*

And from the time that the continual burnt-offering shall be taken away, and the abomination that maketh desolate set up... (Daniel 12:11)

When therefore ye see the abomination of desolation, which was spoken of through Daniel the prophet, standing in the holy place (let him that readeth understand), then let them that are in Judaea flee unto the mountains: let him that is on the housetop not go down to take out things that are in his house: and let him that is in the field not return back to take his cloak. But woe unto them that are with child and to them that give suck in those days! And pray ye that your flight be not in the winter, neither on a sabbath: for then shall be great tribulation, such as hath not been from the beginning of the world until now, no, nor ever shall be. (Matthew 24:15-21)

And he deceiveth them that dwell on the earth by reason of the signs which it was given him to do in the sight of the beast; saying to them that dwell on the earth, that they should make an image to the beast who hath the stroke of the sword and lived. And it was given unto him to give breath to it, even to the image to the breast, that the image of the beast should both speak, and cause that as many as should not worship the image of the beast should be killed. (Revelation 13:14-15)

Near the beginning of his reign over all the earth, near the start of the last 3½ years of this age, the Antichrist will desolate the temple in Jerusalem. This will occur shortly after his death and resuscitation. The Antichrist will sit in the temple saying that he is God. He will claim to be the true God. He will substantiate his claim through miracles and signs, and particularly through his resuscitation.

The Antichrist, by the hand of the false prophet, will set up the abomination of desolation in the holy place of the temple. This abomination of desolation will be an idol set up in the temple

---

* New American Standard Bible

as a great blasphemy to God and the Jewish religion.* This event will mark the beginning of the great tribulation to the Jews.† The false prophet will force the Jews to worship the idol. The choice given to so many at that time will be to bow before the idol of Antichrist or die. What a terrible and fearful situation that will be.

The Antichrist will also stop the animal sacrifices, oblations, and offerings of the reinstituted Levitical service in Jerusalem. He will completely end the Jewish worship of God. Yet, this will be altogether of God. God will stop the worship having as its basis a rejection of Him as embodied in His Son. At that time, in the words of Isaiah, "He who kills an ox is like he who slays a man; He who sacrifices a lamb, like he who breaks a dog's neck; He who offers a meal offering is like he who offers the blood of swine; He who burns incense is like he who blesses an idol."[2] How repulsive the Jewish worship during the endtime will be to God! Eventually God will use the Antichrist to dismantle it.

In the Gospels the Lord uttered a warning concerning the abomination of desolation. He said that when the abomination is seen standing in the holy place, then those who are in Judea should flee to the mountains. They should not turn back to pick up any clothing or other goods, but flee immediately. To whom was the Lord addressing these words of warning? Certainly it was not to the Jews as a whole, since they have rejected both Him and the New Testament. Nor was it to the believing Gentiles, for there should be very few, if any, non-Jewish Christians in Israel at the time of the end. This word was uttered for the believing remnant of Israel—for the 144,000 who will be sealed just prior to the setting up of the abomination of desolation. At that time these newly saved Jews will heed these words of the Lord. They will see the abomination of desolation set up in the temple, perhaps by means of television or some other form of mass media. They will know that this is a sign for them to flee, for they will have

---

* This abomination of desolation was typified by the idol Antiochus Epiphenes set up in the temple about 168 B.C. When he defiled the temple with his idol, he also offered swine upon the altar of the temple.

† The time of trial that comes upon the whole earth begins with the sixth seal, but the great tribulation to the Jews begins with the setting up of the abomination of desolation in the temple. (See the footnote on the great tribulation on page 22.)

been so instructed by those who brought them to Christ. When this occurs, these believers among the Jews will flee to the mountains to avoid the intense suffering that will occur in Israel at the beginning of the great tribulation.

To what mountains will these Jewish believers flee? They cannot be the mountains in Judea, because the believers in Judea are the ones who are to flee. The only other mountains nearby Jerusalem and Judea are those to the south around Mt. Sinai, those across the Jordan River in the country of Jordan, and those to the north in Galilee and southern Syria. It is doubtful that the 144,000 will flee to Mt. Sinai. This very arid and inhospitable region is now in Egyptian hands. Additionally, there is no record of the Lord and His disciples ever having visited that area. It is possible that the 144,000 could flee into the mountains of Jordan. This view is held by some. However, it seems unlikely that Jordan would freely and immediately accept so many Jewish refugees, as the peril of those times will demand.* When the Lord spoke about the mountains, those listening should have understood Him to mean those mountains located in Galilee north of Judea. This area is now called the Golan Heights, part of northern Israel. It may be that this region will be somewhat spared from the intense suffering during the beginning of the tribulation, and thus provide a place of refuge for the newly saved Israelites.

In the Gospels, whenever the Lord went to the mountains outside of Judea it was to Galilee in northern Israel. This area is around Caesarea Philippi, the place to which the Lord traveled to reveal Himself to His disciples.[3] Caesarea Philippi was far from the strong religious influence centered in Jerusalem in the Lord's day. It was away from Judaism, away from the thick, cloudy atmosphere that prevented people from seeing who the Lord was. It was to this spot, at the foot of Mt. Hermon, that the Lord took the disciples to show them that He was the Christ, the Son of the living God.[4] In these mountains the Lord was transfigured before Peter, James, and John, and His divinity unveiled.[5] Here the disciples received the clear vision of who the dear Lord Jesus is.

---

* On the other hand, we are told that Edom, Moab, and the foremost of the children of Ammon, all of which are part of present day Jordan and the West Bank of Israel, will in some way slip away from the hand of the Antichrist (Dan. 11:41).

He is the Son of God. He is God embodied. He is God expressed. He is God shining. He is the One who fulfills the law and the prophets, as typified by Moses and Elijah. He is the One in whom the Father is well-pleased. He is the One we should look to and hear. He is the only One upon whom we should set our eyes!

This vision of Jesus was given in the northern mountains of Israel. It is very possible that during the beginning of the tribulation the Lord will bring His seekers once more to northern Galilee, near Caesarea Philippi* at the base of Mt. Hermon. He will lead His disciples away from the blinding religious atmosphere that even today enshrouds Jerusalem. There the sealed 144,000 will receive the vision of Christ—the incarnate God, the crucified, resurrected, and ascended man. There, apart from the religious influence dominating the rest of Israel, these newly saved believers will be brought into an intimate knowledge of Christ. Perhaps they will be accompanied by Moses and Elijah. This time apart in the mountains will be filled with prayer and seeking after the Lord. During this time they will gain all that is needed for their testimony during the remainder of the tribulation.

The Fifth Trumpet

And I saw, and I heard an eagle, flying in mid heaven, saying with a great voice, Woe, woe, woe, for them that dwell on the earth, by reason of the other voices of the trumpet of the three angels, who are yet to sound. And the fifth angel sounded, and I saw a star from heaven fallen unto the earth: and there was given to him the key of the pit of the abyss. And he opened the pit of the abyss; and there went up a smoke out of the pit, as the smoke of a great furnace; and the sun and the air were darkened by reason of the smoke of the pit. And out of the smoke came forth locusts upon the earth; and power was given them, as the scorpions of the earth have power. And it was said unto them that they should not hurt the grass of the earth, neither any green thing, neither any tree, but only such men as have not the seal of God on their foreheads. And it was given them that they should not kill them,

---

* This may indicate that the Golan Heights will not be given back to Syria, but will remain in the hands of Israel until the Lord's second coming.

but that they should be tormented five months: and their torment was as the torment of a scorpion, when it striketh a man. And in those days men shall seek death, and shall in no wise find it; and they shall desire to die, and death fleeth from them. And the shapes of the locusts were like unto horses prepared for war; and upon their heads as it were crowns like unto gold, and their faces were as men's faces. And they had hair as the hair of women, and their teeth were as teeth of lions. And they had breastplates, as it were breastplates of iron; and the sound of their wings was as the sound of chariots, of many horses rushing to war. And they have tails like unto scorpions, and stings; and in their tails is their power to hurt men five months. They have over them as king the angel of the abyss: his name in Hebrew is Abaddon, and in the Greek tongue he hath the name Apollyon. (Revelation 8:13-9:11)

That which the palmer-worm hath left hath the locust eaten; and that which the locust hath left hath the canker-worm eaten; and that which the canker-worm hath left hath the caterpillar eaten. ... For a nation is come up upon my land, strong, and without number; his teeth are the teeth of a lion, and he hath the jaw-teeth of a lioness. (Joel 1:4, 6)

Blow ye the trumpet in Zion, and sound an alarm in my holy mountain; let all the inhabitants of the land tremble: for the day of Jehovah cometh, for it is nigh at hand; a day of darkness and gloominess, a day of clouds and thick darkness, as the dawn spread upon the mountains; a great people and a strong; there hath not been ever the like, neither shall be any more after them, even to the years of many generations. A fire devoureth before them; and behind them a flame burneth: the land is as the garden of Eden before them, and behind them a desolate wilderness; yea, and none hath escaped them. The appearance of them is as the appearance of horses; and as horsemen, so do they run. Like the noise of chariots on the tops of the mountains do they leap, like the noise of a flame of fire that devoureth the stubble, as a strong people set in battle array. At their presence the peoples are in anguish; all faces are waxed pale. They run like mighty men; they climb the wall like men of war; and they march every one on his ways, and they break not their ranks. Neither doth one thrust another; they march every one in his path; and they burst through the weapons, and break not off their course. They leap upon the city; they run upon the wall; they climb up into the houses; they enter in at the windows like a thief. The earth quaketh before them; the heavens tremble; the sun and the moon are darkened, and the stars withdraw their shining. And Jehovah uttereth his voice before his army; for his camp is very great; for he is strong that executeth his word; for the day of Jehovah is great and very terrible; and who can abide it? (Joel 2:1-11)

But when ye see Jerusalem compassed with armies, then know that her desolation is at hand. Then let them that are in Judaea flee unto the mountains; and let them that are in the midst of her depart out; and let not them that are in the country enter therein. (Luke 21:20-21)

The great tribulation is composed mainly of three great woes. The first of these is the fifth trumpet that will sound near the beginning of the tribulation. This will happen about the same time that the abomination of desolation is being set up in the temple. It will be marked by armies surrounding Jerusalem in preparation for its destruction.* The abomination of desolation, with the accompanying persecution of the Jews by the armies invading Israel in the woe of the fifth trumpet, will be the principal cause of the great tribulation to the Jews during the endtime.

The fifth trumpet will be the first judgment to strike mankind directly. The previous four trumpets and the sixth seal will only indirectly touch man. Though many men will die during these judgments, the judgments themselves are leveled against the earth, trees, grass, heavens, oceans, and waters. With the fifth trumpet, God begins to touch men directly.

---

* Many people believe that the verses in Luke 21, which speak of Jerusalem being surrounded by armies and destroyed, refer to the destruction of Jerusalem in A.D. 70 by the Roman armies under Titus. While it is possible that a partial fulfillment to these verses occurred at that time, the complete and ultimate fulfillment of this portion of the Word waits for the time of the great tribulation. In this passage the surrounding of Jerusalem by armies, with its being given over to the Gentiles for its destruction, is coupled with the Lord's second coming. Verse 25 joins the occupation of Jerusalem by the Gentiles to the Lord's physical return to the earth. This indicates that these verses will not be fulfilled completely until the time of the end.

In addition, the first four trumpets and the sixth seal, though causing great destruction upon the earth, will continue but a short time. Their aftereffects will be long-lasting, but the actual judgments themselves will be relatively brief. When the fifth trumpet sounds, it will last for five *months*. For these reasons the fifth trumpet is considered the first of the woes, being far more severe than the previous judgments from God.

When the fifth trumpet sounds, a plague of locusts will come forth from the opened pit of the abyss to torment mankind. These are *not* physical locusts. They will *not* be like those of the plague that struck Egypt in Moses' time.[6] First of all, these locusts come up from the abyss, which is the place of spirits. This is the place under the earth to which the Lord Jesus descended in His death. It is the temporary holding place for the dead. Since these locusts come up from the abyss they cannot be physical locusts. Second, these locusts have a king over them, the angel* of the abyss, who is called Abaddon and Apollyon.† Physical locusts do not have a king over them. Third, these locusts sting; physical locusts do not. Finally, the locusts have men's faces and look like horses. From all these facts it is clear that the locusts of the fifth trumpet are not a kind of physical insect.

These locusts should be like those described in Joel 1. There, the armies of the Gentiles that desolate Israel are called locusts. In Joel 1 four different kinds of locusts are depicted. These refer to the armies of the four empires that would destroy the Jews—the Babylonians, Medo-Persians, Greeks, and, in particular, the Romans. These armies swarm over everything, just as locusts do.

---

* The word "angel" does not always refer to the God-created spiritual ministers, such as Michael or Gabriel. The word "angel" can also refer to any one who is a messenger. Thus, the Lord Jesus Himself is said to be an "angel" numerous times in Revelation (7:2; 8:3-5; 10:1, 5; 18:1). In the Old Testament He appeared various times as the "angel of Jehovah" (e.g., Ex. 3:2; Jud. 13:13-20). Furthermore, in Revelation the Spirit spoke to the "angels" of the seven churches (2:1, 8, 12, 18; 3:1, 7, 14). These angels are not the ministering spirits, but rather the shining stars among the believers (Rev. 1:20). Thus the word "angel," as used in Revelation 9:11, should not always be taken in the commonly understood way. Here it refers to the Antichrist as the messenger of destruction, who will come forth from the abyss.

† This angel of the abyss is the coming Antichrist, or more properly, the spirit of the coming Antichrist.

They devour all that is in their path. They find their way into everything—every hole, every hiding place, every closet, every secret area. Nothing can stop nor dissuade them. Because of this they are described as locusts. Thus, the term "locusts" is used in Joel, and also in Revelation, to indicate a particular kind of swarming plague.

Who then are these locusts? They are described as armies prepared for battle. Furthermore, their king is the one who comes up from the abyss, the Antichrist. Thus, these locusts must be the armies of the Antichrist. But they will not be ordinary armies. They will be demon-possessed. This is indicated by the description of the locusts. They are said to have tails like scorpions with stings, symbolizing demons.[7] Just as the spirit of Nero will come forth from the abyss to inhabit the body of the Antichrist, so the demonic spirits from the abyss will possess his armies. Like scorpions, they will be violent and venomous, fierce and unstoppable.

The description of the locusts is very informative. They are said to be like horses prepared for battle. That is, they will be armored horsemen. They will have crowns of gold. These will be the battle helmets of the horsemen. They will have men's faces. This reveals that they are not physical insects or horses alone, but horse*men*. They will have hair like women.* They will have teeth like lions. This description is used for Nebuchadnezzar and the Antichrist as well. This indicates that the horsemen will be a fierce, cruel, and vicious people, ripping men and nations apart. They will have breastplates of iron. That is, they will be clad in nearly impenetrable battle armor. Their sound will be like the chariots of many horses. No doubt, the Antichrist's armies will include many "chariots." Their tails will be like scorpions with stings. We cannot say what these stings will be. Perhaps they will be some kind of excruciatingly painful weapon, or even something demonic and supernatural.

During that time the armies of the Antichrist will have only one intent. They will not harm the grass or the trees. Their only

---

* The confusion between the sexes is already prevalent on the earth today. This depiction in Revelation may not only say something about the kind of people the Antichrist's followers will be, but also about the Antichrist himself (see, for example, Dan. 11:7 and Rev. 11:8).

desire and their sole mission will be to torment mankind. They will mainly cause suffering to the people of Israel.* However, there will also be great persecution wherever the Antichrist's armies are.

The fifth trumpet will be a strong judgment from God to the godless, Christ-rejecting, sinful Jews. By that time Jerusalem will have become so evil that it is called Sodom and Egypt.[8] It is also termed the place where the Lord Jesus was crucified. Therefore, because of their rejection of Christ, their sodomitical sinfulness, and their evil, Egyptian worldliness, God will send the strongest judgment upon them. This will come through the Antichrist and his armies. During this time the Antichrist will use every available means to coerce the Jews and others to worship him and his image. Yet, God will wisely use this torment to soften the Jews to the gospel which will be preached to them during the remainder of the tribulation.

The torment of the fifth trumpet will last for five months. During this time the Antichrist will torture those in Israel. The torment of the affliction from the Antichrist's demon-possessed armies will be so intense, so excruciating, that men will earnestly long to die. The pain from the sting of these locusts will not be like that of a bee sting, which comes and then quickly goes. Rather, the wounds the locusts inflict will be long-lasting, severe, and intense. Men will writhe in pain when "stung." They will desire to die because of the severe torment they will have to endure, but death will flee from them. For five months men will suffer non-lethal, yet unbearable pain and indescribable agony.

How is it that the armies of the Antichrist could enter Israel? Israel has an exceptionally strong military. It not only outmatches all the Arab armies together, but is probably more than the equal of most European countries as well. The armies of an invading European force would face an extremely difficult battle were they to invade Israel. Israel would certainly fight for its existence to prevent such an incursion, perhaps even using nuclear weapons in its national defense. Yet, throughout the Bible there is no mention of any kind of battle between Israel and the Antichrist at

---

* The fact that the 144,000 sealed Jews of Israel will not be hurt by the Antichrist's armies shows that Israel is the focus of this particular woe.

the start of the tribulation. How can this be? Perhaps the Antichrist's armies will already be in Israel at that time, as peace keepers for the seven-year pact between the Antichrist and the Jews.

It may be that after the covenant between the Antichrist and Israel is signed, many of the armies of the Antichrist will be stationed in Israel to guarantee peace between it and its Arab neighbors. The Levitical service will be reinstituted, and the temple will be rebuilt. Sacrifices will be offered upon the altar before the temple in Jerusalem. The apparent success of the pact may prompt Israel to issue the Antichrist an official invitation to visit Jerusalem and the temple. This may occur about the time of one of the Jewish feasts, such as the Passover. Perhaps at the time that he is in Israel the Antichrist will be slain. It may be that a religious zealot, perceiving the evil person of the Antichrist, will assassinate him. Satan will then release the spirit of Caesar Nero along with many demons from the abyss. The Antichrist will be miraculously revived, and his armies possessed by the demons. The Antichrist's armies will certainly be evil and godless—they will be open to receive the demons—but the demons possessing them will make them all the more evil and vicious. Immediately after his resuscitation the Antichrist will consolidate his power and organize his forces. He will then take the opportunity offered by his own death to persecute the Jews. In a very short time he will gather his armies to surround Jerusalem. He will sit himself in the temple declaring that he is God. Through the false prophet he will erect an idol to himself in the holy place of the temple. The wise among the Jews, no doubt including the sealed 144,000, will see these signs and flee to the mountains from the intense suffering about to begin. There they will be instructed and prepared for their testimony during the remainder of the tribulation. The Antichrist will then immediately start to torment the Jews through his armies, in order to force them to worship him as God. This will continue for five months. How dreadful a place Israel will be during the great tribulation.

Israel Destroyed

For thus saith Jehovah: We have heard a voice of trembling, of fear, and not of peace. Ask ye now, and see whether a man doth travail with child: wherefore do I see every man with his hands on his loins, as a woman in travail, and all faces are turned into paleness? Alas! for that day is great, so that none is like it: it is even the time of Jacob's trouble; but he shall be saved out of it. (Jeremiah 30:5-7)

... and there shall be a time of trouble, such as never was since there was a nation even to that same time... (Daniel 12:1)

And there was given me a reed like unto a rod: and one said, Rise, and measure the temple of God, and the altar, and them that worship therein. And the court which is without the temple leave without, and measure it not; for it hath been given unto the nations: and the holy city shall they tread under foot forty and two months. (Revelation 11:1-2)

But when ye see Jerusalem compassed with armies, then know that her desolation is at hand. Then let them that are in Judaea flee unto the mountains; and let them that are in the midst of her depart out; and let not them that are in the country enter therein. For these are days of vengeance, that all things which are written may be fulfilled. Woe unto them that are with child and to them that give suck in those days! for there shall be great distress upon the land, and wrath unto this people. And they shall fall by the edge of the sword, and shall be led captive into all the nations: and Jerusalem shall be trodden down of the Gentiles, until the times of the Gentiles be fulfilled. (Luke 21:20-24)

And he deceiveth them that dwell on the earth by reason of the signs which it was given him to do in the sight of the beast; saying to them that dwell on the earth, that they should make an image to the beast who hath the stroke of the sword and lived. And it was given unto him to give breath to it, even to the image to the breast, that the image of the beast should both speak, and cause that as many as should not worship the image of the beast should be killed. And he causeth all, the small and the great, and the rich and the poor, and the free and the bond, that there be given them a mark on their right hand, or upon their forehead; and that no man should be able to buy or to sell, save he that hath the mark, even the name of the beast or the number of his name. (Revelation 13:14-17)

And it shall come to pass, that in all the land, saith Jehovah, two parts therein shall be cut off and die; but the third shall be left therein. (Zechariah 13:8)

For I will gather all nations against Jerusalem to battle; and the city shall be taken, and the houses rifled, and the women ravished; and half of the city shall go forth into captivity, and the residue of the people shall not be cut off from the city. (Zechariah 14:2)

... my people and for my heritage Israel, whom they have scattered among the nations: and they have parted my land, and have cast lots for my people, and have given a boy for a harlot, and sold a girl for wine, that they may drink. (Joel 3:2-3)

The five months of torment inflicted by the Antichrist during the fifth trumpet will merely be the beginning of his destruction of Israel. The whole 3½ years of the great tribulation is called the time of Jacob's trouble. There will be no other suffering to Israel to compare with that time. When we consider some of the destruction that has taken place in the holy land, as when Babylon devastated it in 586 B.C. and Titus destroyed it in A.D. 70, this is all the more remarkable. When Nebuchadnezzar razed Israel there was hardly a soul left—only the poor remained to keep the land. When Rome destroyed Jerusalem in A.D. 70 not one stone of the temple was left upon another, and Jerusalem was carried away captive. At both these times the suffering was so intense and the famine so great that parents even ate their children.[9] When we read Josephus' eyewitness account of what occurred in A.D. 70, it is hard to imagine that such calamities could befall a people. Yet, the time of the great tribulation will bring far greater torment, persecution, and death.

Jerusalem will be given over to the Gentiles for 42 months, during which it will be destroyed. This will be the "times of the Gentiles" spoken of by the Lord in Luke 21. For the third time in history Jerusalem will be taken from Jewish hands, each time due to the Jews' rejection of God. During this 42 months the false prophet will cause untold agony among the Jewish people. He will force them to receive the mark of the beast on their forehead or their hand under threat of death. Many of those who do not receive the mark will be killed. Those who do will eventually be thrown into the lake of fire for eternity.[10] Those who do not have the mark of the beast will not be able to buy or sell. This will be particularly true in Israel, the area under the control of the false prophet. There will be hunger and deprivation both in Israel and Europe.

Those 3½ years will be a time of unparalleled destruction and torment. Israel will be in a complete shambles. Her cities will be destroyed. Many Jews will be massacred. The women will be ravished. The people will be enslaved. Her children will be sold in exchange for prostitutes. The Jews will be scattered throughout the whole earth yet once again. They will die miserable deaths. Two thirds of the Jews will be killed. Only one third will survive that time of fiery trial that they might repent, believe, and be saved.

The abomination of desolation spoken of in Matthew 24, the fifth trumpet portrayed in Revelation 9, and Jerusalem being given over to the Gentiles as revealed in Luke 21 are three views of one event. All these are different aspects of the Antichrist's persecution and destruction of Israel during the great tribulation. This destruction starts with the desolation of the temple by the idol of abomination. It continues for five months with the demon-possessed armies of the fifth trumpet. It proceeds throughout the great tribulation for the complete destruction of Israel. It will end with Israel completely and utterly hopeless, just before the Lord's return to earth.

God's Testimony in Israel

And I will give unto my two witnesses, and they shall prophesy a thousand two hundred and threescore days, clothed in sackcloth. These are the two olive trees and the two candlesticks, standing before the Lord of the earth. And if any man desireth to hurt them, fire proceedeth out of their mouth and devoureth their enemies; and if any man shall desire to hurt them, in this manner must he be killed. These have the power to shut the heaven, that it rain not during the days of their prophecy: and they have power over the waters to turn them into blood, and to smite the earth with every plague, as often as they shall desire. ... these two prophets tormented them that dwell on the earth (Revelation 11:3-6, 10)

And I heard the number of them that were sealed, a hundred and forty and four thousand, sealed out of every tribe of the children of Israel... (Revelation 7:4)

Behold, I send you forth as sheep in the midst of wolves: be ye therefore wise as serpents, and harmless as doves. But beware of men: for they will deliver you up to councils, and in their synagogues they will scourge you; yea and before governors and kings shall ye be brought for my sake, for a testimony to them and to the Gentiles. But when they deliver you up, be not anxious how or what ye shall speak: for it shall be given you in that hour what ye shall speak. For it is not ye that speak, but the Spirit of your Father that speaketh in you. And brother shall deliver up brother to death, and the father his child: and children shall rise up against parents, and cause them to be put to death. And ye shall be hated of all men for my name's sake: but he that endureth to the end, the same shall be saved. But when they persecute you in this city, flee into the next: for verily I say unto you, Ye shall not have gone through the cities of Israel, till the Son of man be come. (Matthew 10:16-23)

In the time of her greatest distress God will not forsake Israel. The merciful Lord will still preserve for Himself a testimony that Israel might be saved. This testimony will first be announced by the two witnesses, Moses and Elijah. On the negative side they will call forth plagues on the evil and wicked world. They will devour their enemies by fire. They will bring drought upon the earth and parch it during the days of their testimony, and whatever water remains they will turn into blood. Israel, with the whole world, will suffer intensely from the resultant lack of water. By their frequent plagues the two witnesses will torment the whole earth. Those who dwell on the earth and reject God will hate them and desire to destroy them.

On the positive side, the two witnesses will testify to Israel concerning Christ. They will testify about His incarnation as a man, His human living, His redemptive and life-releasing death,

His regenerative resurrection, His ascension and enthronement in the heavens, and His second coming. They will also prophesy concerning the kingdom of God and the coming Millennium. Furthermore, they will condemn Satan, the Antichrist, the false prophet, and those who follow them.

In conjunction with the two witnesses, the 144,000 sealed Jews will also testify concerning Christ to Israel during the great tribulation. They should receive instruction and preparation for this testimony during the five months of the fifth trumpet, when they flee to the mountains from the persecution of the Antichrist. After that, they will spread the gospel to all Israel. As the Lord sent His disciples out two by two in His day, so shall He send the 144,000 to testify to everyone in Israel.[11] They will go out two by two to every city and to every door. They will go to every Jewish household in Israel. Toward those who reject the gospel they will brush off the dust of their feet as a testimony against them. With those who are open to the gospel, they will abide, speaking Christ, relaying what they have received from the Lord. They will be preparing Israel for her salvation at the time of the Lord's return. It will not be until they have gone through every city of Israel that the Lord Jesus will come back.

The 144,000 will meet fierce opposition as they bring the gospel to the Jews in Israel. They will be given up to death by members of their own family. They will be persecuted in the synagogues. They will be rejected again and again. Yet, in this time of cruel and inhuman treatment, they will not lose a hair of their heads.[12] In fact, through this severe persecution they will gain their souls. They will reign with Christ during the Millennium.[13]

During this time many of them, perhaps even all, will be martyred. The Antichrist and the false prophet will seek to destroy them in every place. Their own families and friends will turn against them, handing them over into death. Yet, in spite of the death of massive numbers among them, they will be faithful to the Lord to testify concerning Him. They will be emboldened by the empowering seven Spirits to stand against every kind of persecution. They will testify of all that Christ is, has accomplished, and will do at His second coming. That such a large number—144,000—is required to preach the gospel to the small nation of Israel during a period of more than three years indicates how many of them will die. Yet, they will not be deterred by the Antichrist, by the false prophet, by the opposing Jews, or even by their own relatives from bringing Christ into that godless land. It is through their testimony and the testimony of the two witnesses that all of Israel will be prepared to receive salvation at the time of the Lord's return.

The Antichrist's Persecution of Religion

And he opened his mouth for blasphemies against God, to blaspheme his name, and his tabernacle, even them that dwell in the heaven. And it was given unto him to make war with the saints, and to overcome them: and there was given to him authority over every tribe and people and tongue and nation. ... If any man hath an ear, let him hear. If any man is for captivity, into captivity he goeth: if any man shall kill with the sword, with the sword must he be killed. Here is the patience and the faith of the saints. ... And it was given unto him to give breath to it, even to the image to the beast, that the image of the beast should both speak, and cause that as many as should not worship the image of the beast should be killed. (Revelation 13:6-7, 9-10, 15)

Here is the patience of the saints, they that keep the commandments of God, and the faith of Jesus. And I heard the voice from heaven saying, Write, Blessed are the dead who die in the Lord from henceforth: yea, saith the Spirit, that they may rest from their labors; for their works follow with them. (Revelation 14:12-13)

And I saw as it were a sea of glass mingled with fire; and them that come off victorious from the beast, and from his image, and from the number of his name, standing by the sea of glass, having harps of God. (Revelation 15:2)

I beheld, and the same horn made war with the saints, and prevailed against them... (Daniel 7:21)

And it waxed great, even to the host of heaven; and some of the host and of the stars it cast down to the ground, and trampled upon them. (Daniel 8:10)

... he shall destroy the mighty ones and the holy people. (Daniel 8:24)

And the king shall do according to his will; and he shall exalt himself, and magnify himself above every god, and shall speak marvellous things against the God of gods; and he shall prosper till the indignation be accomplished; for that which is determined shall be done. Neither shall he regard the gods of his fathers, nor the desire of women, nor regard any god; for he shall magnify himself above all. (Daniel 11:36-37)

... when they have made an end of breaking in pieces the power of the holy people, all these things shall be finished. (Daniel 12:7)

During the great tribulation the Antichrist will not only persecute the Jews, he will also persecute all religions. The Antichrist, as a person who is one with Satan in every respect, will hate God and everything to do with God. He will reject God, Christ, and everything that is worshipped. He will persecute the believers, especially those in Europe and Israel. He will in some way wear them down, tormenting and torturing them. Many will be martyred. Yet, with their martyrdom they will be counted worthy to reign with Christ during the coming age. Throughout all of the Antichrist's empire there will be intense suffering. This persecution will force many to flee from his kingdom. The Antichrist's persecution of religion will not be limited to the Jews and the believers. He will also persecute everyone who is in any way related to religion, including Catholics, Methodists, Episcopalians, Lutherans, and all Protestants, whether genuine believers or not. Every religious organization will be destroyed and brought to naught. The tribulation will be a time of terror to everyone who in any way worships God.

During this time some of the unbelievers will aid the persecuted saints. They will help the Christians who are suffering in prison, the ones who are wounded, and those who are hungry. They will also assist the Jews as they are scattered among the nations. This help, arranged by a sovereign God, will enable many of God's people to survive the great tribulation.

However, by the end of the tribulation it will seem as if the Antichrist has won in his battle with God. He will put down the saints and destroy the power of the holy people. He will martyr many, if not all, of the believing Jews in Israel and Christians throughout his empire. He will kill the two witnesses, Moses and Elijah,[14] and destroy all religions within his realm. It will appear as if there is no God, but only the Antichrist and Satan.

The Wilderness

And the woman fled into the wilderness, where she hath a place prepared of God, that there they may nourish her a thousand two hundred and threescore days... And when the dragon saw that he was cast down to the earth, he persecuted the woman that brought forth the man child. And there were given to the woman the two wings of the great eagle, that she might fly into the wilderness unto her place, where she is nourished for a time, and times, and half a time, from the face of the serpent. And the serpent cast out of his mouth after the woman water as a river, that he might cause her to be carried away by the stream. And the earth helped the woman, and the earth opened her mouth and swallowed up the river which the dragon cast out of his mouth. (Revelation 12:6, 13-16)

Due to the suffering of those times multitudes of Christians will flee from the Antichrist's empire. They will flee en masse from the torment of Satan, the Antichrist, and others into a safe haven, possibly the United States. Every means possible will be used to escape the storm of tribulation that will sweep Europe like wildfire. It is probable that similar persecutions will occur in the Far East and elsewhere.

Though the earthquake of the sixth seal and the judgments of the first four trumpets will cause immense destruction on earth, and probably greatly damage the West Coast of the United States, much of the US will remain somewhat habitable. A large portion of the South and Midwest will remain arable. Food produced in the rich soil of those regions will sustain the saints, even though conditions will be extremely difficult. It may be that at that time the Lord will bless the United States with a God-fearing president and Congress who will, in the divine mercy and compassion, open the doors of the US to this great flock of immigrants. Though the United States will be suffering great hardship, this president will be moved to give refuge to the persecuted saints.

The wilderness will have been already prepared by that time. It may be that during the first 3½ years of Daniel's seventieth week some of the saints will be enlightened to know what is happening on earth. They will foresee the suffering that will occur during the great tribulation, and prepare accordingly. For so many believers to be sustained during the entire tribulation, there will be the need for vast amounts of physical food to allow the saints to live.

The preparation of the wilderness will more importantly involve the readying of spiritual food. The reason that the majority of believers will be left behind to pass through the great tribulation is their spiritual immaturity. This, in turn, is due to the lack of proper spiritual nourishment. What is needed for their maturity is not simply an outward situation of suffering, but much more the proper spiritual food. This food will be supplied by the proper spiritual literature—literature conveying the divine life in the divine truths.

Today many of God's dear children are suffering from spiritual malnutrition. Many are starving for Christ. Many of us lack the proper spiritual diet. We are eating the wrong food! There is much talk about doctrines, philosophies, social issues, and even political agendas, yet there is an enormous lack of Christ as spiritual food. Our great need, the need of every child of God, is not better teachings, proper philosophies, rituals, political activism, or merely human social involvement. Our great need is Christ—Christ as our food, Christ as our drink, Christ as our spiritual nourishment. Such a Christ causes us to grow to maturity in the divine life. Nothing else can meet the need of today's Christians except Christ Himself as the rich source of supply.

The children of Israel provide an Old Testament picture that depicts our current situation. While the children of Israel were in Egypt they ate leeks, melons, and other Egyptian foods. When the Lord delivered them from Egypt into the wilderness, He changed their diet, giving them manna to eat. Through their years of wandering in the wilderness their tastes, preferences, and desires were slowly transformed by this change in diet. While they were wandering, they still longed to go back to Egypt and, desiring Egyptian food, they murmured against God. Yet, eventually after their long sojourn, they had been purified of their

Egyptian tastes. The heavenly manna had delivered them *subjectively* from Egypt. Their outward deliverance from Egypt was a simple, quick matter; their inward deliverance took many years. After that time in the wilderness they were then ready to enter into the good land to enjoy all its riches—the wheat, barley, figs, pomegranates, grapes, milk, honey, streams, and fountains. All the riches of that wonderful good land became theirs once they had been purified from their Egyptian tastes.

In John 6, the Lord said *He* is the real manna that has come down from heaven.[15] What the children of Israel ate in the wilderness was merely a picture of the reality. Christ Himself is the real manna to be the spiritual food to God's people. He is also the real drink to quench the spiritual thirst of every man.[16] Unfortunately, most of us have had our spiritual "taste buds" damaged by eating so much "Egyptian" food. By being so involved with worldly things our taste for God has been deadened. During the last years of this age, God will once again bring His people into a wilderness. There all the Egyptian, worldly things will be gone. God will feed His people with Christ as the heavenly manna to nourish, sustain, and mature them. That time will be an intensified, 3½ year, spiritual infusion. All the love for the world will be dried up. All the longings and cares for things other than Christ will be ended. All the desires of the flesh and of the soul will be terminated. In their desperate situation, God's children will return to Christ and Christ alone. They will eat and drink of Him, and enjoy Him day by day and even moment by moment, that they might mature as the sons of God. All this will be possible due to the preparation of the proper spiritual food for that time. Through such a wonderful, divine arrangement many of God's children will be perfected to stand before the judgment seat of Christ at His coming.

The Destruction of Religious Babylon

Another parable spake he unto them; The kingdom of heaven is like unto leaven, which a woman took, and hid in three measures of meal, till it was all leavened. (Matthew 13:33)

But I have this against thee, that thou sufferest the woman Jezebel, who calleth herself a prophetess; and she teacheth and seduceth my servants to commit fornication, and to eat things sacrificed to idols. ... But to you I say, to the rest that are in Thyatira, as many as have not this teaching, who know not the deep things of Satan... (Revelation 2:20, 24)

And there came one of the seven angels that had the seven bowls, and spake with me, saying, Come hither, I will show thee the judgment of the great harlot that sitteth upon many waters; with whom the kings of the earth committed fornication, and they that dwell in the earth were made drunken with the wine of her fornication. And he carried me away in the Spirit into a wilderness: and I saw a woman sitting upon a scarlet-colored beast, full of names of blasphemy, having seven heads and ten horns. And the woman was arrayed in purple and scarlet, and decked with gold and precious stone and pearls, having in her hand a golden cup full of abominations, even the unclean things of her fornication, and upon her forehead a name written, MYSTERY, BABYLON THE GREAT, THE MOTHER OF THE HARLOTS AND OF THE ABOMINATIONS OF THE EARTH. And I saw the woman drunken with the blood of the saints, and with the blood of the martyrs of Jesus. And when I saw her, I wondered with a great wonder. And the angel said unto me, Wherefore didst thou wonder? I will tell thee the mystery of the woman, and of the beast that carrieth her, which hath the seven heads and the ten horns. ... Here is the mind that hath wisdom. The seven heads are seven mountains, on which the woman sitteth ... And he saith unto me, The waters which thou sawest, where the harlot sitteth, are peoples, and multitudes, and nations, and tongues. And the ten horns which thou sawest, and the beast, these shall hate the harlot, and shall make her desolate and naked, and shall eat her flesh, and shall burn her utterly with fire. For God did put in their hearts to do his mind, and to come to one mind, and to give their kingdom unto the beast, until the words of God should be accomplished. (Revelation 17:1-7, 9, 15-17)

And in her was found the blood of prophets and of saints, and of all that have been slain upon the earth. (Revelation 18:24)

And another, a second angel, followed, saying, Fallen, fallen is Babylon the great, that hath made all the nations to drink of the wine of the wrath of her fornication. (Revelation 14:8)

After these things I heard as it were a great voice of a great multitude in heaven, saying, Hallelujah; Salvation, and glory, and power, belong to our God: for true and righteous are his judgments; for he hath judged the great harlot, her that corrupted the earth with her fornication, and he hath avenged the blood of his servants at her hand. And a second time they say, Hallelujah. And her smoke goeth up for ever and ever. And the four and twenty elders and the four living creatures fell down and worshipped God that sitteth on the throne, saying, Amen; Hallelujah. (Revelation 19:1-4)

There are three notorious women in the New Testament. The first is mentioned in Matthew 13. There a woman hid leaven in three measures of fine flour until the whole was leavened. Many Christians think that this parable depicts something good. They believe this portrays Christianity in a good way. However, they ignore the fact that in the Scriptures leaven is *always* bad.

In the Old Testament, offerings were nearly always made to God without leaven.*[17] One feast is even called the feast of unleavened bread.[18] In the Gospels the Lord Jesus told His disciples to beware of the leaven of the Pharisees, the Sadducees, and Herod, referring to their teachings and hypocrisy.[19] In his epistles Paul told us repeatedly to beware of leaven.[20] He said a little leaven leavens the whole lump.[21] The leaven of which he spoke is sinful things, evil companionships, malice, and wickedness.[22] Even keeping the law according to the Old Testament tradition of Judaism was considered leaven by Paul.[23] He told the believers to purge out the leaven that they might become an unleavened lump, that they might become a loaf of sincerity and truth.[24] In Paul's eyes anything other than Christ was a kind of leaven. In every case, then, leaven is an evil thing. The woman,

---

* The only leavened offering in the Old Testament (Lev. 23:17) signifies not Christ, but the church. It depicts the church, composed of fallen, yet redeemed men offered to God on the day of Pentecost. Thus, the leaven in this offering signifies the sin within fallen mankind, from whom some, both Jews and Gentiles, have been redeemed to be the church.

therefore, in Matthew 13 is an evil woman, hiding evil things in the fine flour of Christ.

The second notorious woman is mentioned in Revelation 2. In the epistle to the church in Thyatira the Lord speaks of the woman Jezebel, who causes His servants to commit fornication and to eat things sacrificed to idols. This woman Jezebel claims to be a prophetess speaking for God, yet she is not. She is, in fact, leading the Lord's people astray. She uplifts the deep things of Satan—the satanic rituals, doctrines, and knowledge. These deep things of Satan correspond to the leaven the woman added to the fine flour in Matthew 13. Eventually, the Lord will judge this evil Jezebel, throwing her into great affliction and killing her children.

The third infamous woman in the New Testament is depicted in Revelation 17. She is called *Mystery, Babylon the Great.* She is seen ruling over many peoples, multitudes, nations, and tongues. The kings and peoples of the earth commit fornication with her. She is clothed in purple and scarlet. Interestingly, she is gilded with the same materials with which the New Jerusalem is built—gold, pearl, and precious stones. In her case, however, she is merely gilded, not built, with them. She is merely an imitation of the New Jerusalem. She gives the appearance of being the bride of Christ, yet she is an impostor. In her hand she has a golden cup full of abominations. This is again similar to the fine flour mixed with leaven in Matthew 13. The material of the cup is good, being made of gold, yet within it are abominable things. This woman is also drunk with the blood of the saints. She is renowned for her persecution and slaughter of the genuine believers in Christ. Finally, she sits on seven mountains or hills.

Who are these three woman? These three are actually one and the same. The woman who hid the leaven in the fine flour, the Jezebel of Revelation 2, and Mystery, Babylon the Great are one. I believe all three of these depict the Roman Catholic Church.* What other system, entity, or person upon the face of the earth matches the description of these women?

---

* For a detailed account of the striking resemblance between the doctrines, practices, and appearance of the Roman Catholic Church and ancient Babylon, we refer the reader to the book *The Two Babylons* by Alexander Hislop.

In Matthew 13 the woman mixed leaven with fine flour. Fine flour depicts Christ as the New Testament truth. The Roman Catholic Church does have something of this truth. For example, she confesses that Christ is the Son of God, that He is God incarnated to be a man, that He died for men's sins, that He rose again, and that He ascended to the heavens. Yet, as the woman in Matthew 13 mixed leaven with the fine flour, so the Roman Catholic Church has mixed pagan things with the pure truth of Christ. In the Roman Catholic Church there are many misleading, and even false, doctrines. For example, the Roman Catholic Church talks of purgatory, a place in which the souls of the dead suffer indefinitely for their sins. The truth is that Christ suffered once for all for the sins of mankind.[25] Acceptance of Christ in His person and work of redemption saves us from perishing.[26] There is no other way for us to be saved. No suffering by man other than Christ's redemptive death can atone for sins.[27]

Within the Catholic Church is the worship of Mary, whom they call the "mother of God." She is said to have been immaculately conceived. The Roman Catholic Church declares that she was a virgin for her entire life, and that upon her death she was "assumed" into heaven. These assertions all are heresies. God does not have a mother; only the *man*, Jesus, has a mother. Christ in His divinity is eternal, without beginning or ending.[28] Mary was not conceived immaculately. She was born of typical human parents, inheriting sin as every other human.[29] Only Jesus, who was conceived of the divine Father and a human mother, is without sin.[30] Mary was certainly not a virgin her entire life. We are told in many places that she bore offspring other than Jesus of her husband, Joseph.[31] Finally, there is no hint anywhere in the Bible that Mary did anything other than die. She awaits, as do the myriad of God's redeemed, the time of resurrection in the future.

There is much more leaven within the Catholic Church. Consider her holidays. Christ's incarnation is a wonderful, profound, mysterious, and miraculous matter. Yet, within the Roman Catholic Church and even within all Christianity, this divinely human event has been mixed with the celebration of the birth of the sun god to become Christmas.* Christ's resurrection is another mar-velous matter. In this resurrection He was begotten to be the firstborn Son of God, the firstborn among many brothers.[32] In His resurrection the *man*, Jesus, was born to be the Son of *God*! In His resurrection the Lord Jesus also became the life-giving Spirit.[33] Furthermore, in Christ's resurrection God begot us, His many children.[34] These are marvelous, exceptional, wonderful, heavenly matters. Yet, today we see a great mixture concerning Christ's resurrection. We hear of Easter. Easter has as its source Ishtar, the Babylonian goddess of fertility. It is from the ancient Babylonian and Egyptian rites surrounding the worship of the goddess of fertility that the Easter rabbits and Easter eggs come. In the Roman Catholic Church, evil and satanic things have been mixed with Christ's resurrection. This is the leaven mixed with fine flour.

In Revelation 2 the woman, Jezebel, causes many of the Lord's people to sin. First, she causes them to eat idol sacrifices. The "holy communion" of the Roman Catholic Church is such an idol sacrifice. It is generally offered before an idol, and then distributed. In fact, the Roman Catholic Church is a place full of idols and idolatry. Any person with a sensitive conscience who enters a Roman Catholic cathedral would immediately react to the multitude of idols.

In addition, this Jezebel brings the Lord's people into forni-cation. The Roman Catholic Church is full of various kinds of fornication. She is full of spiritual fornication, mixing pagan things with that which is holy and divine. In addition, she is full of physical fornication (sexual deviation) as well, as history and the headlines in today's newspapers have so conspicuously testified.

Where Jezebel is, there are the deep things of Satan. These are the satanic mysteries—the practices, doctrines, and symbols

---

* A check with most any reference source will verify that the source of Christmas was the celebration of the birth of the sun god which occurred right after the winter solstice. When Constantine the Great decreed that everyone born a Roman was a member of the church, he brought many pagan things into Christendom. One of these was the worship of the sun god. This was eventually embraced by the Roman Catholic Church. Today this event still misleads and distracts many believers.

from the evil one himself. Within the Catholic Church are many such things. The worship of the saints is one. Prayers for the dead is another. The rosary and so many other Catholic liturgies are still more. She even interposes her priests as intermediaries between God and man, when only one—the man Christ Jesus—is our intermediary.[35] Consider her confessionals, wherein people confess their sins, not to God, but to her priests. What are all these things? These are the deep things of Satan.

Finally, the Roman Catholic Church claims to speak for God. She calls the dwelling of her pope the Vatican, which means the place of the seer, or the oracle. She asserts that the pope represents Christ on the earth, and speaks with divine authority. Thus, she claims to be a prophetess. Yet, her words are not divine.

The Roman Catholic Church is also the great harlot of Revelation 17. She is seen sitting upon many peoples. The Catholic Church holds hundreds of millions of people under her control. She manipulates and uses them for her own purposes, keeping them under her influence and away from God.

She is also full of political association. This is her spiritual fornication with the kings of the earth. The Catholic Church has become a political entity, sending out ambassadors and being recognized by worldly governments. The genuine church is apart from politics; in her there is room only for Christ.

In Revelation 17 the harlot is clothed in purple, scarlet, and precious things. What more accurate description could be given of the appearance of the Catholic Church? Her pope, cardinals, and bishops array themselves in purple and scarlet. Her cathedrals are full of precious stones and golden objects.

The harlot has a golden cup full of abominations. No one can deny that there is something genuine—"golden"—in the Catholic Church. As mentioned above, many of the things she says concerning Christ are true. Thus, no one could say that the Catholic Church is evil in every respect. But, within her golden "cup" are evil, abominable things. These are her evil practices and doctrines. Thus, her greatest evil is her mixture. She is worse than that which is completely evil, because she deceives people by her good appearance. Who is easily deceived by murderers or other evil doers? But the Catholic Church, by mixing many evil things with a good appearance, is more deceptive and more evil than that which is blatantly wicked.

The Catholic Church is also drunk with the blood of the saints. Throughout history the Roman Catholic Church has been a notorious persecutor of the true believers. She is known to have killed more genuine Christians than the Roman Empire. Her torture of the saints has also been more cruel and brutal. The inhuman things she did during the Inquisition under the hands of Torquemada, the first grand inquisitor, the Jesuits, Dominicans, Franciscans, and others are historical facts. No one can deny her drunkenness. She is drunk with the blood of the saints.*

Finally, this evil woman sits upon seven hills, seven mountains. It is no accident that the Vatican is located within the city of Rome, which is built upon seven hills. When John wrote this he was fully aware that only one city of his time was situated upon seven hills. Thus, there can be no mistake but that this woman is the Roman Catholic Church.

God hates this woman. He hates her as the woman in Matthew 13; He hates her as Jezebel in Revelation 2; He hates her as the harlot in Revelation 17. He hates her to such a degree that He will use the Antichrist, the most vile person, to judge her. The Antichrist, with the ten kings who follow him, will be doing God's mind when he destroys the Roman Catholic Church.† God will use the most evil man to judge this most evil system. Praise Him!

As the great tribulation progresses, the Antichrist and the ten kings will rise up to fight against all religions as depicted in Revelation 14. They will persecute the Jews and the believers. They will especially destroy the Roman Catholic Church. They will have had enough of her interference, her manipulation, and

---

* If the reader has any doubt about these matters, he or she is invited to read the book, *Foxe's Book of Martyrs*, which details some of the persecutions, tortures, and murders of the Catholic Church.

† Because the Roman Catholic Church is evil does not mean that there are no genuine believers within her. Certainly, there are some within the Catholic Church who are children of God—genuine, born-again, blood-washed Christians. What we condemn here, even as the Lord Himself condemns, is not God's children who remain within the Catholic Church, but the system of the Catholic Church itself.

her control of the people. By that time Satan will no longer have any use for her. He will desire the direct worship of himself in the person of the Antichrist. He will no longer tolerate any kind of worship of God. Thus, he will intervene through the Antichrist to destroy Catholicism. The Antichrist and his followers will make the Catholic Church desolate and naked. They will eat her flesh and burn her with fire. This will be "Jezebel's" great affliction spoken of in Revelation 2. By this, Catholicism's children will be killed with death.

The Antichrist and the ten kings will expose the evils of the Catholic Church completely. They will strip her and rob her of her riches. They will then burn her to the ground. The Vatican will be fully destroyed; the Catholic cathedrals throughout Europe will be razed. All the Roman Catholic idols and relics will be burned utterly. Furthermore, her clergy and followers will be slaughtered. It is very likely that the pope, the cardinals, the bishops, priests, and others will all be killed.* Her destruction will be the righteous judgment of God.

This will come as a great shock to Catholics and other religious people worldwide. The Roman Catholic Church will have been completely destroyed, her hierarchy completely demolished. All her idols will be smashed. The great Catholic cathedrals will be utterly destroyed, burned with fire. This evil system will be completely torn down. All of this will occur because "the Lord God who judges her is strong."[36] It is through such a judgment from the powerful, righteous God that all the genuine believers in Catholicism will turn from her wiles, deceptions, and fornications back to Christ Himself.

When the Catholic Church is destroyed there will be rejoicing in the heavens. There will be great joy among those who will have been raptured before that time. No doubt the rejoicing ones will include many† that the Catholic Church martyred throughout

---

* This, however, will not be martyrdom, but God's judgment. We know this to be true because God tells His people to "come out of her," that they not partake of her plagues (Rev. 18:4).

† Those Christians slaughtered by the Catholic Church throughout the Dark Ages, martyred during the Inquisition, and persecuted during the Reformation will be included within the manchild. They will be raptured before the great tribulation. (See *The Rapture of the Manchild* in Chapter 4.)

the centuries. When the Catholic Church is razed by the Antichrist and burned utterly, they will rejoice with exultation, praising God for all that He has done. Even the angelic elders and the living creatures in the heavens will join in this celebration. All will praise God for His judgment. This will be a partial answer to the cry of the martyred saints during the fifth seal. Praise our Lord for His coming judgment upon the Roman Catholic Church!

The Sixth Trumpet

And the sixth angel sounded, and I heard a voice from the horns of the golden altar which is before God, one saying to the sixth angel that had one trumpet, Loose the four angels that are bound at the great river Euphrates. And the four angels were loosed, that had been prepared for the hour and day and month and year, that they should kill the third part of men. And the number of the armies of the horsemen was twice ten thousand times ten thousand: I heard the number of them. And thus I saw the horses in the vision, and them that sat on them, having breastplates as of fire and of hyacinth and of brimstone: and the heads of lions; and out of their mouths proceedeth fire and smoke and brimstone. By these three plagues was the third part of men killed, by the fire and the smoke and the brimstone, which proceeded out of their mouths. For the power of the horses is in their mouth, and in their tails: for their tails are like unto serpents, and have heads; and with them they hurt. And the rest of mankind, who were not killed with these plagues, repented not of the works of their hands, that they should not worship demons, and the idols of gold, and of silver, and of brass, and of stone, and of wood; which can neither see, nor hear, nor walk: and they repented not of their murders, nor of their sorceries, nor of their fornication, nor of their thefts. (Revelation 9:13-21)

And the sixth poured out his bowl upon the great river, the river Euphrates; and the water thereof was dried up, that the way might by made ready for the kings that come from the sunrising. (Revelation 16:12)

Near the middle of the tribulation, sometime after the five months of torment from the locusts of the fifth trumpet, the sixth trumpet will sound. This will be the second of the three great woes that comprise the great tribulation. At that time four angels, who are bound at the river Euphrates, will be released. These are, no doubt, evil angels. They have been held for an unspecified amount of time until the great tribulation. They have been prepared for the hour, day, month, and year. This is the duration of this woe. It will last for an hour, *plus* a day, *plus* a month, *plus* a year, a total of 13 months and 25 hours.

When these angels are released they will do one thing—kill. They are not told to kill; they just like to kill. They are murderous angels. It is their pleasure to kill men. Because of them the third part[*] of men will die.

These angels will slaughter mankind by means of 200 million horsemen, an incredibly large army. These horsemen will have breastplates of fire, hyacinth, and brimstone. These are the colors of their breastplates—fiery red, deep blue or purple, and yellow. They will have heads like lions. They will be fierce. From the mouths of the horses come forth fire, smoke, and brimstone. This may be a reference to modern weapons. The Apostle John, of course, had no word to describe rifles. He merely relayed in the language of his day what he saw in his vision. He may have viewed the firing of present-day rifles. Modern day guns emit fire from the flash of the gunshot, smoke from the burning of the gunpowder, and brimstone, the bullet coming from the muzzle. These three combine together to kill people, just as in John's vision. The fire, smoke, and brimstone coming from the mouths of the horses may refer to the vicinity of the gunshots, as when a rifle is fired from the shoulder of a horseman. Thus, it is possible that the horsemen in the vision of the sixth trumpet will destroy the third of mankind with rifles and other present-day weapons. The tails of the horses will be like serpents with heads. With these they also hurt and maim men. What a dreadful plague these 200 million cavalrymen will be.

---

[*] As with the first four trumpets, "the third part of men" mentioned in Revelation 9 should refer not to a *random* third of the people on the earth, but to that *particular evil* third of mankind.

When the sixth trumpet sounds, God will release the four angels bound at the river Euphrates. These angels are particularly cruel, vicious, and murderous. They will stir up 200 million horsemen, who will come from east of the Euphrates River.* These horsemen will be fully possessed by the devil. The Antichrist's army will have tails like *scorpions*, signifying that they will be demon-possessed. The 200 million horsemen, however, will have tails like *serpents*, signifying Satan himself. Thus, these horsemen are even more evil and satanic than those of the Antichrist. These 200 million horsemen will not merely harm men; rather, they will kill them. Therefore, the second woe will be much worse than the first. Though the first woe touched men directly, it only caused pain. The second woe kills.

The slaughter during the sixth trumpet will last for more than thirteen months. It will be unbelievable, terrifying, and gruesome. The 200 million horsemen will start from the Far East and advance westward toward the Euphrates and the Middle East. They will sweep throughout most of Asia.† The killing from these horsemen will be so bad, so severe that many will think that it simply could not continue. After one hour people will hope that the slaughter is over, yet it will go on for another day. After that day people will long for the murdering to end, but it will proceed for yet another month. After that month of carnage, it will still continue for another whole year. And so, the sixth trumpet will last for the hour, plus the day, plus the month, plus the year.

---

* On the whole earth there are only two countries with a population large enough to field such a cavalry—India and China. Both of these are east of the Euphrates. By the year 2030, both India and China are estimated to have populations of approximately 1.4 billion. Furthermore, even now both these countries have well over 200 million people fit for military service. The army described as part of the sixth trumpet could never have been fielded until very recent times, as there were simply not enough people for any nation to produce such an army. Yet, the Word of God foretold the coming of this army over 1900 years ago.

† It is interesting that by the year 2030 it is estimated that the total population of Asia will be nearly 5 billion, which will amount to well over 50% of the world's population. Asia will be the only continent where one third of the earth's population could be killed by horsemen. This may then indicate where that evil *third* part of the earth is. This may also show where the judgments of the first four trumpets will strike—Asia with the Pacific Ocean.

These hoards from the rising of the sun (i.e., east of the Euphrates) will slaughter everything in their path. They will be headed by the four evil angels and led by the kings* of the east. Massive war will break out across most of the Asian continent. Most of the people in the Asian mainland will die. Very few will escape out of the hands of these horsemen. In addition, many of these 200 million will also die. They will certainly be opposed as they attack. The armies of the nations these horsemen invade will certainly fight back, but the 200 million cavalrymen will be hard to locate and kill. They will be spread out and mobile, unlike columns of tanks and modern troop carriers.

This massive army will sweep westward toward the river Euphrates, the source of the four evil angels. This river forms a boundary between most of Asia and the countries of the Middle East that border the Mediterranean Sea. According to the Old Testament it is actually the northeast boundary of the nation of Israel.[37] Thus, it is a natural line of defense for Israel. Therefore, the real focus of the attack of these 200 million horsemen is not Asia *per se*, but actually the Middle East, and Israel in particular.

What a horrific time this will be. Consider the slaughter that took place in Cambodia during the "killing fields." Consider the slaughters that have occurred in Africa—in Uganda, Ethiopia, and Somalia. Consider the murder in Bosnia, Afghanistan, and elsewhere. All of these pale when compared to the woe of the sixth trumpet. The slaughter† that will take place then will be incomparable. Nothing in human history will match it, except that final battle at Armageddon.

Although this judgment will be so severe and terrible, men will still not repent. In particular, they will not repent of their idolatries. It is significant that idolatry is mentioned here in relation to the sixth trumpet and the slaughter of the third of mankind. Asia is full of idols: Buddhism, Hinduism, Taoism, and Shinto—four of the five major religions in that area—are constituted of idols and false gods. There is much worship of dragons

---

* The word "kings" (plural) may indicate that these 200 million horsemen are comprised of people from more than one country.

† There certainly will be a reason why these horsemen slaughter so many people, but I leave that to the reader to discern.

and serpents. All these things are devilish. In addition, Islam, another great false religion, permeates most of that part of the world. This religion leads men astray from Christ and God. Rather than worshipping God in Christ, Muslims worship their religion. God will use the 200 million horsemen of the sixth trumpet to destroy all these evils. He will utterly destroy the evil of idol worship and the evil of false worship. He will completely eliminate them from the face of the earth.

The reason why God will bring all the judgments of the great tribulation upon the earth is that men would repent. It is God's desire that no man would perish. Yet, He is also a righteous God, unable to indefinitely tolerate evil. Consequently, He will bring His judgments upon the earth to turn men from their wicked ways. Nevertheless, men still would not repent until they are destroyed during the tribulation and at the Lord's second coming.

References

1 Matt. 25:31-46
2 Is. 66:3
3 Matt. 16:13-21
4 Matt. 16:16
5 Matt. 17:1-8
6 Ex. 10:13
7 Luk. 10:19
8 Rev. 11:8
9 Jer. 19:9; The Works of Josephus, Books 6, 7
10 Rev. 14:9-11
11 Matt. 10:16-23
12 Luk. 21:16-18
13 Rev. 20:4
14 Rev. 11:7-8
15 Jn. 6:32-33
16 Jn. 7:37-38
17 Lev. 2:11; 6:16-17; 10:12
18 Ex. 23:15
19 Matt. 16:6, 12; Mk. 8:15
20 1 Cor. 5:6-8
21 Gal. 5:9
22 1 Cor. 5:6-8
23 1 Cor. 5:7
24 1 Cor. 5:7
25 Heb. 7:27
26 Jn. 3:16
27 1 Cor. 15:3; Gal. 1:4; Col. 1:14; Heb. 1:3; 7:26
28 Heb. 7:3
29 Rom. 5:12
30 Luk. 1:35
31 Matt. 12:46-47; 13:55; Jn. 2:12; 7:3; Gal. 1:19
32 Rom. 8:29; Col. 1:18; Heb 1:6; Rom. 1:4
33 1 Cor. 15:45
34 1 Pet. 1:3
35 1 Tim. 2:5
36 Revelation 18:8
37 Gen. 15:18; Deut. 1:7, 11-24; Josh. 1:4

CHAPTER 7

The Time of the End

At the beginning of the great tribulation, due to the judgments of the sixth seal and the first four trumpets, chaos will reign on earth. The earth will be thrown into turmoil and upheaval. This will be but the start of 3½ years of unparalleled suffering. What will follow will be a time of trial unmatched in the history of the creation. The sufferings at that time will come from every side. God will judge the earth, man, and even the heavens. Satan will have been cast to the earth with great wrath, desiring to destroy mankind. The Antichrist, who will have been revived with the spirit of Caesar Nero, will torment man to the uttermost. From every side and in every way man will face unbearable suffering.

During this time it will be extremely difficult to live. There will be enormous tumults everywhere. The physical earth will be in upheaval. All aspects of society will be in confusion. There will be great worldwide shortages of food and a lack of necessities in nearly every place. Throughout the earth men will suffer all kinds of deprivation.

In addition, there will be great persecutions. All religions will be destroyed. The Jews will be decimated. What they will suffer will be worse than what they passed through during World War II. Eventually two thirds of the Jews will be slaughtered.[1] In addition, great numbers of Christians may be martyred.

Throughout these last 3½ years God's judgments will continue. Repeated plagues from the two witnesses will strike the earth. A great drought will fall upon mankind. Earthquakes will probably shake the earth daily. The 200 million horsemen from the Far East will massacre one third of mankind. So very many men will die. Very few will survive until the time of the end, and those who do will survive barely. What an awful, dreadful place the earth will be during the tribulation.

Then the end will come quickly. Just as the Antichrist is at the height of his power, the end will come in a very unexpected way. The godless unbelievers will never foresee the Lord's physical coming to the earth to destroy them. The current age will close at the sounding of the seventh trumpet in but a few days. As the beginning of the tribulation will be marked by the opening of the seventh seal, so its end will be marked by the sounding of the seventh trumpet. This period of time will be extremely complex just as the beginning of the great tribulation will be.

The Breaking of the Power of the Holy People

I beheld, and the same horn made war with the saints, and prevailed against them... (Daniel 7:21)

... he shall destroy the mighty ones and the holy people. (Daniel 8:24)

And one said to the man clothed in linen, who was above the waters of the river, How long shall it be to the end of these wonders? And I heard the man clothed in linen, who was above the waters of the river, when he held up his right hand and his left hand unto heaven, and sware by him that liveth for ever that it shall be for a time, times, and a half; and when they have made an end of breaking in pieces the power of the holy people, all these things shall be finished. (Daniel 12:6-7)

But beware of men: for they will deliver you up to councils, and in their synagogues they will scourge you; yea and before governors and kings shall ye be brought for my sake, for a testimony to them and to the Gentiles. But when they deliver you up, be not anxious how or what ye shall speak: for it shall be given you in that hour what ye shall speak. For it is not ye that speak, but the Spirit of your Father that speaketh in you. And brother shall deliver up brother to death, and the father his child: and children shall rise up against parents, and cause them to be put to death. And ye shall be hated of all men for my name's sake: but he that endureth to the end, the same shall be saved. ... And be not afraid of them that kill the body, but are not able to kill the soul: but rather fear him who is able to destroy both soul and body in hell. Are not two sparrows sold for a penny? and not one of them shall fall on the ground without your Father: but the very hairs of your head are all numbered. (Matthew 10:17-22, 28-30)

But before all these things, they shall lay their hands on you, and shall persecute you, delivering you up to the synagogues and prisons, bringing you before kings and governors for my name's sake. It shall turn out unto you for a testimony. Settle it therefore in your hearts, not to meditate beforehand how to answer: for I will give you a mouth and wisdom, which all your adversaries shall not be able to withstand or to gainsay. But ye shall be delivered up even by parents, and brethren, and kinsfolk, and friends; and some of you shall they cause to be put to death. And ye shall be hated of all men for my name's sake. And not a hair of your head shall perish. In your patience ye shall win your souls. (Luke 21:12-19)

And the dragon waxed wroth with the woman, and went away to make war with the rest of her seed, that keep the commandments of God, and hold the testimony of Jesus... (Revelation 12:17)

And another angel, a third, followed them, saying with a great voice, If any man worshippeth the beast and his image, and receiveth a mark on his forehead, or upon his hand, he also shall drink of the wine of the wrath of God, which is prepared unmixed in the cup of his anger; and he shall be tormented with fire and brimstone in the presence of the holy angels, and in the presence of the Lamb: and the smoke of their torment goeth up for ever and ever; and they have no rest day and night, they that worship the beast and his image, and whoso receiveth the mark of his name. Here is the patience of the saints, they that keep the commandments of God, and the faith of Jesus. And I heard the voice from heaven saying, Write, Blessed are the dead who die in the Lord from henceforth: yea, saith the Spirit, that they may rest from their labors; for their works follow with them. (Revelation 14:9-13)

And I will give unto my two witnesses, and they shall prophesy a thousand two hundred and threescore days, clothed in sackcloth. These are the two olive trees and the two candlesticks, standing before the Lord of the earth. ... And when they shall have finished their testimony, the beast that cometh up out of the abyss shall make war with them, and overcome them, and kill them. (Revelation 11:3-4, 7)

... it cast down truth to the ground... (Daniel 8:12)

By the end of the great tribulation, the Antichrist will subdue or kill all the saints. In Israel the 144,000, who will be sealed at the beginning of tribulation and who will preach the gospel to all of Israel throughout the last 3½ years, will be mostly, if not entirely, martyred. Throughout the rest of the Antichrist's empire Christians will be imprisoned and killed. All the faithful believers living in the Antichrist's empire will be silenced. Even the two witnesses, Moses and Elijah, will die at the hands of the Antichrist, being killed in Jerusalem and lying there for 3½ days. At that time Jerusalem will be so evil, so worldly, and so immoral that it is even called Egypt and Sodom.[2] There these two "lamp-stands," the two "olive trees" who are so full of the Spirit, will be put to death.

The whole earth will rejoice when they are killed. Everyone will see these two witnesses lying dead in the street of Jerusalem. This may be broadcast throughout the Antichrist's empire via television. The earth-dwellers will rejoice and give gifts to one another, because the two witnesses that brought plagues upon the earth will have been killed by the Antichrist. Throughout the ages the despisers of God have rejoiced at the martyring of His prophets, apostles, and even His very own Son. At the endtime these rebellious God-haters will even give gifts to one another to celebrate the slaughtering of God's people. By this, they will bring upon themselves all the innocent blood of God's martyred people from righteous Abel to the two witnesses.[3]

Eventually, the Antichrist will subdue all spiritual opposition. The voice of the truth will be completely silenced. Everyone in the Antichrist's kingdom who speaks for God will have been martyred or imprisoned. Every one of the saints will have been worn down by this consummately evil person. This will be the darkest, the grimmest hour ever upon the face of the earth. Satan and the Antichrist will have "won" the battle. Evil will reign. The whole earth will be under the power of darkness. But this will last for only a moment.

The Seventh Trumpet

And I saw another strong angel coming down out of heaven, arrayed with a cloud; and the rainbow was upon his head, and his face was as the sun, and his feet as pillars of fire; and he had in his hand a little book open: and he set his right foot upon the sea, and his left upon the earth; and he cried with a great voice, as a lion roareth: and when he cried, the seven thunders uttered their voices. ... And the angel that I saw standing upon the sea and upon the earth lifted up his right hand to heaven, and sware by him that liveth for ever and ever, who created the heaven and the things that are therein, and the earth and the things that are therein, and the sea and the things that are therein, that there shall be delay no longer: but in the days of the voice of the seventh angel, when he is about to sound, then is finished they mystery of God, according to the good tidings which he declared to his servants the prophets. (Revelation 10:1-3, 5-7)

And the seventh angel sounded; and there followed great voices in heaven, and they said, The kingdom of the world is become the kingdom of our Lord, and of his Christ: and he shall reign for ever and ever. And the four and twenty elders, who sit before God on their thrones, fell upon their faces and worshipped God, saying, We give thee thanks, O Lord God, the Almighty, who art and who wast; because thou hast taken thy great power, and didst reign. And the nations were wroth, and thy wrath came, and the time of the dead to be judged, and the time to give their reward to thy servants the prophets, and to the saints, and to them that fear thy name, the small and the great; and to destroy them that destroy the earth. And there was opened the temple of God that is in heaven; and there was seen in his temple the ark of his covenant; and there followed lightnings, and voices, and thunders, and an earthquake, and great hail. (Revelation 11:15-19)

And I saw another sign in heaven, great and marvellous, seven angels having seven plagues, which are the last, for in them is finished the wrath of God. ... And after these things I saw, and the temple of the tabernacle of the testimony in heaven was opened... (Revelation 15:1, 5)

And the seventh poured out his bowl upon the air; and there came forth a great voice out of the temple, from the throne, saying, It is done: and there were lightnings, and voices, and thunders; and there was a great earthquake, such as was not since there were men upon the earth, so great an earthquake, so mighty. (Revelation 16:17-18)

... in a moment, in the twinkling of an eye, at the last trump: for the trumpet shall sound, and the dead shall be raised incorruptible, and we shall be changed. (1 Corinthians 15:52)

For this we say unto you by the word of the Lord, that we that are alive, that are left unto the coming of the Lord, shall in no wise precede them that are fallen asleep. For the Lord himself shall descend from heaven, with a shout, with the voice of the archangel, and with the trump of God: and the dead in Christ shall rise first; then we that are alive, that are left, shall together with them be caught up in the clouds, to meet the Lord in the air: and so shall we ever be with the Lord. (1 Thessalonians 4:15-17)

At this very time the seventh angel will trumpet. This will occur very near the end of the great tribulation. As the power of the holy people is completely destroyed, when Moses and Elijah are slain, the seventh trumpet will sound. This trumpet will last a very short time, probably only a period of days. It will be the last of God's judgments upon man during the great tribulation. It will also be the last of the three great woes that will strike man before Christ's return. This trumpet will end the great tribulation and the time of trial that will come upon all those dwelling on the earth.

The seventh trumpet has both positive and negative components. On the negative side it includes the fury of God poured out in the seven bowls,[4] as God's wrath to destroy those who destroy the earth. This is the annihilation of the Antichrist and all the worldly armies at the battle of Armageddon. It also includes the destruction of Satan's kingdom of the world.

The seventh trumpet also contains many positive items. When the seventh trumpet sounds, the mystery of God will be finished. This is that which He spoke through the prophets in the Old Testament and revealed to the apostles in the New Testament. At the time of the sounding of the seventh trumpet, all the prophecies concerning the mystery of God will be fulfilled. This will be the dispensational completion of God's eternal purpose in Christ. It will include the manifestation of the sons of God in glory as the consummation of God's operation in man throughout all the ages. It is for this purpose that God Himself became a man, died, and rose again, that He might bring forth many sons into glory to manifest His divine attributes in human virtues for eternity.

The seventh trumpet includes the resurrection of all the remaining dead believers. It is during this trumpet that all the unresurrected saints from prior ages will arise from the dead. This may include the martyrs from among the 144,000 sealed Jews killed during the great tribulation, along with the two witnesses, Moses and Elijah.* After this resurrection all the remaining believers, whether dead and resurrected, or still living, will be caught up to meet with the Lord in the air. The Word of God is without ambiguity in stating that this resurrection will happen during the last, seventh trumpet.

During the seventh trumpet, a judgment upon the dead will also take place. The word "dead" in Revelation 11:8 should not refer to all the dead generally, since the dead unbelievers are not resurrected and judged until after the Millenium at the great white throne. Rather, it should refer to the dead of God's redeemed people. At that time the Lord will judge all of His redeemed to determine whether they will participate in the millenial kingdom. These redeemed include God's people from the time of the patriarchs,[5] through the time of Israel during the Old Testament,[6] and throughout the church age.[7]

During the seventh trumpet, Christ will descend from the heavens to the air. He will come with all the overcoming believers who were raptured to the heavens before the great tribulation, and with all the holy angels. There He will meet with all the remaining believers who will be caught up to the air to stand before Him.

---

* It may be that the resurrection of Moses and Elijah, along with the martyrs from among the 144,000 sealed Jews killed during the tribulation, occurs a short time *before* the seventh trumpet sounds, since the martyred Jewish believers are pictured before the throne of God in the *heavens* (Rev. 15:2), whereas the saints resurrected during the seventh trumpet are caught up to meet with the Lord in the *air*.

After the believers are caught up to the air, the Lord will reward the faithful ones at His judgment seat. However, as we will see, not all believers will receive a reward. Some will receive a dispensational punishment. Those who are unfaithful to the Lord in the current age will be disciplined that they might be perfected and brought into the eternal glory of the New Jerusalem.

At the time of the seventh trumpet the Lord will also give a reward to the God-fearing unbelievers of the nations. These are those who will heed the preaching of the eternal gospel to fear God during the tribulation. They will not receive the mark of the Antichrist. Since they will not follow him, they will not share his destruction. Furthermore, they will care for the believers during this great time of trial and suffering. Therefore, the Lord will reward them at His coming back.[8]

Finally, the seventh trumpet includes the coming of the kingdom of Christ to the earth. Not only will Satan's kingdom be destroyed, but Christ's kingdom will also come. It is for this that all the God-loving, Christ-seeking saints have prayed, labored, and waited throughout the ages. During the days of the sounding of the seventh trumpet, Christ's kingdom will finally come to the earth in glory and power. Praise Him!

The Bowls of God's Fury

And I saw another sign in heaven, great and marvellous, seven angels having seven plagues, which are the last, for in them is finished the wrath of God. ... And after these things I saw, and the temple of the tabernacle of the testimony in heaven was opened: and there came out from the temple the seven angels that had the seven plagues, arrayed with precious stone, pure and bright, and girt about their breasts with golden girdles. And one of the four living creatures gave unto the seven angels seven golden bowls full of the wrath of God, who liveth for ever and ever. And the temple was filled with smoke from the glory of God, and from his power; and none was able to enter into the temple, till the seven plagues of the seven angels should be finished. (Revelation 15:1, 5-8)

The negative contents of the seventh trumpet are the seven bowls, which are seven plagues—the last to strike man. When these are poured out the fury of God will be finished. The bowls, especially the first four, are similar to the trumpets. However, whereas the first four trumpets were directed against man's environment, the first four bowls are directed against man himself, particularly against the Antichrist and his followers.

The seven bowls are full of the fury of God. Throughout the ages God in His mercy has tolerated sinful, evil man with the desire that man might be brought to repentance and return to God. During the endtime God will become furious with wicked mankind, so furious that no one will be able to enter His heavenly temple. That is, no one will be able to appease God; no one will be able to make intercession for man. By the time of the seven bowls, the age of intercession will be over. No one will be able to placate God until the bowls of His wrath are fully poured out upon man.

The seventh trumpet will sound for a period of days. Since the seven bowls are a part of the seventh trumpet they will be poured out in at most a few days. The first bowl will be poured out. It will be followed immediately by the second, then the third, then the fourth, fifth, sixth, and seventh. Bowl after bowl will be poured out upon evil man without any respite or lull. These plagues will be designed to decimate all of God's enemies throughout the Antichrist's kingdom. After being poured out, they will continue to affect mankind until the physical return of the Lord Jesus. They will weaken Christ's opposers for the battle at Armageddon. By the time the Lord Jesus physically returns, the Antichrist's kingdom will be diseased, afflicted, and suffering great torment. The final destruction of the Antichrist, his armies, and his people will then occur quickly.

The First Five Bowls

And I heard a great voice out of the temple, saying to the seven angels, Go ye, and pour out the seven bowls of the wrath of God into the earth. And the first went, and poured out his bowl into the earth; and it became a noisome and grievous sore upon the men that had the mark of the beast, and that worshipped his image. And the second poured out his bowl into the sea; and it became blood as of a dead man; and every living soul died, even the things that were in the sea. And the third poured out his bowl into the rivers and the fountains of the waters; and it became blood. And I heard the angel of the waters saying, Righteous art thou, who art and who wast, thou Holy One, because thou didst thus judge: for they poured out the blood of the saints and the prophets, and blood hast thou given them to drink: they are worthy. And I heard the altar saying, Yea, O Lord God, the Almighty, true and righteous are thy judgments. And the fourth poured out his bowl upon the sun; and it was given unto it to scorch men with fire. And men were scorched men with great heat: and they blasphemed the name of God who hath the power over these plagues; and they repented not to give him glory. And the fifth poured out his bowl upon the throne of the beast; and his kingdom was darkened; and they gnawed their tongues for pain, and they blasphemed the God of heaven because of their pains and their sores; and they repented not of their works. (Revelation 16:1-11)

For, behold, darkness shall cover the earth, and gross darkness the peoples ... (Isaiah 60:2)

The first bowl of God's wrath will be poured out into the earth. This is similar to the first trumpet in that the judgment will be on the earth. With the first trumpet, however, the trees and the greenery of the earth will be damaged. With the first bowl *man* will be afflicted. When the first bowl is poured out, an evil and malignant sore will appear upon the followers of the Antichrist. Throughout the Antichrist's kingdom those who worship the Antichrist's image and bear his mark will be given a new mark—an evil and malignant sore. These lesions should result from some sort of grievous disease that raises dreadful boils on the flesh. This plague will infest the Antichrist's followers, causing extreme pain. It will be like an extremely virulent, quickly spreading cancer. That the sores are malignant indicates that the disease will be unhealable—Satan, the Antichrist, and the false prophet will not be able to cure it. Neither doctors nor sorcerers will be able to heal those afflicted with the disease from the first bowl. The plague of these sores may be similar to the boils with which God afflicted the Egyptians during the time of Moses.[9] However, this plague will be much worse and far more painful.

It will be God's righteous judgment upon those who receive the Antichrist's mark. They will receive the mark of the evil one, so God will mark them with an evil and malignant sore. They will torment mankind, therefore God will torment them in righteousness with an excruciatingly painful disease.

The second bowl of God's fury will be poured out into the sea.* This is similar to the second trumpet in that the judgment will be toward the sea. While the second trumpet will turn the third of the sea into blood, the second bowl will change the sea into the blood of a dead man. Thus, the judgment of the second bowl will be far more severe than that of the second trumpet. When the second bowl is poured out, the sea will by some means become like the blood of a dead man—congealed and reddish-black. This will kill all the creatures in the sea. What an enormous disaster this will be. This will also be God's righteous judgment upon the Antichrist and his kingdom. The evil followers of the Antichrist for their own interest and gain will slaughter so many men. God will righteously judge them by turning their source of food and the means by which they carry out their evil commerce into the blood of a dead man.

The third bowl will be poured out into the rivers and streams, just like the third trumpet. While the third trumpet makes the rivers and springs poisonously bitter, the third bowl will turn all the waters from which men drink into blood. Men will be given blood to drink. Once again we can see God's righteous judgment upon the Antichrist and his kingdom. During the tribulation, the people of the Antichrist will shed the blood of the saints. They will massacre so many of the believers. Since they will shed so much innocent blood, God will righteously give them blood to drink.†

The fourth bowl will be poured out upon the sun. Like the fourth trumpet, this judgment will be toward the heavenly bodies. During the fourth trumpet the earth will merely be *darkened*.

---

* The judgments of these bowls will be directed towards the Antichrist's empire, as seen in the first and fifth bowls, indicating that the sea here refers to the Mediterranean Sea.

† This plague will be directed toward those who martyr the saints. This indicates that it, along with the other plagues of the seven bowls, will be directed at the Antichrist and his kingdom.

However, the judgment of the fourth bowl will cause the sun to produce intense heat to burn men. During the fourth trumpet, though the atmosphere will be darkened, the sun itself will still shine. During the fourth bowl the sun itself will be changed. Thus, the fourth bowl will be far more severe than the fourth trumpet. At that time the sun will scorch men with fire and great heat. Huge solar flares may be unleashed on the sun. Immense solar eruptions may occur. Evidently, a major structural change will happen within the sun.* The nuclear reactions that fuel the sun will intensify greatly. Enormous amounts of heat and radiation will engulf the earth, making it unbearably hot. The side of the earth facing the sun at that time, which will include the kingdom of the Antichrist, will bear the brunt of this solar onslaught. By this, the sufferings of evil men will be greatly multiplied. In addition to their sores and boils, in addition to their hunger and thirst, they will suffer intense searing by fire. As with the other bowls, the fourth bowl will touch man directly. God's righteous judgment of the fourth bowl will give evil mankind a foretaste of the coming lake of fire. This will be the merciful God's intervention to save men, if possible, from perishing for eternity. Even in God's fury He will judge with the hope of bringing men to repentance. Yet, despite all these plagues men would still not repent.

When the fifth bowl is poured out it will strike the throne of the beast, the heart of the Antichrist's kingdom. This will bring thick darkness to all of the Antichrist's empire. This darkness will not be typical. It will cause excruciating pain. The pain will be so great that men will gnaw their tongues. This will be yet another righteous judgment from God. Since the Antichrist's kingdom will be altogether in spiritual darkness, God will give them darkness to dwell in. In addition, the Antichrist and his followers tormented others, particularly Israel, with unbearable pain. Therefore, at the time of the fifth bowl God will repay them with unbearable pain. This will be the most excruciating, most intense pain possible for men to suffer. This will be the awful judgment upon the Antichrist and his followers. Yet, they still will not

---

* It may be that through this change the sun will shine seven times more brightly during the Millennium as prophesied in Isaiah 30:26.

repent. In spite of their dreadful pain, sores, and thirst—in spite of all the plagues—these evil ones become still more evil. At that time they will blaspheme the God of heaven for these judgments.

By then there will be nothing more that God can do to bring men to repentance. God's only recourse will be to destroy all these vilely rebellious men. Thus, the stage will be set for the battle at Armageddon and the final tumultuous upheavals on earth that will occur during the sixth and seventh bowls.

The Sixth Bowl

And the sixth poured out his bowl upon the great river, the river Euphrates; and the water thereof was dried up, that the way might by made ready for the kings that come from the sunrising. And I saw coming out of the mouth of the dragon, and out of the mouth of the beast, and out of the mouth of the false prophet, three unclean spirits, as it were frogs: for they are spirits of demons, working signs; which go forth unto the kings of the whole world, to gather them together unto the war of the great day of God, the Almighty. ... And they gathered them together into the place which is called in Hebrew Har-magedon. (Revelation 16:12-14, 16)

And Jehovah will utterly destroy the tongue of the Egyptian sea; and with his scorching wind will he wave his hand over the River, and will smite it into seven streams, and cause men to march over dryshod. (Isaiah 11:15)

But tidings out of the east and out of the north shall trouble him; and he shall go forth with great fury to destroy and utterly to sweep away many. And he shall plant the tents of his palace between the sea and the glorious holy mountain; yet he shall come to his end, and none shall help him. (Daniel 11:44-45)

Son of man, set your face toward Gog of the land of Magog, the prince of Rosh, Meshech, and Tubal, and prophesy against him ... After many days you will be summoned; in the latter years you will come into the land that is restored from the sword, whose inhabitants have been gathered from many nations to the mountains of Israel which had been a continual waste; but its people were brought out from the nations, and they are living securely, *all of them. And you will go up, you will come like a storm; you will be like a cloud covering the land, you and all your troops, and many peoples with you. Thus says the Lord GOD, It will come about on that day, that thoughts will come into your mind, and you will devise an evil plan, and you will say, I will go up against the land of unwalled villages. I will go against those who are at rest, that live securely, all of them living without walls, and having no bars or gates; to capture spoil and to seize plunder, to turn your hand against the waste places which are not inhabited, and against the people who are gathered from the nations, who have acquired cattle and goods, who live at the center of the world. Sheba, and Dedan, and the merchants of Tarshish, with all its villages, will say to you, Have you come to capture spoil? Have you assembled your company to seize plunder, to carry away silver and gold, to take away cattle and goods, to capture great spoil? Therefore, prophesy, son of man, and say to Gog, Thus says the Lord GOD, On that day when my people Israel are living securely, will you not know it? And you will come from your place out of the remote parts of the north, you and many peoples with you, all of them riding on horses, a great assembly and a mighty army; and you will come up against my people Israel like a cloud to cover the land. It will come about in the last days that I shall bring you against My land, in order that the nations may know Me when I shall be sanctified through you before their eyes, O Gog.* (Ezekiel 38:2, 8-16)*

And I saw the beast, and the kings of the earth, and their armies, gathered together to make war against him that sat upon the horse, and against his army. (Revelation 19:19)

The sixth bowl will be poured upon the river Euphrates. This great river originates in Turkey, runs through Syria and Iraq, and empties into the Gulf of Arabia. It forms a great natural barrier between middle Asia and the countries bordering the Mediterranean. When this bowl is poured out the Euphrates will be dried up. This will not be a minor event, for it is considered a plague by God. The amount of water transported by the Euphrates is enormous. For it to dry up implies some sort of major geological

---

* New American Standard Bible

upheaval. This bowl will likely be accompanied by great topological changes throughout Asia Minor and the Middle East. By these upheavals the mighty Euphrates will be broken up and greatly altered. In addition, an intense, hot wind will strike it.[*] In a very short time the Euphrates River will be altogether gone. This will make way for the 200 million horsemen[†] (at least those of them who remain alive) to cross the Euphrates on their way to Israel. They will be able to pass over dry shod. They will be led by the kings[‡] from the rising of the sun (i.e., from east of the Euphrates), firstly to invade the Middle East, and then to fight at the battle of Armageddon.[§]

At the time of the end, three evil spirits—demons—will come forth from Satan, the Antichrist, and the false prophet. These spirits will go out sometime before the great battle at Armageddon with the sole purpose of gathering all the armies of the earth to war. They will gather armies from three directions— Gog and Magog will come down from the north, the 200 million horsemen will sweep across from the east, and the armies of the Antichrist will come from the west and south. The armies of the earth will come to battle each other for the riches of the Middle

---

[*] Perhaps as a result of the searing heat from the fourth bowl.

[†] The drying up of the Euphrates River will not only prepare the way for the 200 million horsemen, but will also later allow any Jews scattered to the east of the Euphrates to return to Israel to enjoy the Lord's reign during the Millennium (Is. 11:10-16).

[‡] Some think that the kings mentioned in Revelation 16:12 are Jews who will return to Israel at the start of the Millennium. However, this cannot be. First of all, the Jews who return to Israel at that time will not be kings. Rather, they will be priests to the nations in the earthly part of the millennial kingdom. It is the overcoming believers who will be the kings over the earth during the Millennium. Furthermore, according to the context, the kings mentioned here are those who will be gathered from throughout the earth for the great battle at Armageddon (vv. 14, 16). These, no doubt, must be the kings of the satanic world who will be destroyed by the Lord Jesus at His return. Thus, "the kings from the rising of the sun" must be earthly kings, the ones who will lead the 200 million horsemen from the Far East as they sweep across Asia. This is con- firmed by the mention of the Euphrates River in the two passages which refer to the 200 million horsemen and the kings from the rising of the sun (Rev. 9:14- 16; 16:12).

[§] Since Armageddon is mentioned here (vv. 14, 16), the battle of Armageddon should occur about this time.

East and control of the earth. They will think that the victor in this battle will reign over the whole earth. Yet, it is God who will be gathering them. The demons will do God's bidding to bring the armies of the earth to Armageddon where they will be destroyed by the Lord at His second coming.

Gog and Magog will sweep down from the uttermost parts of the north. Knowledgeable Bible scholars recognize that Gog and Magog refer to Russia and her allies. Moscow itself lies directly north of Israel. Thus, Gog and Magog, which are said to lie in the remote parts of the north, could be none other than Russia. Russia will plan and prepare for an invasion of the Middle East for some years. It will be their plot to invade a prosperous Israel while it is at peace.* It will be their desire to plunder the enormous wealth in the Middle East. For this reason they will sweep down from the north into the mountains of Israel.

The 200 million horsemen will come from the Far East. They will destroy most of the Asian continent on their way to Israel. When they reach the Euphrates River the sixth bowl will be poured out upon the Euphrates enabling them to cross over into the Middle East for the final battle at Armageddon. They will proceed from the Euphrates toward Israel to invade the holy land and fight with the Antichrist.

According to Daniel 11 the Antichrist himself will be south of Israel in the area of Egypt at that time.[10] Tidings from the north and east will trouble him. The tidings from the north should refer to the invading Russian hordes; the tidings from the east should refer to the coming of the 200 million horsemen. Troubled by these reports the Antichrist will go forth with great wrath to make war. He will summon all the forces from Europe and the rest of his kingdom to the Middle East for this final battle.

Israel will be overflowing with armies. Seemingly, it will cease to exist as a nation. It will be ravished and demolished by the evil military forces from all the earth. From the east, hundreds of millions of horsemen will be sweeping across to Israel; from the north, untold numbers of Russian horsemen will be storming down; from the west and south, all of the Antichrist's armies will be invading. There they will camp, planning their battle against

---

* That is, this planning will take place before the tribulation starts.

one another. However, they will actually be awaiting their destruction at the hand of the coming Christ. What a desperate, unspeakably hopeless situation this will be to the Jews in the holy land. It will seem to them that their only lot will be utter destruction.

The Resurrection of the Two Witnesses

And I will give unto my two witnesses, and they shall prophesy a thousand two hundred and threescore days, clothed in sackcloth. ... And when they shall have finished their testimony, the beast that cometh up out of the abyss shall make war with them, and overcome them, and kill them. And their dead bodies lie in the street of the great city, which spiritually is called Sodom and Egypt, where also their Lord was crucified. And from among the peoples and tribes and tongues and nations do men look upon their dead bodies three days and a half, and suffer not their dead bodies to be laid in a tomb. And they that dwell on the earth rejoice over them, and make merry; and they shall send gifts one to another; because these two prophets tormented them that dwell on the earth. And after the three days and a half the breath of life from God entered into them, and they stood upon their feet; and great fear fell upon them that beheld them. And they heard a great voice from heaven saying unto them, Come up hither. And they went up into heaven in the cloud; and their enemies beheld them. And in that hour there was a great earthquake, and the tenth part of the city fell; and there were killed in the earthquake seven thousand persons: and the rest were affrighted, and gave glory to the God of heaven. (Revelation 11:3, 7-13)

As all the armies from throughout the earth are gathering in Israel, on the very last day of the great tribulation, after lying 3½ days in the street of Jerusalem, the two witnesses, Moses and Elijah, will be resurrected. After they are resurrected the voice of the Lord Jesus will call them to Himself. They will be caught up to the air to meet with the Lord. This may occur at the same time as the rapture of all the other believers remaining on the earth.

In the same hour that the two witnesses are resurrected and raptured another great earthquake will strike the earth. This is the third great earthquake prophesied in Revelation. The first will occur at the opening of the sixth seal, the second at the opening of the seventh seal, and the third after the rapture of Moses and Elijah. At that time seven thousand men will die. Literally, the Bible says that seven thousand *names* of men will die. That is, seven thousand names among men, or famous people, will perish in this earthquake. It is not that only seven thousand people will die, but that a vast multitude will perish among whom are seven thousand well-known men. If seven thousand famous people die at that time, it may be that a total of hundreds of millions of people perish in this great quake.

This particular earthquake, however, will focus upon famous people. Many people of renown are against God. They are absolutely for themselves and their own fame. In their lives all glory goes to themselves, not to God. By that time most of the famous people will be exposed—they will have allied themselves with the Antichrist. They will become the Lord Jesus' open opposers. Consequently, the judgment of this great earthquake will be specifically towards them. God will judge the famous. Many of the great idols among men will be destroyed by this shaking of the earth. This should include politicians, businessmen, military leaders, scientists, artists, and famous people from all walks of life. God will intervene to judge these God-forsaking, self-promoting men of renown, those who will celebrate the most when the two witnesses, Moses and Elijah, are slain.

During this earthquake the tenth part of the great city—Jerusalem—will be destroyed.* Jerusalem is supposed to be the holy city. Yet, by that time it will have become "Egypt," "Sodom," and the "great" city. It will be remembered as the place of the Lord Jesus' crucifixion, signifying the Jews' rebellion against God and murder of His Son. Consequently, God will judge it, demolishing the tenth part of it. The mentioning of Jerusalem here may indicate that many of the famous will not only be allied with the Antichrist, but companying with him in Israel and the Middle East. Many of them may be destroyed in Jerusalem itself. While they are rejoicing and giving gifts to one another, celebrating the destruction of the two witnesses who plagued the earth, before their very eyes these same witnesses will be resur-

---

* This may indicate that Jerusalem will be the epicenter of this quake.

rected and raptured. Then they themselves will be slain by this great earthquake.

After being shocked by the resurrection and rapture of Moses and Elijah, and after being terrified by God's judgment with this great earthquake, the Jews who remain in Israel will finally start to turn their heart back to God to glorify Him. Finally, after so many calamities, they will give the Lord a way to intervene to bring them to repentance.

The Destruction of Rome

And I heard another voice from heaven, saying, Come forth, my people, out of her, that ye have no fellowship with her sins, and that ye receive not of her plagues: for her sins have reached even unto heaven, and God hath remembered her iniquities. Render unto her even as she rendered, and double unto her the double according to her works: in the cup which she mingled, mingle unto her double. How much soever she glorified herself, and waxed wanton, so much give her of torment and mourning: for she saith in her heart, I sit a queen, and am no widow, and shall in no wise see mourning. Therefore in one day shall her plagues come, death, and mourning, and famine; and she shall be utterly burned with fire; for strong is the Lord God who judged her. And the kings of the earth, who committed fornication and lived wantonly with her, shall weep and wail over her, when they look upon the smoke of her burning, standing afar off for the fear of her torment, saying, Woe, woe, the great city, Babylon, the strong city! for in one hour is thy judgment come. And the merchants of the earth weep and mourn over her, for no man buyeth their merchandise any more; merchandise of gold, and silver, and precious stone, and pearls, and fine linen, and purple, and silk, and scarlet; and all thyine wood, and every vessel of ivory, and every vessel made of most precious wood, and of brass, and iron, and marble; and cinnamon, and spice, and incense, and ointment, and frankincense, and wine, and oil, and fine flour, and wheat, and cattle, and sheep; and merchandise of horses and chariots and slaves; and souls of men. And the fruits which thy soul lusted after are gone from thee, and all things that were dainty and sumptuous are perished from thee, and men shall find them no more at all. The merchants of these things, who were made rich by her, shall stand afar off for the fear of her torment, weeping and mourning; saying, Woe, woe, the great city, she that was arrayed in fine linen and purple and scarlet, and decked with gold and precious stone and pearl! for in an hour so great riches is made desolate. And every shipmaster, and every one that saileth any wither, and mariners, and as many as gain their living by sea, stood afar off, and cried out as they looked upon the smoke of her burning, saying, What city is like the great city? And they cast dust on their heads, and cried, weeping and mourning, saying, Woe, woe, the great city, wherein all that had their ships in the sea were made rich by reason of her costliness! for in one hour is she made desolate. Rejoice over her, thou heaven, and ye saints, and ye apostles, and ye prophets; for God hath judged your judgment on her. And a strong angel took up a stone as it were a great millstone and cast it into the sea, saying, Thus with a mighty fall shall Babylon, the great city, be cast down, and shall be found no more at all. And the voice of harpers and minstrels and flute-players and trumpeters shall be heard no more at all in thee; and no craftsman, of whatsoever craft, shall be found any more at all in thee; and the voice of a mill shall be heard no more at all in thee; and the light of a lamp shall shine no more at all in thee; and the voice of the bridegroom and of the bride shall be heard no more at all in thee: for thy merchants were the princes of the earth; for with thy sorcery were all the nations deceived. And in her was found the blood of prophets and of saints, and of all that have been slain upon the earth. (Revelation 18:4-24)

At this time the city of Rome will be burned and utterly destroyed. This may happen due to the same earthquake that destroys the seven thousand famous men. Rome will be brought down into ruin. Near the beginning of the tribulation the Roman Catholic Church, the mysterious, religious Babylon, will be burned by the Antichrist and his followers. At the end of the great tribulation, the city of Rome—the material Babylon and capital of the Antichrist's empire—will be demolished and burned by God. All the merchants, captains, and seamen, and all the kings and those who became rich through their commercial relationship with Rome will stand far off and watch her smoke ascend as she burns to the ground. This will be God's judgment upon this great, evil city. It is there that the blood of so many saints has and will be shed. It is there that the Antichrist himself will make his capital. Consequently, God will judge this city by fire.*

References

[1] Zech. 13:8
[2] Rev. 11:8
[3] Matt. 23:34-35
[4] Rev. 15:7
[5] Matt. 8:11
[6] Dan. 12:1-2, 13
[7] Rom. 14:10; 2 Cor. 5:10
[8] Matt. 25:34-40
[9] Ex. 9:9-10
[10] Dan. 11:42-44

---

* Eventually, Rome will be cast into the sea, swallowed up forever, never to be seen again (Rev. 18:21). This may happen during the last and greatest earthquake of the tribulation, which will occur at the pouring out of the seventh bowl.

CHAPTER 8

The Judgment Seat of Christ

The subject of this chapter, the judgment seat of Christ, is a difficult matter to propound because of the inaccurate understanding of God's salvation held by many believers. Many Christians believe that once they have been saved there could never be a problem between them and the Lord. According to their understanding, if they were to die they would immediately go to a heavenly paradise. If they were to remain on the earth until the Lord's second coming, they would be raptured into the Lord's joy and glory for eternity. This understanding is unscriptural. But, because many believers cling to these concepts, it is difficult for them to see the truth revealed in the Bible. Their misunderstanding concerning the Christian life, death, heaven, the rapture, and eternal salvation are like tinted lenses that color what they see. If we read the Bible through such darkened glasses, then the extremely weighty and sobering matters, such as the need for growth in life, the proper service to the Lord, and the judgment seat of Christ, become obscured. For this reason, when the matter of the judgment seat of Christ is discussed it may evoke an incredulous response and immediate denial from some Christians. Nevertheless, according to the Word of God there is a *judgment seat* before which *every* believer must stand.[1] This truth is crucial to our Christian life and experience.

Many Christians are not clear concerning the matter of salvation. Some believe that once they have been saved, they are eternally saved. Unfortunately, they add to this truth the misconception that a person who has been saved could never have a problem with God. Others proclaim that salvation is not eternal. They believe that they may be saved one day, lost the next, and then saved yet again on the following day. This is a tumultuous experience of salvation, like being on a storm-tossed sea. One day it is high—"I am saved!" Another day it is low—"I am lost!"

Ones who hold this belief misinterpret verses related to the punishment of believers *after* they have been saved.

These misconceptions are two extremes. Both of them have some support from verses in the Bible, yet they both also overlook, reject, or misinterpret other verses in the Bible. The truth lies in between these two extremes. Once a person is saved, he is always saved. Nevertheless, such a one may still be disciplined and punished by the Lord. However, his eternal destiny is secured. The truth in the Bible is that all believers will eventually enjoy their part in the New Jerusalem—not a one will be lost. Yet, many will suffer some kind of punishment and discipline from the Lord. This is the only way to reconcile all the verses in the Bible, both those speaking of eternal security and those relating to the punishment of the believers.

Eternal Security

Verily, verily, I say unto you, He that heareth my word, and believeth him that sent me, hath eternal life, and cometh not into judgment, but hath passed out of death into life. (John 5:24)

All that which the Father giveth me shall come unto me; and him that cometh to me I will in no wise cast out. (John 6:37)

... even as he chose us in him before the foundation of the world, that we should be holy and without blemish before him in love: having foreordained us unto adoption as sons through Jesus Christ unto himself, according to the good pleasure of his will, to the praise of the glory of his grace, which he freely bestowed on us in the Beloved... (Ephesians 1:4-5)

Before we speak about the judgment seat it is first necessary to lay a proper foundation concerning salvation and eternal security. According to the Bible, all believers in Christ are eternally secured. The reason believers may not be assured of their salvation is due to an inadequate understanding of what salvation is. Salvation is not merely a change of outward state. It is not simply a matter of going to heaven and not going to hell. It is not a matter of being transferred into a heavenly mansion. It is absolutely not a matter of going to a wonderful "place." This is not what the Bible means when it refers to salvation.

Salvation is actually a profound *life* matter.[2] On the one hand, God Himself puts *us into Christ*.[3] By being in Christ we are identified with Christ to partake of all God's blessings in Him. By such a standing before God we enjoy Christ's place of blessing before the Father, as well as forgiveness of sins through Christ's death.[4]

At the same time, God puts *Christ into us*.[5] Thus, God in Christ as the Spirit becomes our inward divine life.[6] By this transaction we are begotten of God to become God's children.[7] We share God's divine life, God's divine nature, and even His divine glory.[8] These wonderful, divine facts can never be undone.

Once we are of God in Christ we can never be taken out of Christ.[9] Though we may be severed from Christ in our practical daily experience of Him, nevertheless for eternity we are in Christ. A substandard daily experience can never change the eternal, spiritual reality of our being in Christ. Furthermore, once we are born of God, we can never become unborn. Once a child is born he can never stop being the son of his father. Whether this child is bad or good is unrelated to whether he is a son. Even the most evil son is still a son. Thus, every son of God has been begotten of God to be His child, no matter how he behaves. Even in the extreme case where one wants to stop being a son, it is too late! The divine birth of the children of God can never be undone or nullified.

Thus, God's children always remain His children. Because we are children, God would never throw us into the lake of fire for eternity. Consequently, the sons of God could never perish.[10] We are in Christ and Christ is within us forever. Our sense of Him may change. This is variable. When we love the world, commit sin, or rebel against the Lord we may lose His presence and the sense of His life flowing within us. Nevertheless, whether we sense Him or not, He is still in us and we in Him. He will never leave nor forsake us.[11] This eternal fact is independent of our experience.

Thus, the salvation of the believers is assured. It is secured by God in various ways. All the believers have been predestinated by God the Father unto sonship. In eternity past before creation, the Father, according to His good pleasure, chose all the believers in Christ, and according to His selection predestinated us to become His sons. Before anything was, before we were born, before we ever sinned, before we even received Christ, we had already been predestinated by our Father to become His sons. Eventually, our being God's children is initiated and carried out by God according to His choosing and predestination, not by us.[12] Nothing can undo or annul this.

Our eternal salvation is also secured by the love of God. Because God loves us, He would do anything and everything necessary to save us. Even when we were dead in sins, our Father God loved us with a great love.[13] According to such a love, God became a man and died for our sins.[14] He terminated everything, whether negative or positive, that could separate us from Him. Through such a death there is no person, thing, or matter in all the universe that can separate us from God's love in Christ.[15] Even we ourselves cannot separate us from God. Thus, the unlimited and unchanging love of God guarantees our salvation.

Our salvation is also secured by the life of God. We have been regenerated to be the children of God.[16] It is not possible to be "de-regenerated." The children of God are forever the children of God. Thus, the divine birth in the divine life guarantees our eternal salvation.

A further guarantee of our eternal salvation is the righteousness of God.[17] It is conceivable that God's love towards us could fluctuate, given our condition at times. However, God's righteousness cannot. His throne is built upon His righteousness.[18] God's righteousness must remain for eternity and cannot be subject to any kind of variation. Were God to act unrighteously in any way His throne would fall. God judged Christ on our behalf.[19] All of our sins were borne by Jesus in His body when He hung on the cross.[20] There, He who knew no sin was made sin for us.[21] The judgment that was due for all the sins of all mankind fell upon this one man, Jesus. Christ's resurrection is proof that God accepted Christ's vicarious death on our behalf.[22] Thus, according to God's righteousness, man may freely come to God in Christ.[23] Any man may be received by God and also receive God by accepting what Christ has accomplished on the cross. Since God has accepted Christ's sacrifice as full payment for all debts owed to Him, it would be unrighteous of Him to ask that these debts be repaid, that they be paid a second time. Christ has already paid every debt in full. God could not righteously require that these debts be paid again. Thus, once any man has accepted Christ in His person and work, God is bound by His own righteousness to secure the salvation of such a one for eternity.

Furthermore, the salvation of the believers is guaranteed by the word and promise of God. The Lord has spoken that those who believe in Him will never perish.[24] God's word is His guarantee. He has given His unshakable promise that those who come to Him would be saved from perdition. It is not possible for God to lie.[25] Since the eternal God has spoken, it will surely come to pass. Thus, His word with His promise guarantees our eternal destiny.

In addition, our salvation is guaranteed by the faithfulness of God. God is unchanging, never varying. He is the same yesterday, today, and forever.[26] Because God is faithful He will do all that He has said.[27] Because God is faithful He would never let any of His children perish.

Finally, the salvation of the believers is guaranteed by the power of God. Though God might love us, give His word to us, and be faithful, if He did not have the power to support and guarantee His promise, our eternal security would be in doubt. Our eternal salvation is ensured both by the hand of our Lord Jesus and the hand of the Father.[28] Who is more powerful than Jesus? All authority in heaven and earth is His.[29] Can anyone overpower Him, or take us from His hand? Furthermore, our Father is greater than all, and no one can snatch us from His hand. By the power of these two hands, the Son's hand of grace and the Father's hand of love, our salvation is secured eternally. By all these, we can peacefully rest in full assurance knowing that we have been born of God and saved from the judgment of the coming great white throne.

Dispensational Punishment

According to the grace of God which was given unto me, as a wise masterbuilder I laid a foundation; and another buildeth thereon. But let each man take heed how he buildeth thereon. For other foundation can no man lay than that which is laid, which is Jesus Christ. But if any man buildeth on the foundation gold, silver, costly stones, wood, hay, stubble; each man's work shall be made manifest: for the day shall declare it, because it is revealed in fire; and the fire itself shall prove each man's work of what sort it is. If any man's work shall abide which he built thereon, he shall receive a reward. If any man's work shall be burned, he shall suffer loss: but he himself shall be saved; yet so as through fire. Know ye not that ye are a temple of God, and that the Spirit of God dwelleth in you? If any man destroyeth the temple of God, him shall God destroy; for the temple of God is holy, and such are ye. (1 Corinthians 3:10-17)

For the time is come for judgment to begin at the house of God: and if it begin first at us, what shall be the end of them that obey not the gospel of God? (1 Peter 4:17)

Although the salvation of the believers is eternally secured, there still may be problems between some believers and the Lord. Although we, God's children, are saved from eternal perdition in the lake of fire, it may be that we will be saved *through* fire. Although we are eternally secured, we may still suffer a loss. Paul the Apostle was emphatic that no believer could be separated from the love of God.[30] Yet, he was equally emphatic that we may suffer loss and be saved through fire. No matter how the fire and loss of which Paul speaks in 1 Corinthians 3 is interpreted, no one can deny that whoever suffers this loss and fire will experience discipline, punishment, and some kind of affliction. Whatever these may be, they are certainly not pleasant.

The Lord disciplines every one of His children to varying degrees according to their need. He disciplines us because He loves us.[31] If it were not for His wise discipline we all would be spoiled. His discipline brings us into full salvation by causing us to partake of His holiness.[32] His desire is not merely that we would be saved from eternal damnation in the flames of the lake of fire. Rather, He desires the more that we would partake of, experience, and enjoy His divine, holy nature in every part of our being. The issue of this participation is our full salvation.

Discipline from the Lord can occur at various times in the Christian life. This certainly happens during this age in our present-day lives. Simply consider our day by day experience. Consider the trials we encounter each day. Many of these are the

Lord's chastisement of us. These should be regarded as discipline from a loving and wise Father.

If we do not accept and benefit fully from the Lord's discipline to us during this current age, and should we remain alive until the Lord's coming, then we will receive a further discipline from the Lord in the form of the great tribulation. Many believers think that every Christian will be taken from the earth before the great tribulation. However, according to the Word of God this is untrue. As we have already seen in detail,* many believers will be left to pass through that time of trial. This, surely, will be a very hard discipline from the Lord.

Finally, if during our present life, whether now or in the great tribulation, we do not mature properly and serve the Lord in a faithful, prudent way, then we will receive from the Lord a punishment during the coming kingdom age. During that one thousand years, all Christians who have not matured suitably will receive the consummate discipline from the Lord to prepare them for participation in the New Jerusalem.

There are numerous examples of blood-washed, regenerated Christians having problems with the Lord in the New Testament. In 1 Corinthians 3 there were those who built with wood, grass, and stubble. According to the Apostle Paul's word, these would suffer loss and be saved through fire. In the same book, Paul dealt with an incestuous brother who was handed over to Satan, that at least his spirit might be saved at the Lord's return (though the other parts of his being might suffer some kind of destruction).[33] Again, in the same epistle Paul speaks of those who are sick and others who have died because they have partaken of the Lord's table unworthily.[34] Certainly the weakness, sickness, and death were disciplines from the Lord. In his epistle to Timothy, Paul speaks of delivering certain ones to Satan that they might be taught not to blaspheme.[35] He furthermore mentions being deserted by all those in Asia.[36] Even some of Paul's coworkers, such as Barnabas and Demas, had great problems with the Lord.[37] We should not think that simply because we have been saved from eternal perdition everything will be wonderful in our Christian

---

* See, for example, Chapter 3, *Concerning the Rapture.*

lives. No! There may be various problems between us and the Lord, and these problems can result in many kinds of discipline.

Discipline from the Lord does not relate to eternal salvation or eternal perdition in the lake of fire. It is altogether a matter of reward or punishment, particularly during the coming Millennium. The reward and punishment given by the Lord at His judgment seat is a dispensational matter. That is, it lasts only for a period of time, the one thousand years of the kingdom. Perdition is a matter of being thrown into the lake of fire for eternity. There is no end to that. What the Lord pronounces at His judgment seat concerns the status and portion of the believers during the Millennium only. At that time those who have matured in the divine life and served the Lord faithfully during their Christian life will enjoy a reward from Him. However, those who are immature in the divine life, those who have been unfaithful, slothful, and evil in their service to the Lord will suffer a discipline, one that has the goal of bringing them to maturity.

God is the wisest of fathers. What wise father would not discipline his children? Which of us would not punish our sons and daughters according to their need, to adjust and perfect them in their disposition, character, attitude, and behavior? Consider, for example, students bringing home their grades to their father. To the one who receives A's the father would say, "Well done! Here are the keys to my car. You may use it during this coming summer." To the one who receives C's the father would give neither reward nor severe punishment. To the one who fails the wise father would say, "Slothful son! Because you failed you must go to summer school." Sometimes a child is so unruly, mischievous, and rebellious that the parents are forced to "ground" him, send him to his room, or even give him a proper spanking to deal with him.

If we would deal with our children in this manner, how much more wisely would God discipline His children? Many say, "God loves us. How could He harm us in any way? How could He leave us on the earth during the tribulation, or put us into outer darkness during the Millennium?" This is foolish talk. Yes, God loves us and God could never harm His children. But, this is exactly why He disciplines us. He sends the trials, tribulations, and punishments *because* of His love and care for us. It would be an unloving father who did not discipline and punish His children. And, it is only the spoiled believer who rejects God's discipline.

God's discipline is a sign of His love. Those whom He loves He chastises, that they might become partakers of His holiness, that they would not be spoiled or eternally damaged. In fact, to be a child without discipline is to be without love. The most unloving parent is the one who does not discipline his or her children. A lack of discipline spoils and damages the children, perhaps irreparably.

God would not allow this to happen. In one way or another He will save His children from every kind of damage. He will discipline us in every age. In this current age He arranges many situations to discipline, chastise, and deal with us, that we might become partakers of His holiness through His divine nature. If we reject the Lord's discipline during this age, then at the time of the Lord's return He will leave us on the earth, that we might suffer many severe trials and afflictions during the great tribulation. All the sufferings the believers pass through at that time are meant to perfect and mature them. Nevertheless, at the judgment seat of Christ there will still be many Christians unprepared for the kingdom age and the New Jerusalem. They will not be matured in life or equipped to reign with the Lord. They will not know Christ as their life or the proper priestly service to the Lord. Within them many elements, such as rebellion, sin, lust, greed, ambition, and pride, will remain untouched and unpurged. Many will have very little growth in Christ. They will be spiritual babes. How could a baby reign with the Lord during the Millennium? This is not only an impossibility, it is an absurdity. Therefore, at that time Christ will pass judgment upon all the believers according to their need. Many will be punished in some way by the Lord during the Millennium, that they might be matured in Him.

The Maturing of the Saints

Wherefore leaving the doctrine of the first principles of Christ, let us press on unto perfection; not laying again a foundation of repentance from dead works, and of faith toward God...
(Hebrews 6:1)

For whom the Lord loveth he chasteneth, And scourgeth every son whom he receiveth. ... For they indeed for a few days chastened us as seemed good to them; but he for our profit, that we may be partakers of his holiness. All chastening seemeth for the present to be not joyous but grievous; yet afterward it yieldeth peaceable fruit unto them that have been exercised thereby, even the fruit of righteousness. (Hebrews 12:6, 10-11)

Our present life is the proper time for us, the believers, to grow in Christ unto maturity. It is the Lord's heart's desire that every one of His children would redeem the time that they would ripen as God's harvest before the time of the great tribulation. However, only some will heed the Lord's word and consider His warnings. Only some are willing to pay the "price"* to mature in the current age.[38] Very few are willing to suffer the loss of all things and count them but refuse, that they might gain Christ.[39] Very few are willing to deny the soul and love Christ above all things.[40] Very few love not the world.[41] Many Christians are seeking things other than Christ—things such as fame, power, money, worldly amusement and entertainment, and self-gratification. Because many Christians do not cooperate with the Lord to grow in Him, only those who do pay the price to mature will be taken by the Lord before the time of the tribulation.

Those believers who are not full-grown by the beginning of the tribulation will be left on the earth. That time for them will be a time of ripening through suffering and discipline. The great tribulation will be sent to the remaining believers from the loving, caring God to bring them into maturity. Thus, God will allow Satan and the Antichrist to persecute the believers. God will also bring the earth into great upheaval. These persecutions and the calamities on the earth will combine to cause intense suffering to the believers during the tribulation. This will be allotted by the loving Lord, that many of the believers on the earth may mature during that time and consequently not suffer a dispensational punishment from the Lord during the Millennium. The great tribulation will be a period to mature the believers before they have to stand before the judgment seat of Christ and give account for their Christian life.

---

* This "price" is meager indeed when compared to the glory gained.

The Rapture of the Majority of the Believers

Behold, I tell you a mystery: We all shall not sleep, but we shall all be changed, in a moment, in the twinkling of an eye, at the last trump: for the trumpet shall sound, and the dead shall be raised incorruptible, and we shall be changed. (1 Corinthians 15:51-52)

For this we say unto you by the word of the Lord, that we that are alive, that are left unto the coming of the Lord, shall in no wise precede them that are fallen asleep. For the Lord himself shall descend from heaven, with a shout, with the voice of the archangel, and with the trump of God: and the dead in Christ shall rise first; then we that are alive, that are left, shall together with them be caught up in the clouds, to meet the Lord in the air: and so shall we ever be with the Lord. (1 Thessalonians 4:15-17)

And I saw, and behold, a white cloud; and on the cloud I saw one sitting like unto a son of man, having on his head a golden crown, and in his hand sharp sickle. And another angel came out from the temple, crying with a great voice to him that sat on the cloud, Send forth thy sickle, and reap: for the hour to reap is come; for the harvest of the earth is ripe. And he that sat on the cloud cast his sickle upon the earth; and the earth was reaped. (Revelation 14:14-16)

... for they are spirits of demons, working signs; which go forth unto the kings of the whole world, to gather them together unto the war of the great day of God, the Almighty. (Behold, I come as a thief. Blessed is he that watcheth, and keepeth his garments, lest he walked naked, and they see his shame.) And they gathered them together into the place which is called in Hebrew Harmugedon. (Revelation 16:14-16)

And this is the will of him that sent me, that of all that which he hath given me I should lose nothing, but should raise it up at the last day. For this is the will of my Father, that every one that beholdeth the Son, and believeth on him, should have eternal life; and I will raise him up at the last day. ... No man can come to me, except the Father that sent me draw him: and I will raise him up in the last day. (John 6:39-40, 44)

The rapture of the majority of the saints is the final reaping of God's harvest. This will occur at the very end of the tribulation, after 1,260 days of trial.[42] This part of the rapture should occur on the last day of this age. About the time that the sixth bowl is poured out, as the earthly armies are being gathered together to Armageddon for the outpouring of God's wrath, all the believers left on the earth will be gathered to the air to meet with Christ. Thus, two harvests will occur at one time. The matured believers will be wheat for God's house. The earthly armies will be the grapes of God's wrath to be tread upon by the Lord at the time of His physical appearing. The believers will be gathered to the air, while the earthly armies are being gathered to Armageddon. This gathering of the saints will occur immediately prior to the battle of Armageddon, just before the final, massive tumult of the seventh bowl.

The rapture of the majority of believers to the air will be preceded by the resurrection of all the remaining dead saints. This is the resurrection of life mentioned in John.[43] It differs from the resurrection of judgment that will occur at the end of the Millennium. The resurrection of judgment is for the *unbelievers*; the resurrection before the Millennium is a resurrection to life for the *believers*. The ones participating in this resurrection will never perish in the lake of fire, but according to the Word of God they may suffer some sort of discipline from the Lord.

This resurrection should include all the later overcoming saints—the believers who have been martyred during the great tribulation.[44] By their martyrdom they will overcome the Antichrist and his mark, the false prophet, and Satan. They will participate in Christ's millennial reign. This resurrection could also include the two witnesses, Moses and Elijah, who will have been slain three and a half days prior.[45] It will include all the Old Testament saints.[*] This resurrection will also include all the New Testament saints who were not resurrected before the tribulation.[†]

---

[*] All the Old Testament saints that remain in Paradise (i.e., the pleasant section of Hades) will be resurrected on the last day of the current age. Concerning this the Word of God is clear. Abraham, Isaac, Jacob, and the other patriarchs, along with Daniel and the other Old Testament overcoming saints will participate in the kingdom during the Millennium (Matt. 8:11; Dan. 12:13; Heb. 11).

[†] See *The Rapture of the Manchild* in Chapter 4.

Then all the saints, both the resurrected dead saints and the living saints remaining on earth, both those of the Old Testament as well as those of the New Testament, will be caught up together to meet with Christ in the air. Even at that time, however, the Lord will still come as a thief. Even after the 3½ years of tribulation, at the very time when the last trumpet is sounding, many saints will still be immature and unaware of the Lord's imminent appearing. Many will still be found "naked," unclothed before Christ. The Lord warns the believers then on earth about the necessity of keeping their garments. To keep our garments is to experience Christ by living a life that expresses Him. By such a living, He becomes our practical daily covering in our everyday living. Such a "garment" is needed by the believers to stand before the Lord at His judgment seat. Otherwise the shame of our nakedness will be manifested before all.

The Judgment Seat of Christ

Verily, verily, I say unto you, He that heareth my word, and believeth him that sent me, hath eternal life, and cometh not into judgment, but hath passed out of death into life. (John 5:24)

For we must all be made manifest before the judgment-seat of Christ; that each one may receive the things done in the body, according to what he hath done, whether it be good or bad. (2 Corinthians 5:10)

Behold, I come as a thief. Blessed is he that watcheth, and keepeth his garments, lest he walked naked, and they see his shame. (Revelation 16:15)

At that time all the believers will stand before the judgment seat of Christ in the air. Every believer will give account to the Lord. The overcomers who were raptured to the heavens before the great tribulation will descend with the Lord from the heavens to the air. They, with the Lord, will meet together with the remaining believers who will be raptured to the air at the end of the tribulation. At that time *every* believer will stand before the Lord's judgment seat.

At the judgment seat the Lord will judge every saint in righteousness. The judgment seat should not be confused with the throne of grace.[46] During this age the Lord sits upon the throne of grace, dispensing mercy and grace to His children who come forward to Him, that He might supply their every need in their daily lives. Christ sits on the throne of grace during this age, the age of grace. But at the end of the tribulation, when the saints meet with the Lord in the air, the age will have changed from the age of grace to the age of the kingdom. The time for the Lord's dealing with us in grace will be over. The kingdom age in righteousness will have begun. At the judgment seat the saints will give account, not to the merciful and gracious Lord, but to the righteous Judge.[47] That will be the time for judgment according to righteousness.

Some believers use John 5:24 to say that the saints could never be judged by the Lord. According to this verse, the believers have passed out of death into life and will never enter into judgment. This verse is absolutely true. However, what is spoken of here is not the judgment at the judgment seat of Christ, but the judgment at the great white throne.[48] At the great white throne, the Lord judges the unbelievers to determine their eternal destiny. All the believers have passed out of *that* judgment. There is no danger of any believer suffering eternal perdition. Nevertheless, every believer will stand before the judgment seat of Christ and be judged by the Lord according to righteousness. This is not for eternal salvation or perdition. Rather, it is to determine whether we will receive a reward or a punishment during the Millennium. Both John 5:24 and 2 Corinthians 5:10 are true because they refer to different judgments. John 5:24 refers to the judgment of the great white throne unto eternal perdition. Second Corinthians 5:10 speaks of the judgment at the judgment seat of Christ for a reward or a punishment during the Millennium.

At the judgment seat, the Lord will judge every one of the believers for all they have done as a Christian. Each one of us will receive in our body the things we have done, whether good or bad. This will be the judgment for reward or punishment. If, since believing, we have been faithful to follow the Lord and take care of the Lord's interests on the earth according to the grace He has apportioned to us, then we will receive a reward.[49] If, on the other hand, we have been foolish, slothful, and even evil in our Christian conduct and service, then we will receive a punishment from the Lord for the evil we have done.[50] This punishment will be a discipline from the Lord as a chastisement to correct, perfect, and mature us.

The Lord will judge every believer for everything he has said and done. Every negative item in the lives of the believers, including motives, intents, and desires—all the things that have not been thoroughly dealt with by the Lord—will be made manifest. In addition, every positive aspect of the believers lives will also be made manifest. Then the Lord will render judgment to each one according to their works. Some will receive a reward for their godly living and faithful service to the Lord; others will receive a punishment. The rewards and punishments given to the believers by the Lord will be of varying degrees, just as their service in faithfulness or slothfulness in unfaithfulness is of varying degrees.

A number of the believers will receive the highest reward. Some will mature before the great tribulation, such as the ones taken in Matthew 24, the overcoming ones in the church in Philadelphia, and the manchild. In addition, others will be persecuted and martyred during the great tribulation. All of these will be counted by the Lord as overcomers. With them there will be no problem at the judgment seat. Rather, they will be ushered into the joy of the Lord and reign with Him during the millennial kingdom.

The Lord will allot a punishment to a number of the remaining believers to discipline them. At the judgment seat, some Christians will be found lacking; some still will not be filled with Christ. They will still be filled with lust, greed, ambition, the world, naturalness, sinfulness, and various other spots, wrinkles, and blemishes. Many will be nearly void of Christ within. They will have been saved, having received Christ as their initial salvation. However, many will have very few experiences of Christ since their regeneration. Consequently, the Lord will find them lacking.

Every believer has received Christ as the garment of salvation.[51] Christ is the One into whom God has put us.[52] In such a Christ we stand before God as His redeemed. But, this is merely Christ as our objective righteousness. This has nothing to do with our actions and behavior *after* being saved. Every Christian can boast of Christ as his objective righteousness. However, some are clothed with Him as their experiential, subjective righteousness. We all need a second garment. We need Christ—not only objectively, but also subjectively. We need to experience Christ daily. As this Christ within us is enjoyed, lived out, and expressed He becomes a second garment, a garment of subjective righteousness. It is this garment, called "the righteous acts of the saints" or "the righteousnesses of the saints" in Revelation 19:8, that will enable us to stand before Christ unashamed at the judgment seat.

Christians who are nearly void of Christ in experience will be put to shame. The shame of their nakedness, of their real inward condition, will be exposed for all to see. Their sinfulness, naturalness, and lack of Christ—the One who is the only genuine and truly valuable content—will be manifested. Without such a Christ we are simply naked before God.

Whatever our condition is, it will be brought to light at the judgment seat. Our inward being will be displayed openly. This will become a great shame to those believers who have not properly prepared for the Lord's second coming. Everything we have done, especially our treatment of the other believers, our spouse, our children, our parents, and our coworkers—every relationship, both with man and God—will be brought to light and judged. How we have handled all that has been entrusted to us will also be judged. Our inward condition will be fully exposed before the bright, penetrating light of the Lord's appearing. The lot of many believers at the judgment seat will be shame and discipline.

There are very many portions in the Word that present details concerning the judgment seat. This is one of the most important matters in the New Testament, even though it is overlooked by the many. It is crucial for our present and future spiritual welfare to examine many of these portions in the Word.

The Parable of the Ten Virgins

Then shall the kingdom of heaven be likened unto ten virgins, who took their lamps, and went forth to meet the bridegroom. And five of them were foolish, and five were wise. For the foolish, when they took their lamps, took no oil with them: but the wise took oil in their vessels with their lamps. Now while the bridegroom tarried, they all slumbered and slept. But at midnight there is a cry, Behold, the bridegroom! Come ye forth to meet him. Then all those virgins arose, and trimmed their lamps. And the foolish said unto the wise, Give us of your oil; for our lamps are going out. But the wise answered, saying, Peradventure there will not be enough for us and you: go ye rather to them that sell, and buy for yourselves. And while they went away to buy, the bridegroom came; and they that were ready went in with him to the marriage feast: and the door was shut. Afterward came also the other virgins, saying, Lord, Lord, open to us. But he answered and said, Verily I say unto you, I know you not. Watch therefore, for ye know not the day nor the hour (Matthew 25:1-13)

... for I espoused you to one husband, that I might present you as a pure virgin to Christ. (2 Corinthians 11:2)

Let us first consider the parable of the ten virgins in Matthew 25. Many Christians believe that the five foolish virgins mentioned in this parable are unbelievers and that the five wise virgins are believers. Consequently, they think that the punishment spoken of in these verses could never apply to them. However, whenever we interpret the Word of God we must do so without any preconceived notion, with a sober mind and a pure spirit, and according to the Bible itself.

First, all ten of the ones mentioned here are called virgins. It is not that some of the virgins are real and the others false. Rather, it is simply that some are wise and the others are foolish. Whether wise or foolish, all are virgins. The unbelievers are never considered virgins by the Lord. It is only the believers in Christ who have been espoused to Him as chaste virgins. Therefore, to say that virgins refer to unbelievers is not according to the Bible itself.

In this parable all the virgins are going forth to meet the bridegroom, who depicts the Lord Jesus. However, in actuality none of the unbelievers are going forth to meet Him as the bridegroom. In fact, the unbelievers are running away from the Lord, not going toward Him.

It is also said of these virgins that they slept, rose at midnight, and went to meet with the bridegroom. This is a reference to the death and resurrection of the believers. In a number of places in the New Testament the death of the believers is referred to as sleep.[53] Their awakening is their resurrection. Here, all ten virgins awake at the same time to meet the Lord. That is, they are resurrected together. However, the believers are resurrected before the Millennium, while the unbelievers are not resurrected until after the Millennium.[54] This is another indication that the foolish virgins are not unbelievers.

In this parable all the virgins have some oil. All ten virgins have oil in their *lamps*. However, the five wise virgins also take oil in their *vessels*. When all the virgins arise, it appears to the foolish ones that their lamps are going out. The fact that their lamps are *lit* indicates that they already have some oil. Oil here refers to the Holy Spirit. He is the oil that fills the believers. When a man is born of the Spirit to be a child of God, the Holy Spirit enters into him to indwell him. By this, the Spirit becomes the "oil" within every new believer's lamp. No unbeliever has this supply. No unbeliever has the Holy Spirit indwelling him. Every believer receives the Spirit through faith at the time of initial salvation. Thus, the *lit* lamps of each of the ten virgins indicate again that all ten, whether wise or foolish, are believers.

The foolish virgins are told to go buy oil from those who sell it. This could not in any way be referring to salvation. If this were referring to the unbelievers receiving the redemption of Christ for salvation from eternal perdition in the lake of fire, it would mean that this salvation can be bought, that in some way we can earn God's salvation by our works. The Bible, however, clearly states that salvation is the free gift of God received by us through faith. Therefore, the foolish virgins cannot denote unbelievers in need of redemption.

Furthermore, the foolish virgins are told to go buy oil from those who sell. But, this occurs after their resurrection. Indeed, they return, knock at the door, and ask to enter into the wedding feast. This shows that they had gained a supply of oil in their vessels. While they went away to buy the oil, however, the door was shut. While they were gaining the extra supply of oil needed to enter the wedding feast, the door to the feast was closed* to them. However, the fact that these foolish virgins can and do gain oil designates them as believers. Whether or not they had oil before, by the end of the parable they had gained at least some oil. Could any unbeliever be said to have the oil of the Holy Spirit in any amount? Thus, this is another clear indication that the five foolish virgins are believers.

Finally, we are never told that the five foolish virgins are cast into the lake of fire for eternity. Rather, they are only kept from the enjoyment of the wedding feast. Though they do lose the exceedingly precious and intimate enjoyment of Christ as the bridegroom during the millennial kingdom, they will not be thrown into the lake of fire as unbelievers will be. Thus, from all of these facts it is abundantly clear that all ten of these virgins are believers.

With this as a basis, let us consider what this parable means. Since this word is spoken to the believers, what is its significance to us? All believers are considered to be virgins by the Lord. We all have some amount of the Spirit as "oil," which we gained from the Lord when we first believed. However, after believing we may behave either foolishly† or wisely. After their regeneration the foolish ones gain no extra oil with which to fill their vessel. The wise ones pay a price during their lifetime to gain that extra supply of oil. What does this mean practically in our experience?

According to the Bible man is composed of three parts—spirit, soul, and body. When God created man, He formed him out of the dust of the ground—this formed man's *body*. He breathed into man the breath of life—this formed man's human *spirit*. Then man became a living *soul*.[55] Thus, Paul in 1 Thessalonians prayed that our whole spirit *and* soul *and* body would be preserved blameless unto the coming of the Lord.[56] He also told us that our spirit and soul could be divided one from the other.[57]

---

* Thus, it is not only a matter of gaining an extra supply of oil, but also of when the supply is gained.

† Some believers may say that the Lord would never call the believers foolish, using Matthew 5:22 to justify such an assertion. However, this is an unfounded interpretation of the Bible. Paul himself calls the believers in Galatia foolish (Gal. 3:1). Therefore, it is indeed possible for genuine Christians to be considered foolish by the Lord.

Therefore, man is of *three* parts. The spirit and the soul are not the same; these words are not synonyms.

God's salvation is a process. It starts when we first believe, continues throughout our whole lifetime, and ends when we are transfigured. This process corresponds to the three parts of our being. In our initial salvation we are born of God the Spirit in our human spirit. We are joined in our spirit to the Holy Spirit to become one spirit.[58] This is the first step of the complete process of salvation.

The next phase is that of sanctification with transformation. This occurs in our soul. Paul tells us to be transformed by the renewing of our mind. Our mind is a part of our soul, along with our emotion and will. Throughout our Christian life our experience should be one of enjoying the sanctification, renewing, and transformation of our soul, that we might be remade from an old creation to a new creation. This is a lifelong process.

God's complete salvation consummates with the maturity of the divine life within, our conformity to Christ in every way, and the transfiguration of our physical body. Thus, there are three stages to God's salvation—the initial stage, the progressing stage, and the stage of consummation—and each of these stages corresponds with a part of our being.

Proverbs 20:27 tells us that the spirit of man is the lamp of the Lord. In addition, in Romans 9 Paul tells us that we ourselves—that is, our souls—are vessels of the Lord.[59] So in the parable of the ten virgins, the lamps refer to the human spirit within man while the vessel refers to man's soul. When we receive Christ, the Holy Spirit enters within our human spirit to beget us as children of God.[60] This entry of the Holy Spirit is the filling of the "lamp" with "oil." Every genuine believer has the Holy Spirit as oil in his lamp. Thus, every genuine believer shines with some amount of light; every real Christian has a lamp that is burning.

However, from the time of our initial salvation there is a need for the Spirit within our human spirit to spread into our soul, into our mind, emotion, and will. By this, we are renewed in the spirit of the mind[61] and transformed into the image of the Lord from the Lord Spirit.[62] In the words of this parable, we need to gain oil in our "vessel" as well as in our "lamps." When the Lord returns, our real condition before Him will be manifested. If we have the Spirit only within our spirit then our lamp will shine very dimly. It will appear to be going out. This will indicate that we have an inadequate supply of the oil of the Holy Spirit. If, however, we also gain oil within our vessel, then we will have the rich and bountiful supply of the Spirit.[63] We will shine brightly in the brilliance of the Lord's presence at His coming. The brightness of His presence will bring our real inward condition to light.

Thus, this parable is a warning—not to the unbelievers, but to the believers. It is a warning to us that this present age is for us to gain oil in our vessels. It is not the time for us to enjoy the world or so many pleasures on the earth. Rather, this present time is for us to pay some price to gain oil in our vessels.

The oil we gain in our spirit at the time of our salvation is free. However, the spreading of the oil into every part of our soul costs a price. What could we possibly pay for the Holy Spirit? It is not that we pay something in return for the Spirit. We pay a price to *allow* the Spirit to fill us. What is this price? It is the denying of our self, the laying down of our soul-life, the hating of all our natural affections, the forsaking of the world, the laying aside of our family and friends for the gospel's sake, and the suffering of the loss of all things and counting them as refuse, that we might gain Christ.[64] All of these are a cost to us; they involve some suffering on our side. Yet, by paying this "price" and continually turning to Christ to gain Him in His rich supply in our soul, we become the wise virgins who receive an extra supply of oil in our vessels.

When the Lord Jesus returns He will bring every believer before His judgment seat. He will not judge us according to whether we have been saved or not, for only saved ones will be there. Rather, He will judge us by whether we have gained an adequate supply of the Spirit. Those who have will enter into the wedding feast, to enjoy Christ in exultation for the thousand years of the kingdom. Those who have not gained the needed supply of the Spirit will be left outside the glory of the kingdom in darkness, as a dispensational punishment for that thousand years. By this, they will be chastised and disciplined for their negligence in their Christian life, that they might be prepared to enter into the New Jerusalem as mature sons of God for eternity.

As believers in Christ, what should our realization and concern be during this age? We should not be those who live in a self-deceiving fantasy, thinking that everything will be fine at the Lord's return, that the Lord would never punish any of His children. On the contrary, the Lord disciplines those whom He loves and chastises every child whom He receives.[65] We must consider whether we are gaining the extra supply of the Spirit to make us wise virgins. Are we those who, day by day, moment by moment, behold and reflect the Lord to be transformed into His image from one degree of glory to another?[66] Are we those in whom the word of Christ is dwelling richly?[67] Are we those who have given every bit of ground within our hearts to the wonderful Spirit of Jesus Christ, that He might deposit in us all His divine and human riches for our maturity in His life? These are today's crucial matters, and it is by these that the Lord will reward or punish us at His return.

Workers of Lawlessness

Not every one that saith unto me, Lord, Lord, shall enter into the kingdom of heaven; but he that doeth the will of my Father who is in heaven. Many will say to me in that day, Lord, Lord, did we not prophesy by thy name, and by thy name cast out demons, and by thy name do many mighty works? And then will I profess unto them, I never knew you: depart from me, ye that work iniquity. (Matthew 7:21-23)

Life and service go together. The parable of the ten virgins concerns maturity in life. To buy the oil is to grow in life, to be transformed into the Lord's image, to have the very Triune God Himself as the Spirit saturating every part of our being. There is, however, another side to the Christian life—the side of service. Life and service go together. To be a Christian without service to the Lord is to be dead in practicality. We may have the Lord in us as the eternal life, but this life must be lived out in service. If we think we are expressing the divine life, yet do not serve the Lord in a proper manner, we deceive ourselves. The life of Christ lived out from us is manifested in service. The Son of Man came to serve.[68] This same One now lives in us. When He lives through us, that is our service to God.

On the other hand, to serve without life is to have dead works.[69] The proper service to the Lord is that which comes forth from the divine life within us. Any work or service that lacks the divine life as its source is disowned by the Lord. This is why He will say to many of those who do great miracles, "I never knew you." Many cast out demons, heal, and do many great works of power, yet the Lord may say, "I never knew you." The Lord may disown all that they have done. Their works are not allowed by Him. Their works did not have Him as their life-source.

These two, life and service, go hand in hand. The divine life issues in Christian service. Christian service is the expression of the divine life. The divine life is the content; Christian service is the living. To be a proper Christian, one who will be received by the Lord at the judgment seat, we must properly care for both these aspects of our Christian life. How we are judged at the judgment seat of Christ depends upon how we live after becoming a Christian. If we serve the Lord faithfully, wisely, and properly we will receive a reward. If we are unfaithful and slothful we will receive a punishment. This punishment is not to suffer in the lake of fire for eternity. It is to receive a dispensational discipline from the Lord, a discipline that lasts for one thousand years.

Some would argue that Matthew 7:21-23 is addressed to the unbelievers. However, this cannot be the case. In these verses the servants of Christ call Him, "Lord, Lord." The unbelievers never address Jesus as Lord.* Furthermore, those depicted in these verses cast out demons and do many great works in the Lord's name. Do the unbelievers do works of power in the Lord's name?[70] Therefore, these verses must refer to believers.

Very few people understand what the proper service to the Lord is. Some think it is doing great works. However, according to these verses many who do great works will be cast out of the Lord's presence. According to the New Testament, the proper service to God is to *feed* His people. In John 21 the Lord told Peter this emphatically three times.[71] If Peter loved the Lord, then he must feed and care for the Lord's lambs and sheep. In Matthew

---

* To address Jesus as Lord actually makes us believers (Rom. 10:13-14; 1 Cor. 12:3).

24:45 the Lord reiterates this thought: the wise and faithful servant is the one who *feeds* God's household at the proper time. God's people are hungry. They need Christ as their spiritual food. God's servants should minister Christ as food to all God's children that they may be fed, nourished, and thereby grow in life. Anything else, even if it is *for* God, is not acknowledged by the Lord as service to Him. His sole desire is that His people be fed and cared for.

In this regard there are many warnings in the New Testament. The Lord repeatedly admonishes us that how we serve Him will determine how He treats us at the judgment seat.[72] In Matthew 7 the Lord says that many will come to Him, asking Him whether they had cast out demons, prophesied, and done many great works in His name. The Lord will tell them to depart from Him, that they are workers of lawlessness (i.e., iniquity). Their works were not what the Lord desired.

Many today seek to do great works for God. They desire to have a large following and perform many marvelous things to make themselves prominent and famous. Their thought may be that by doing such great deeds they will have something about which to boast before the Lord. This, however, is altogether against the principle of the New Testament. The life Christ has deposited within us is a fruit-bearing life.[73] What God does today is according to the principle of this life. He desires not great works with huge numbers, but fruit.[74] Fruit comes through slow, constant labor. The Lord lived and worked on the earth according to this principle. He told the demons not to make Him known when they declared Him the Son of God.[75] He would strictly charge those whom He healed to speak of the healing to no one.[76] When people sought to make Him a king, He withdrew.[77] The Lord never sought a great work. He withdrew from fame and publicity. He did everything in His power to keep Himself hidden. This was because He desired to bear fruit to God, not to do a great work. God Himself, embodied in the man Jesus, after 33½ years on the earth and after 3½ years of constant ministry, produced only about 120 followers who were faithful to Him after His death.[78] The Lord Jesus was truly restricted by the principle of a fruit-bearing life.

The Apostle Paul lived similarly. Although he did more than any other apostle, and although he completed the Word of God, he nevertheless lived a life under a constant restriction.[79] He was restricted by his vision of God's New Testament economy* and move. He was restricted by the Spirit who indwelt him. Paul never sought to make a name for himself, to become a somebody, to have a huge following, to build up his own work, or to rule over his own "empire." What Paul did was in Christ and unto Christ.[80] When some said that they were of Paul, Paul rebuked them for being divisive.[81] Paul declared himself to be nothing and Christ to be everything.[82] He espoused all the believers to Christ Himself.[83] Paul was a pure-hearted servant who ministered spiritual food to God's people as a loving slave of the Lord.[84] At the end of his life, though nearly all forsook him, Paul had the assurance that he would receive a crown of righteousness from the Lord at the judgment seat.[85]

We must faithfully and honestly examine our condition and situation today according to the light in God's Word. When we look at the situation today in Christianity, what do we see? Today many have become famous by promoting themselves, their works, and their "ministry." Is such service under the restricting hand of the Lord? Would the Lord allow such service? Today many build great edifices supposedly in the Lord's name. Is it for these that Christ died? Is this the Lord's desire in His New Testament move? Today many do great, and apparently miraculous, works, and by such works draw attention to themselves to gather a following. By exacting funds from this following they make a handsome living for themselves. They take the money from these people to build their own "empire." Are such actions according to the Lord's heart's desire and by the divine life? Will such deeds be acknowledged by the Lord? Today some even play rock music for Jesus. Will the Lord acknowledge such "service" as His own at the end of this age? According to the Word of God, in that day many will come to the Lord claiming they have done great things for Him. The Lord never contradicts their statement.

---

* God's economy is His household administration to dispense all of His riches in Christ into His redeemed people for the accomplishing of His eternal purpose (1 Tim. 1:4; Eph. 3:9).

Yes, they did do great things. But the things they did were not of God. They did them supposedly *for* God, but they were not *of* God. They did not have Christ as life as their source. In actuality the ones doing these things were not building God's kingdom, but their own. In that day the Lord will call many of those who are doing great things today "workers of iniquity" or "workers of lawlessness." What they are doing is not allowed by Him. He neither allows it, acknowledges it, nor is in it. The Christian service of many will be condemned by the Lord in that day as rebellion against His restricting hand and as a damage to His New Testament move to accomplish His purpose.

To those who do such things, no matter how great, the Lord will issue a punishment. They will be cast out of the Lord's presence into darkness. Rather than enter into the glory of the millennial kingdom to reign with Christ, many will be put out of that glory. Though eventually they will inherit the New Jerusalem for eternity, the kingdom age will be a time of suffering in darkness to them. This is the Lord's clear warning to His children.

Wise Servants and Evil Servants

Who then is the faithful and wise servant, whom his lord hath set over his household, to give them their food in due season? Blessed is that servant, whom his lord when he cometh shall find so doing. Verily I say unto you, that he will set him over all that he hath. But if that evil servant shall say in his heart, My lord tarrieth; and shall begin to beat his fellow-servants, and shall eat and drink with the drunken; the lord of that servant shall come in a day when he expecteth not, and in an hour when he knoweth not, and shall cut him asunder, and appoint his portion with the hypocrites: there shall be the weeping and the gnashing of teeth. (Matthew 24:45-51)

And the Lord said, Who then is the faithful and wise steward, whom his lord shall set over his household, to give them their portion of food in due season? Blessed is that servant, whom his lord when he cometh shall find so doing. Of a truth I say unto you, that he will set him over all that he hath. But if that servant shall say in his heart, My lord delayeth his coming; and shall begin to beat the menservants and the maidservants, and to eat and drink, and to be drunken; the lord of that servant shall come in a day when he expecteth not, and in an hour when he knoweth not, and shall cut him asunder, and appoint his portion with the unfaithful. And that servant, who knew his lord's will, and made not ready, nor did according to his will, shall be beaten with many stripes; but he that knew not, and did things worthy of stripes, shall be beaten with few stripes. And to whomsoever much is given, of him shall much be required: and to whom they commit much, of him will they ask the more. (Luke 12:42-48)

In both Matthew and Luke the Lord Jesus talks about faithful and slothful servants. The Gospel of Matthew, according to its Jewish flavor, was written with the Jewish believers in view.[86] The Gospel of Luke, on the other hand, was written by Luke—who was very possibly a Gentile—to a Gentile.[87] However, whether to Jews or Gentiles, the words of the Lord Jesus are strikingly similar. In both these sections of the Word there are faithful and slothful servants. In both instances, the faithful ones are rewarded, whereas the slothful ones are severely disciplined. Who are these servants?

Some say the faithful ones are Christians, whereas the slothful ones are unbelievers. Can this be true? First, consider this: are the unbelievers ever considered to be the Lord's servants? Only the believers are considered the servants of Christ, purchased by Him on the cross for priestly service to God.[88] Furthermore, the servants in these two sections of the Word were appointed to feed God's household. It is evident from the rest of the New Testament that God's household is the church. Are any unbelievers appointed by God to nourish His church? Do any of them have the supply of Christ needed to feed the believers in Christ? Certainly not. The Lord's words are clear. All the servants here, whether faithful or slothful, are believers. They simply behave differently in their Christian service.

The Lord's servants are assigned to do only one thing. They are not directed to do great works. They are not appointed to build religious empires. They are not commissioned to become famous or prosperous. They are not led to do anything great. The Lord's assignment for them is simply to feed His people, to nourish them with the proper food at the proper time. This was the Lord's word to Peter. In John 21 He told Peter that if he loved Him he should feed His sheep.[89] He did not direct Peter to start a great religion. He exhorted him to feed His people. Similarly, the Lord's charge to us according to His heart's desire is that we would feed God's people, according to our spiritual capacity in the divine life.[90] This is pure and genuine service to God. This is the stewardship the Lord recognizes as His own. This is what the Lord will reward at His return.

Some of the Lord's people take these warnings with utmost seriousness. They endeavor to pour out something of the Christ they have gained in their experience to God's people for their spiritual growth, building up, and maturity. At the Lord's second coming He will reward these faithful believers who feed His sheep, by giving them responsibility over all things. They will share in Christ's reign over the nations during the Millennium.

On the other hand, some of the believers, by their slothfulness and unfaithfulness, manifest that they are evil in heart. These know that the Lord will return soon, yet have no fear of His judgment at the judgment seat. Rather, they use the Lord's seeming delay as an excuse to spend their time indulging themselves in worldly pleasures and worldly endeavors, just as the unbelievers do. Today the unbelievers are drunk with the pleasures of the world. Some dear Christians have joined in this revelry, and thus have been usurped by the world. In addition, they mistreat the other believers by abusing them spiritually and psychologically. Like the Pharisees of old, they self-righteously condemn and abuse their fellow slaves, while they indulge in worldly pursuits for fame, fortune, and power. At the Lord's coming back He will cut these slaves apart. This refers to their being opened within and exposed. He will also have them lashed according to the degree of their responsibility in their unfaithfulness. He will cast them into outer darkness where there will be weeping and gnashing of teeth. This darkness will be a place outside the bright, shining light of the glory of the millennial kingdom. There, these evil servants—those believers who have behaved unfaithfully—will weep for not having heeded God's Word. They will gnash their teeth in regret for how they have behaved. They will weep in anguish for being kept from the joy of the coming kingdom, ruing their actions in the present age. They will suffer a temporal discipline, a punishment that will be like that of the unbelievers in nature. That dispensational chastisement will be most unpleasant to the unfaithful believers. It will be a thousand years of discipline without grace. This is the Lord's stern and severe warning to us all that we should not be ensnared by the world and mistreat the brethren.

Knowing these things then, what shall we do? Who among us could ever be a faithful servant? Only the Lord Jesus Himself is qualified to be such a one. What shall we do? We should fall upon our knees and cry out to the Lord for mercy—mercy to shine on us in our improper service, mercy to bring us to a thorough repentance, mercy that He would grow in us to become the faithful One, mercy that He would grace us to live a life that He could approve and for which He could reward us in the day of His second coming. By His mercy we must repudiate any haughty thought of self-righteous worth in person and deed. We should put aside not only every failure, but also every apparent success to seek the Lord and be delivered from all kinds of evil and slothfulness in service, that we might feed His people with Christ Himself for their spiritual enrichment. We must seek to be filled with Christ in His unsearchable riches[91] for our own nourishing, that we might have something with which to feed others. We should also seek the Lord that He would become in us the faithful One to pour out the divine life to meet the need of each of God's people. It is only such a life laid down for the service of God's household that the Lord will reward at His second coming.

Faithful Servants and Slothful Servants

For it is as when a man, going into another country, called his own servants, and delivered unto them his goods. And unto one he gave five talents, to another two, to another one; to each according to his several ability; and he went on his journey. Straightway he that received the five talents went and traded with them, and made other five talents. In like manner he also that received the two gained other two. But he that received the one went away and digged in the earth, and hid his lord's money. Now after a long time the lord of those servants cometh, and maketh a reckoning with them. And he that received the five talents came and brought other five talents, saying, Lord, thou deliveredst unto me five talents: lo, I have gained other five talents. His lord said unto him, Well done, good and faithful servant: thou hast been faithful over a few things, I will set thee over many things; enter thou into the joy of thy lord. And he also that received the two talents came and said, Lord, thou deliveredst unto me two talents: lo, I have gained other two talents. His lord said unto him, Well done, good and faithful servant: thou hast been faithful over a few things, I will set thee over many things; enter thou into the joy of thy lord. And he also that had received the one talent came and said, Lord, I knew thee that thou art a hard man, reaping where thou didst not sow, and gathering where thou didst not scatter; and I was afraid, and went away and hid thy talent in the earth: lo, thou hast thine own. But his lord answered and said unto him, Thou wicked and slothful servant, thou knewest that I reap where I sowed not, and gather where I did not scatter; thou oughtest therefore to have put my money to the bankers, and at my coming I should have received back mine own with interest. Take ye away therefore the talent from him, and give it unto him that hath the ten talents. For unto every one that hath shall be given, and he shall have abundance: but from him that hath not, even that which he hath shall be taken away. And cast ye out the unprofitable servant into the outer darkness: there shall be the weeping and the gnashing of teeth. (Matthew 25:14-30)

He said therefore, A certain nobleman went into a far country, to receive for himself a kingdom, and to return. And he called ten servants of his, and gave them ten pounds, and said unto them, Trade ye herewith till I come. But his citizens hated him, and sent an ambassage after him, saying, We will not that this man reign over us. And it came to pass, when he was come back again, having received the kingdom, that he commanded these servants, unto whom he had given the money, to be called to him, that he might know what they had gained by trading. And the first came before him, saying, Lord, thy pound hath made ten pounds more. And he said unto him, Well done, thou good servant: because thou wast found faithful in a very little, have thou authority over ten cities. And the second came, saying, Thy pound, Lord, hath made five pounds. And he said unto him also, Be thou also over five cities. And another came, saying, Lord, behold, here is thy pound, which I kept laid up in a napkin: for I feared thee, because thou art an austere man: thou takest up that which thou layedst not down, and reapest that which thou didst not sow. He saith unto him, Out of thine own mouth will I judge thee, thou wicked servant. Thou knewest that I am an austere man, taking up that which I laid not down, and reaping that which I did not sow; then wherefore gavest thou not my money into the bank, and I at my coming should have required it with interest? And he said unto them that stood by, Take away from him the pound, and give it unto him that hath the ten pounds. And they said unto him, Lord, he hath ten pounds. I say unto you, that unto every one that hath shall be given; but from him that hath not, even that which he hath shall be taken away from him. But these mine enemies, that would not that I should reign over them, bring hither, and slay them before me. (Luke 19:12-27)

The servants in these two parables also refer to the believers. First, as we have already seen, the unbelievers are never considered servants of the Lord. Second, the Lord has never delivered His spiritual money to the unbelievers. It is the believers who, at the time of their regeneration, receive a spiritual gift from the Lord to invest for the Lord's gain. Finally, the evil slaves in these parables are not thrown into the lake of fire. Rather, they are put into outer darkness to suffer a temporary punishment for their slothfulness in service. It is clear, therefore, that all the servants in these two parables refer to the believers.

In the previous section we saw two types of service to the Lord. First, there are good and faithful servants who feed the Lord's household at the proper time. These will receive a reward from the Lord at His coming. Second, there are evil servants who beat their fellow slaves, and eat and drink with the drunken. These will be cut asunder and lashed by the Lord as a punishment when He returns. Because of this strong word of warning some believers might think that it is better to do nothing than to risk being punished by the Lord. They may think that by hiding their spiritual gift the Lord could not condemn them for beating their fellow slaves. Some believe the Lord is very hard in His demands, expecting a return where He neither sowed nor invested. Consequently, they hide the Lord's talent to avoid the risk of losing it. However, the Lord is wise in His dealing with His people.

The Lord Jesus knows the case of every one of His children. He knows that some of His servants will improperly associate with the drunken and beat their fellow slaves, so He issues them a stern warning of the coming judgment. He also leaves no ground for any of us to hide the spiritual gift He has given. It is not enough simply to do nothing negative. The Lord expects what He has given to be returned with a profit. In the spiritual realm if there is no positive increase, that is failure. Stagnation is unacceptable to the Lord. Consequently, the Lord also issues a very strong warning to those who would hide their spiritual talent. Not only will the ones who abuse their fellow slaves be cast into the outer darkness, but also those who do not spiritually profit from what the Lord has given. If we do not increase the Lord's gift He considers us to also be unprofitable and worthy of punishment. Those who hide their talent suffer the same discipline as those who eat and drink with the drunken: they are cast into the outer darkness where they will weep and gnash their teeth.

At the time of our regeneration the Lord deposited His divine life into us, making us His children. This divine life has a spiritual capacity. Every member of the Body of Christ has some function.[92] Not one member can say that he or she is functionless or giftless. Every one of us has at least one "talent." The Lord desires that we use the gift He has given us to produce an increase. The Lord desires that each of us trade with the spiritual "money" He has entrusted to us. This is to exercise the spiritual gift He has given. By this exercise, our spiritual function is perfected and also multiplied to the other members of Christ's Body. Other believers profit from the proper spiritual exercise of each member's talent. This is to gain a spiritual increase. Furthermore, by enjoying the exercise of others' spiritual talents we ourselves are increased in our spiritual capacity as well. By such "trading" between the members of Christ, our spiritual talent is multiplied—multiplied into the other members of the body, and multiplied within us as well. Such an exercise of the spiritual gifts is for and unto the building up of the Body of Christ.

Many members of Christ have hidden their spiritual talent. Consider the millions of believers who sit speechless and passive in pews on the Lord's day, with their spiritual gift deadened and buried. This is the hiding of the talent depicted in Matthew 25 and Luke 19. Consider the myriad believers who never speak a word of the gospel, never prophesy the truths in the holy Word, and never pour forth of the spiritual life within them. This is the burying of the Lord's spiritual money. Will the Lord reward these believers at the judgment seat for their passivity? According to these two parables in Matthew and Luke, absolutely not. The Lord will label such believers evil and slothful. He tells them that they should at least have invested their spiritual talent with those who could help them to bear some profit for Him. The Lord's warning here is extremely strong. It is not enough to do nothing negative. We must produce a spiritual, divine, positive increase for the Lord.

The reward to the faithful servants in these verses is exceptional. On the one hand, it is to enter into the joy of the Lord. This is to enter into the exceeding joy of Christ in the millennial kingdom. There, all the overcoming saints will enjoy the unsearchably rich Christ in His innumerable attributes and virtues to the fullest extent for one thousand years. This reward also includes reigning with Christ during the Millennium. This is to rule over many things or to reign over the cities on the earth as co-kings of Christ. How wonderful will the reward be during the next age to those who are faithful in this age.

Saved through Fire

According to the grace of God which was given unto me, as a wise masterbuilder I laid a foundation; and another buildeth thereon. But let each man take heed how he buildeth thereon. For other foundation can no man lay than that which is laid, which is Jesus Christ. But if any man buildeth on the foundation gold, silver, costly stones, wood, hay, stubble; each man's work shall be made manifest: for the day shall declare it, because it is revealed in fire; and the fire itself shall prove each man's work of what sort it is. If any man's work shall abide which he built thereon, he shall receive a reward. If any man's work shall be burned, he shall suffer loss: but he himself shall be saved; yet so as through fire. (1 Corinthians 3:10-15)

The Apostle Paul in 1 Corinthians 3 speaks an extraordinarily strong word to the believers. He tells us that only one foundation has been and can be laid—that is Christ Himself. However, each of us builds upon that foundation in some manner. Our whole Christian life is a kind of building upon the Christ deposited within us at the time of our rebirth. The crucial matter to a believer is not whether a foundation has been laid—every believer shares Christ as this foundation. Rather, the critical matter is how we build upon the Christ we have already received.

The Apostle tells us that we may build with gold, silver, and precious stone, or with wood, grass, and stubble. Whatever we build will be tested by fire. A fiery trial will come to expose the source and element of the materials with which we build. If today we build with precious materials—gold, silver, and precious stones, which cannot be destroyed by fire—then we will receive a reward at the Lord's second coming. On the other hand, if we build with corruptible materials—wood, grass, or stubble—our work will be destroyed by the fiery trial, and we will suffer loss. To suffer loss does not mean to perish eternally in the lake of fire. Rather, it means to suffer a loss at the judgment seat of Christ, to be disciplined by the Lord at His coming back. Nevertheless, the one suffering such a discipline will be saved, but saved *through fire*.

What are the precious materials with which we should build? Gold, silver, and precious stone refer to the Triune God in His person and work. Gold signifies the divine nature of the Father—eternal, incorruptible, and inestimably precious. Silver speaks of the redemptive work of the Son—perfect, complete, and exceedingly valuable. Precious stone speaks of the transforming work of the Spirit—unfading, incapable of being defiled, and flawless. The proper building is with these materials, with the Triune God Himself: the Father as the source, the Son as the accomplishment, and the Spirit as the application. Only the Triune God Himself can pass through the fiery trial that will test the work of every believer. It is with these materials that we, the believers, must build.

The wood, grass, and stubble signify the natural life, the flesh, and that which is earthly. To build with these materials is to live a life based upon natural concepts and strength, fleshly desires and actions, or earthly and worldly resources and methods. Anything in the believers' daily work and living that is composed of these materials will be consumed by fire. We may think that it does not matter what materials we build our life and work with. We may consider that success is of paramount importance. But God's view is not the human view. He does not look at the outward result, but rather the essence, element, and source of our work and living. His concern is *with what* we build. Consequently, He will test the material of our building by fire to manifest its true nature.

We must be honest, genuine, and frank when we examine the condition of today's Christianity. We must look at the situation among today's Christians, seeking neither to accuse nor excuse, but rather desiring to receive light from the Lord, that we might be fully exposed before Him and thereby brought on to maturity. What do we see when we look at the condition of today's Christians? To a very great degree we see works that have as their source fleshly ambition, pride, and self-exaltation. We see works carried out according to natural thought, opinion, and concept, thus leading to division upon division, with strife and enmity. Today very little among Christians has passed through the cross of Christ and been brought into resurrection. What do we see today? We see worldliness brought into Christian meetings, gatherings, and organizations, and not only condoned, but even encouraged. There is apparently no thought that the entire world, the things of the world, and all that belongs to the world have been condemned by God and are of no use in God's building.[93] Rock music, theatrics, and so many other things of the earth and world are esteemed highly among some of today's Christians. Believers rarely take into account the source, the essence, and the element of their work. Rather, their primary concern seems to be whether an activity will produce something that can in some way be construed as a spiritual success. Very little of what we see today will be acknowledged by the Lord as being wrought of the divine nature, Christ's redemptive work, and the transformation of the Holy Spirit.

The Lord today is longsuffering towards the believers. The day is soon coming, however, when God will test every man's work by fire. The great tribulation will be a time of trial by fire for everything on the earth, including the work of every Christian. What we have done, what we have built, even what we are will be put to the test by fiery trial. Only that which is of and in the Triune God will last. Only that which is constituted according to the Triune God's operation in life will pass through that test. Many believers will suffer loss according to the Apostle Paul's word in 1 Corinthians 3. At the judgment seat of Christ, many believers will have to confess that what they built in their lives was something of the flesh, of the natural man, and of the world. Consequently, they will suffer a loss rather than receive a reward at the judgment seat. They will be given a temporal, dispensational discipline because of their failure in the Christian life. Nevertheless, they themselves will be saved. Yet, even their salvation will be accomplished through some kind of fire.

Some may argue that the fire spoken of by the Apostle Paul in these verses is not a physical fire. However, whether this fire is physical or metaphorical means very little. Whatever this fire, do any of us want to be saved *through* it? Therefore, we do well to heed the Apostle's word concerning how we build, in order that we would not have to be saved through fire. May the Lord grant us all mercy, that we would cooperate with the Triune God to build with Him as the materials to produce that which is pleasing to Him. If we build with these materials, even as the Apostle Paul did, then at the Lord's return the very work we have wrought will become a great reward to us. The divine deposit that we have imparted to others will return to us multiplied as a wonderful reward for our enjoyment during the kingdom. And, the very Christ that we have gained will become our rich portion during the triumphant celebration of the overcomering believers with Christ in the Millennium.

The Righteous Judge

Know ye not that they that run in a race run all, but one receiveth the prize? Even so run; that ye may attain. And every man that striveth in the games exerciseth self-control in all things. Now they do it to receive a corruptible crown; but we an incorruptible. I therefore so run, as not uncertainly; so fight I, as not beating the air: but I buffet my body, and bring it into bondage: lest by any means, after that I have preached to others, I myself should be rejected (1 Corinthians 9:24-27)

... and be found in him, not having a righteousness of mine own, even that which is of the law, but that which is through faith in Christ, the righteousness which is from God by faith: that I may know him, and the power of his resurrection, and the fellowship of his sufferings, becoming conformed unto his death; if by any means I may attain unto the resurrection from the dead. Not that I have already obtained, or am already made perfect: but I press on, if so be that I may lay hold on that for which also I was laid hold on by Christ Jesus. (Philippians 3:9-12)

Therefore let us also, seeing we are compassed about with so great a cloud of witnesses, lay aside every weight, and the sin which doth so easily beset us, and let us run with patience the race that is set before us... (Hebrews 12:1)

I have fought the good fight, I have finished the course, I have kept the faith: henceforth there is laid up for me the crown of righteousness, which the Lord, the righteous judge, shall give to me at that day; and not to me only, but also to all them that have loved his appearing. (2 Timothy 4:7-8)

The day is very near when the Lord Jesus will sit upon His judgment seat to judge all the believers in righteousness. At that time the age of grace will have ended. The time for dealing with God's people according to grace will be over. At the judgment seat, the Lord will sit as the *righteous Judge,* not as the graceful Savior. He will judge each of us in righteousness. This will *not* be to determine whether we participate in the New Jerusalem or the lake of fire; rather, the Lord will give a *reward* or *punishment* to each of the believers according to the works they have done after being saved.

At the judgment seat of Christ, each and every believer will stand before the Lord and be fully manifested both in person and deed, whether good or bad. Everything concerning our Christian life will be fully exposed. The Lord's bright appearing will bring everything concerning us into the light. There will be no possibility of hiding. There will be an end to every delusion and any kind of deception. Our true nature and the true nature of our deeds will be completely revealed.

According to 2 Timothy, at the judgment seat those who love the Lord's appearing will receive a reward. This does not mean that anyone who had some kind of anticipation about the Lord's second coming will be rewarded when He appears. Rather, in these verses the Lord's appearing refers to His appearing to His believers *today* in spirit. The Lord today desires to appear to each of His children every day, again and again. Those who love this appearing love the light. Today the Lord's appearing to us is in and with light. Those who love His appearing love the shining, penetrating light of the Lord's presence. These receive His exposing and dealing today concerning themselves and their deeds. By the time the Lord returns, these believers will have already been fully illuminated by the light of the Lord's penetrating presence. They will have been under the Lord's shining their entire Christian life. Consequently, they with their deeds will have been fully dealt with. All their inward motives will have been purified. Their ambitions, lusts, and self-desires will have been purged away. At the time of the Lord's coming there will be no need for the Lord to deal with them further. They will have been fully prepared to enter into the millennial kingdom to reign with the Lord. Therefore, they, with the Apostle Paul, will receive a reward at the judgment seat.

At the Lord's judgment seat there will also be many Christians who during their daily lives did not love the Lord's appearing. These hide themselves daily from the Lord's presence and from the penetrating rays of His shining. They do not receive Him as light to expose the true character of their deeds. They, themselves, remain untouched and undealt with. Their deeds remain unpurified. Whether they hide themselves in the world or in Christian work, the true nature of their deeds remains unexposed to the purifying light of the Lord. In that day all the lusts, ambitions, desires for material gain, self-glorification, self-motives, and pride will be manifested. Since all these hidden things will still remain untouched, these believers will require a further dealing from the Lord to purify them and impart to them a full measure of the divine life, that they might be qualified to enter the New Jerusalem at the end of the Millennium. They will receive the recompense for the bad they have done during their Christian lives as a punishment and a discipline. Though the Lord loves all of God's children even to the point of dying for them, nevertheless as the righteous Judge He will reward each according to their works. Many, in that day, will suffer being put away from the glory of the Lord's radiant presence during the millennial kingdom. They will weep and gnash their teeth during the millennial kingdom, ruing and regretting their negligence and indulgence during the present age. It is the Lord's desire that all of God's children reign as kings with Him during the coming thousand-year kingdom. However, many of God's children will not be qualified for that time, having refused the Lord's dealing in this age.

Paul saw the need to gain Christ at every opportunity and in every situation. He was never satisfied to remain in his current condition. He never considered himself to have gained enough of Christ to be counted worthy of a reward at the judgment seat. In 1 Corinthians, Paul said he was running the Christian race for the prize. Later in his ministry, when he wrote Philippians, perhaps only three or four years before his martyrdom, Paul was still running the race. He was still striving to attain the goal for the prize. Even when he wrote the book of Hebrews shortly before his death he was still running the race. It was not until the time of his death, at his martyrdom, that Paul could declare triumphantly, "I have fought the good fight; I have finished the course; I have kept the faith." May we all have a heart such as Paul's. May we all run with endurance the race set before us, to obtain the prize of the reward from the Lord at His judgment seat. The Lord grant us all mercy to receive such grace from Him in this age.

Five Warnings

Therefore we ought to give the more earnest heed to the things that were heard, lest haply we drift away from them. For if the word spoken through angels proved stedfast, and every transgression and disobedience received a just recompense of reward; how shall we escape, if we neglect so great a salvation? which having at the first been spoken through the Lord, was confirmed unto us by them that heard... (Hebrews 2:1-3)

Take heed, brethren, lest haply there shall be in any one of you an evil heart of unbelief, in falling away from the living God: but exhort one another day by day, so long as it is called To-day; lest any one of you be hardened by the deceitfulness of sin: for we are become partakers of Christ, if we hold fast the beginning of our confidence firm unto the end... Let us fear therefore, lest haply, a promise being left of entering into his rest, any one of you should seem to have come short of it. ... There remaineth therefore a sabbath rest for the people of God. ... Let us therefore give diligence to enter into that rest, that no man fall after the same example of disobedience. For the word of God is living, and active, and sharper than any two-edged sword, and piercing even to the dividing of soul and spirit, of both joints and marrow, and quick to discern the thoughts and intents of the heart. And there is no creature that is not manifest in his sight: but all things are naked and laid open before the eyes of him with whom we have to do. (Hebrews 3:12-14; 4:1, 9, 11-13)

Of whom we have many things to say, and hard of interpretation, seeing ye are become dull of hearing. For when by reason of the time ye ought to be teachers, ye have need again that some one teach you the rudiments of the first principles of the oracles of God; and are become such as have need of milk, and not of solid food. For every one that partaketh of milk is without experience of the word of righteousness; for he is a babe. But solid food is for fullgrown men, even those who by reason of use have their senses exercised to discern good and evil. Wherefore leaving the doctrine of the first principles of Christ, let us press on unto perfection... For as touching those who were once enlightened and tasted of the heavenly gift, and were made partakers of the Holy Spirit, and tasted the good word of God, and the powers of the age to come, and then fell away, it is impossible to renew them again unto repentance; seeing they crucify to themselves the Son of God afresh, and put him to an open shame. For the land which hath drunk the rain that cometh oft upon it, and bringeth forth herbs meet for them for whose sake it is also tilled, receiveth blessing from God: but if it beareth thorns and thistles, it is rejected and nigh unto a curse; whose end is to be burned. (Hebrews 5:11-14; 6:1, 4-8)

... let us draw near with a true heart in fulness of faith, having our hearts sprinkled from an evil conscience: and having our body washed with pure water, let us hold fast the confession of our hope that it waver not; for he is faithful that promised: and

let us consider one another to provoke unto love and good works; not forsaking our own assembling together, as the custom of some is, but exhorting one another; and so much the more, as ye see the day drawing nigh. For if we sin wilfully after that we have received the knowledge of the truth, there remaineth no more a sacrifice for sins, but a certain fearful expectation of judgment, and a fierceness of fire which shall devour the adversaries. (Hebrews 10:22-27)

Therefore let us also... lay aside every weight, and the sin which doth so easily beset us, and let us run with patience the race that is set before us, looking unto Jesus the author and perfecter of our faith... and ye have forgotten the exhortation which reasoneth with you as with sons, My son, regard not lightly the chastening of the Lord, Nor faint when thou art reproved of him; For whom the Lord loveth he chasteneth, And scourgeth every son whom he receiveth. It is for chastening that ye endure; God dealeth with you as with sons; for what son is there whom his father chasteneth not? ... Furthermore, we had the fathers of our flesh to chasten us, and we gave them reverence: shall we not much rather be in subjection unto the Father of spirits, and live? For they indeed for a few days chastened us as seemed good to them; but he for our profit, that we may be partakers of his holiness. All chastening seemeth for the present to be not joyous but grievous; yet afterward it yieldeth peaceable fruit unto them that have been exercised thereby, even the fruit of righteousness. ... looking carefully lest there be any man that falleth short of the grace of God; lest any root of bitterness springing up trouble you, and thereby the many be defiled; lest there be any fornication, or profane person, as Esau, who for one mess of meat sold his own birthright. For ye know that even when he afterward desired to inherit the blessing, he was rejected; for he found no place for a change of mind in his father, though he sought it diligently with tears. ... See that ye refuse not him that speaketh. For if they escaped not when they refused him that warned them on earth, much more shall not we escape who turn away from him that warneth from heaven... Wherefore, receiving a kingdom that cannot be shaken, let us have grace, whereby we may offer service well-pleasing to God with reverence and awe: for our

God is a consuming fire. (Hebrews 12:1-2, 5-7, 9-11, 15-17, 25, 28-29)

In His epistle to the Hebrews the Apostle Paul* delivers five strong warnings. There has been much confusion among Christians regarding these warnings. In order to have a proper understanding of their intent and meaning, certain misconceptions must be cleared away. We must first consider whether this book was written to believers or unbelievers. It is clear from the language of this book that the recipients were believers in Christ. Paul calls them "brothers," even "holy brothers," thus indicating that they, with him, were partakers of the divine life and nature of the Father.[94] Repeatedly Paul includes himself as one of those to whom the warnings are addressed saying, for example, "How shall *we* escape if *we* have neglected so great a salvation." Furthermore, the ones who received this epistle had been enlightened, had tasted of the heavenly gift, had become partakers of the Holy Spirit, and had tasted the good word of God and the powers of the age to come. Thus, it is abundantly clear that the receivers of this epistle were believers and that Paul's warnings were addressed to them. Consequently, the warnings in the book of Hebrews are for all believers.

Knowing that this epistle was written to believers, some interpret its warnings to mean that believers can lose their salvation, that they may indeed perish in the lake of fire. This, however, contradicts other portions of the New Testament. Such an understanding also ignores the context of the epistle to the Hebrews. In order to understand the warnings in this book, we must have a clear view of the background and intent of this epistle. We must also clearly see God's New Testament economy in His salvation for man.

Many of the Hebrew believers had been saved shortly after the Lord's death, some time after 32 A.D.[95] At that time they en-

---

* The apostle Paul is the evident writer of the epistle to the Hebrews. Only he was qualified to write such a high, deep, and profound epistle. Only he abounded in the revelation and riches of Christ to the degree revealed in this book. None of the other apostles had such a qualification. That Paul wrote this epistle is further confirmed by the mentioning of Timothy, Paul's intimate companion, in verse 13:23 of this book.

joyed a very good beginning in the Lord, giving up all things, including their Judaistic background, to follow Him, seek Him, and grow in Him.[96] Over time, Judaism had gradually crept back into the church in Jerusalem; its strong religious influence enticed many of the believers back to its rituals. The believers in Jerusalem then became zealous—not for Christ, but for the law. A good number of them had fallen away from the New Testament principle of grace back to the Old Testament principle of works by law. Some had even gone back to offering animal sacrifices according to the Levitical practice. The entire church in Jerusalem was in great danger of falling away from the truth of God's New Testament economy by returning to the Old Testament practices, which had been done away with by Christ on the cross.[97] Therefore, the Apostle Paul wrote this very strong word to annul the influence of Judaism and encourage the Hebrew believers on in God's New Testament way.

We must also see that God's salvation starts with the receiving of Christ in His work and person. His work saves us from sin and its result.[98] His person regenerates us with Himself as the divine life to make us children of God.[99] God's salvation continues throughout our whole life, as the divine life spreads to our soul. This salvation eventually consummates in the redemption of our body at the time of the Lord's second coming.[100] Salvation is not just a matter of being saved from the lake of fire for eternity; it is also a matter of being saved from the self, the world, the natural man, as well as the flesh with its passions and lusts.[101] In addition, God's salvation is not merely *from* negative things; it is also *to* something most positive. God's salvation brings us into the divine sonship in which we participate in all that the Son of God is, has, has done, and will do.[102] We become joint heirs with Christ of God Himself.[103] This salvation is neither narrow nor small, but broad, profound, and great. Paul calls it "so great a salvation."

Every one who receives the Lord has partaken of God's salvation, but only to a degree. Once a person has been saved from the lake of fire, he is always saved. Once a person has been regenerated to become a son of God, he remains a son of God forever. Yet, there is still the need for each one of us to go on from that initial salvation, to grow and mature in the divine life, that we might partake of God's consummate salvation and participate in the millennial kingdom as full-grown sons of God, to be kings over the earth with Christ. It is indeed possible for one who is saved not to reach the ultimate goal of God's salvation in this age. Such a one is still saved from the lake of fire, yet has fallen short of God's full salvation. Therefore, this one will not participate in the millennial kingdom as a reward in the next age.

With this background as a basis, we can now interpret the Apostle's warnings to the Hebrew believers and to all Christians in general. Paul says, "How shall we escape if we neglect so great a salvation?" The salvation here is God's operation in grace throughout our lives to bring us into the glory of the sons of God.[104] If we neglect the subjective operation of the Spirit to accomplish God's salvation within us, how can we escape an adverse judgment by the Lord at His judgment seat at the end of this age? If today we neglect the Spirit's subjective working and turn instead to the world, the law, or some other thing, then at the judgment seat the Lord will certainly count us worthy of punishment. We will not escape that judgment at the judgment seat of Christ.

In chapters 3 and 4 of Hebrews, Paul tells us that there remains a Sabbath rest for the people of God. That Sabbath rest refers to the coming millennial kingdom in which we will rest in and with Christ and enjoy to the full all that God is in Christ. That will be the time of ultimate rest and satisfaction. In order to enter into that Sabbath rest, however, we must not fall away from the living God and come short of that rest. We must hold fast the beginning of the assurance firm to the end. In other words, the Lord began His operation in us by grace through faith. That operation begot in us an assurance of the coming day of full salvation. We must continue in this grace, which is nothing other than God Himself in Christ, and hold it fast. By this, we allow God to become everything in us that He could complete His full salvation. We then enter into the millennial kingdom as our Sabbath rest. If we disobey God's word to us in this regard, not heeding His warning to remain in grace unto the consummation of His salvation, then, like the children of Israel who were strewn throughout the wilderness and who did not enter into the rest of the good land, we also will not enter into the rest and enjoyment of the millennial kingdom.[105] Rather, we will suffer a kind of destruction and loss, as the children of Israel did.

In chapter 6* Paul speaks an even stronger word of warning. He cautions his readers, including us, that we must be those who leave the word of the beginning of Christ and are brought on to maturity. If we do not do this and bring forth fruit suitable to mature sons of God, then we, like ground which brings forth thorns and thistles, are near to a curse. This does not mean that believers will be cursed for eternity, but rather that they will suffer some discipline and punishment that is *close* to being cursed. There will be a kind of burning to purge the believers of any remaining thorns and thistles. It is the thorns and thistles that are burned, not the ground. Similarly, it is the deeds, actions, motives, and desires of the believers that will be consumed by the coming fire. The believers themselves, however, can never be cursed or perish.

In chapter 10† the Apostle once again exhorts us to hold fast the confession of our hope unwavering. This is to remain in

---

* The Apostle also says in these verses in chapter 6, "… it is impossible for those who … have fallen away, to renew themselves again unto repentance, crucifying again for themselves the Son of God and putting Him to an open shame." This does not mean that those of whom the Apostle spoke were no longer saved. It means it is impossible to go back to the beginning of our salvation, to repent from the dead works of keeping the law to the New Testament principle of salvation by grace. Once that has been done, it has been done once for all. It is impossible to redo it. Therefore, we must simply go on from wherever we are to mature in Christ. "Crucifying again for themselves the Son of God" refers to the Hebrew believers going back to the animal sacrifices of Judaism and thus making the crucifixion of Christ of no practical effect in their lives.

† In chapter 10 Paul also says, "… when we sin willfully after receiving the knowledge of the truth there no longer remains a sacrifice for sins." To sin willfully refers to the believers in Jerusalem abandoning their assembling together as the church and falling back into Judaism. This was the willful sin of which Paul spoke. He tells the back-sliding Hebrew believers that there no longer remains a sacrifice for sins. This does not mean that their willful sin could not be forgiven by the Lord. Rather, Paul is indicating that the animal sacrifices to which the Hebrew believers had fallen back were of no more effect with respect to forgiving sins. They had been replaced once for all by Christ's death on the cross. The animal sacrifices were no longer efficacious in God's eyes. Therefore, the Hebrew believers should not go back to them. They should not give up the meeting of the church to fall back to animal sacrifices, which were no longer a part of God's move on the earth.

God's New Testament economy of grace so that He could become everything to us subjectively, both for our daily living and for the church life. Paul exhorts us to come out of any kind of religious practice, including the keeping of the law back to God's New Testament covenant of grace. If we would not, if we would continue to fall away, Paul warns us that all that remains is a certain fearful expectation of judgment and fierceness of fire. This fire will consume the adversaries, the unbelievers. It will also be used by God to purify many of the unfaithful believers. Once again this is not to perish eternally in the lake of fire. It is, however, to be judged, punished, and disciplined by the Lord for our unfaithfulness during this age of God's grace. These words are very similar to the ones spoken by the Apostle in 1 Corinthians 3. There the unfaithful believer is saved, yet he is saved *through fire*.[106] Similarly, here there is an expectation of fire that will consume the adversaries, yet not cause the believers to perish.

Finally, in chapter 12 Paul gives one final word of warning to the believers. He tells us all not to faint at the Lord's discipline and not to fall away from the dispensation of grace to other things. We must go on and come forward. God's discipline in this age is that of a loving Father, that we might partake of His holy nature. Paul warns us not to partake of evil things such as fornication, but to hold fast the grace of God. Even one meal of the flesh may cause us to lose the reward of the coming kingdom, just as Esau's lust for food caused him to lose his inheritance, which he could not renew even though he repented in tears. When the time of the judgment seat comes, it will be too late to repent for the kingdom. We must repent from everything other than Christ today, to come back to the One who is our grace and our all, to enjoy Him, be disciplined by Him, purged by Him, and filled with Him. By this, we are transformed to be built with others for the fulfillment of God's eternal purpose in the church. Then we can partake of the reward in the coming kingdom. If we would not repent today then God will not be to us the merciful, gracious Father, but a *consuming fire* to devour everything that is impure, sinful, natural, fallen, worldly, and earthly. That consuming fire will leave nothing but what is of God in Christ. Today we can come to the One who meets us in grace at His throne, to supply our need during this time of purifying through discipline. If we choose not to, then we will suffer Christ's adverse judgment and the consuming of fire at the judgment seat.

We must be impressed that the book of Hebrews was written to believers, not unbelievers. We must be impressed that it speaks not of losing salvation, but of a coming judgment for discipline and punishment. These warnings should sober us and awaken us out of any kind of delusion and deception. How we live today affects our standing at the judgment seat for the coming age. We are accountable for everything we do—for every word, for every action, and for all the motives and desires within us. We will give an account of these to the Lord at His judgment seat. If our person and deeds have not been judged and purified by the Lord in this age, then we will suffer a grievous loss and terrible punishment by the Lord during the coming age. If we stand in the grace given to us, enjoying Christ in His operation for our salvation, that we might be led into glory by the Captain of our salvation, then in the coming age we will enjoy the glory, rest, satisfaction, and kingship in Christ.

He Who Has an Ear, Let Him Hear

He that hath an ear, let him hear what the Spirit saith to the churches. To him that overcometh, to him will I give to eat of the tree of life, which is in the Paradise of God. (Revelation 2:7)

He that hath an ear, let him hear what the Spirit saith to the churches. He that overcometh shall not be hurt of the second death. (Revelation 2:11)

He that hath an ear, let him hear what the Spirit saith to the churches. To him that overcometh, to him will I give of the hidden manna, and I will give him a white stone, and upon the stone a new name written, which no one knoweth but he that receiveth it. (Revelation 2:17)

And he that overcometh, and he that keepeth my works unto the end, to him will I give authority over the nations: and he shall rule them with a rod of iron, as the vessels of the potter are broken to shivers; as I also have received of my Father: and I will give him the morning star. He that hath an ear, let him hear what the Spirit saith to the churches. (Revelation 2:26-29)

He that overcometh shall thus be arrayed in white garments; and I will in no wise blot his name out of the book of life, and I will confess his name before my Father, and before his angels. He that hath an ear, let him hear what the Spirit saith to the churches. (Revelation 3:5-6)

Because thou didst keep the word of my patience, I also will keep thee from the hour of trial, that hour which is to come upon the whole world, to try them that dwell upon the earth. I come quickly: hold fast that which thou hast, that no one take thy crown. He that overcometh, I will make him a pillar in the temple of my God, and he shall go out thence no more: and I will write upon him the name of my God, and the name of the city of my God, the new Jerusalem, which cometh down out of heaven from my God, and mine own new name. He that hath an ear, let him hear what the Spirit saith to the churches. (Revelation 3:10-13)

Behold, I stand at the door and knock: if any man hear my voice and open the door, I will come in to him, and will sup with him, and he with me. He that overcometh, I will give to him to sit down with me in my throne, as I also overcame, and sat down with my Father in his throne. He that hath an ear, let him hear what the Spirit saith to the churches. (Revelation 3:19-22)

In the second and third chapters of Revelation, the Lord Jesus gives seven strong words of exhortation to seven of the churches in Asia Minor. In each of these epistles He issues a call to the believers to *overcome* the degraded condition of the church where they were.

Many think that all Christians are overcomers. They use certain verses in 1 John to justify this understanding.[107] They feel that since all believers must be overcomers, the exhortations and warnings given by the Lord in Revelation 2-3 are not applicable to them. The unreasonableness and illogic of such a view is extraordinary. Let us reasonably consider the book of Revelation and, in particular, chapters two and three.

It is an indisputable fact that the book of Revelation was written to the seven churches in Asia Minor.[108] Not only were the first three chapters written to the churches, the whole book also was.[109] Revelation was not written for Gentile unbelievers, nor for Jews. It was written for the churches. Now we know that the churches are composed only of genuine, born-again believers. The churches are the local expression of the one universal church, which is the Body of Christ. As such, the genuine churches include as their members only the genuine believers. Therefore, the book of Revelation was written to the genuine believers in the churches. Not only are the second and third chapters of Revelation for the believers; the whole book is God's speaking to His children.

Revelation presents to us the ascended Christ in His loving care and concern for His testimony—the churches—coming as the seven Spirits and shining in the dark degradation of the church in this age to illuminate, expose, purify, purge, infuse, strengthen, and empower the believers, that they might become partakers of God's full salvation and thus participate in the New Jerusalem as God's corporate expression for eternity. Accordingly, this book contains many exhortations, rebukes, warnings, and encouragements to adjust, supply, and transform the believers in the churches, bringing them from their present degradation into that divine glory prepared for them from eternity past. This is the character of this book in its intention to save us from our fallen, degraded condition. Thus, the seven epistles in the second and third chapters of this book, which contain the loving reproof of the ascended Christ as a surgical operation to excise the rottenness and corruption that has crept into the church, fit seamlessly with the rest of Revelation in character and intent. As with the whole book of Revelation, the epistles in these chapters are for the believers' reproof, correction, instruction, supply, and sanctification.

Furthermore, in these two chapters the Lord Himself speaks the clearest and most emphatic word as to whom the intended audience for these seven epistles is. Seven times He says, "He who has an ear, let him hear what the Spirit says to the churches." The Spirit here is not speaking to the unbelievers or to the Jewish nation, but to the churches, which are composed of believers. Thus, the one who has an ear to hear must be a believer. In like manner, the ones who do not have an ear to hear must also be believers. Therefore, it is unfounded, illogical, and contrary even to common sense to believe the exhortations and warnings in these seven epistles do not apply to the believers. What is written here is *only* for the believers! Thus, according to these verses the believers may be either overcoming or defeated Christians. Many believers do not live a proper Christian life. They are thus defeated, suffering in the degradation and corruption of the church. Others, who heed the speaking Spirit, are enabled by the Lord's grace to live that life which overcomes all degradation and brings them into the glory of the coming kingdom age. These seven epistles were written to supply this enabling grace to the hearing believers.

With the understanding that these epistles were written to us, the genuine believers in Christ, let us now examine the warnings and encouragements within them. In His epistle to the church in Ephesus, the Lord warns the believers that they had left their first love. This was the beginning of the Church's degradation: leaving Christ as the first, best love.[110] In our Christian life Christ must be the preeminent One, having the first place in all things. He should have the first place in our hearts, being preeminent in everything that concerns us. We should love Him above all else. Leaving Him as the preeminent One, even for something as good as Christian work, results in degradation. The Lord exhorts us all to return to our first love, to remember the love we once had for Him, to repent from every other love.

As both a warning and an encouragement, the Lord says that He will give the one who overcomes to eat of the tree of life in the Paradise of God. This reward refers to Christ Himself as our sweet, nourishing, strengthening, and life-giving source of supply for our full enjoyment in the coming Millennium. The overcoming saints among the Christians will enjoy Christ to the highest degree during the coming thousand-year kingdom. There will be no limit to their enjoyment of Christ's riches in the Paradise of God,* which is the New Jerusalem.

On the one hand, this word should encourage and strengthen us to turn back to the Lord as our first love. On the other hand, it should serve as a warning to awaken us to the fact that it is possible to miss the enjoyment of Christ as the tree of life in the

---

* This Paradise is different from the one to which the Lord and the thief went after their deaths (Luke 23:40-43). That Paradise is the pleasant section of Hades (see footnote on Hades on page 34.). The Paradise in Revelation 2:7 refers to the New Jerusalem where the tree of life is (Rev. 22:2).

Millennium. Just as the five foolish virgins will not be allowed to enter into the wedding feast,[111] so also many dear, genuine believers in Christ will forfeit the high enjoyment of Christ as the tree of life during the kingdom age. As the overcoming believers will be rewarded with Christ as the tree of life in the Paradise of God, so the defeated ones will suffer the loss of this enjoyment as a punishment.

The Lord exhorts those in the church in Smyrna to remain faithful in their suffering circumstances even unto death. The believers in Smyrna were greatly persecuted; many of them were martyred. Throughout the ages there have been many other believers who have been slain for the Lord's sake. To all of these, the Lord speaks words of comfort: they will be rewarded in the resurrection with a crown of life; they will not be touched by the second death, which is the lake of fire.[112] To be untouched by the second death is to have had our being fully dealt with, perfected, and uplifted by the divine nature in this age, and thus not require any further dealing from the Lord in the next age *after resurrection*. However, many genuine Christians will require further discipline from the Lord even after resurrection.

Consider those who have *not* been faithful unto death. Consider those who have lived a life of worldly enjoyment in the lust of the flesh, or those who have backslidden. Consider those who have done many great works, yet apart from Christ. After resurrection, for many believers there will still be the need for further dealing. Many genuine Christians will be touched by the second death. This does not mean that any Christian could perish in the lake of fire for eternity. It does mean, however, that a Christian may suffer some punishment by being touched by the fire of the lake of fire. This is also similar to Paul's word in 1 Corinthians where he says that we may be saved, yet so as *through fire*.[113] In Hebrews, Paul reminds us that we could be near a curse, having nothing but a certain fearful expectation of fire. Paul also warns us that our God is a consuming fire.[114] Thus, it is possible for believers to suffer being touched by fire even after death and resurrection. This is a fearful, sobering word. We should not take lightly the Lord's warning in these verses.

The Lord encourages the believers in Pergamos to overcome the satanic presence among them with its corruption, fornication, and idol worship by offering them a twofold reward: hidden manna and a white stone with a new name written on it. The hidden manna is that which was laid up in a golden pot within the ark of the testimony in the Holy of Holies before God.[115] The Lord Jesus Himself is the true manna that came down out of heaven. Thus, to enjoy the hidden manna is to partake of the nourishing Christ in the deepest and most intimate way in God's presence. Only the overcoming saints will enjoy this portion of Christ during the coming age. The other believers will suffer the loss of it.

The Lord also rewards the overcoming saints in Pergamos with a white stone and a new name. A white stone is a stone that has been approved, a stone that is acceptable to God for His building, the New Jerusalem. To be given a white stone is to be one who has been fully transformed from the "clay" of the natural man into precious materials for God's building. To have a "new name" is to have a personal, hidden, intimate, and eternal experience of Christ according to which the Lord calls us by a new name. This reward is only for the overcoming saints. The defeated ones will instead suffer a discipline from the Lord's hands.

It is worthwhile noting that the hidden manna, the white stone, and the new name, as well as the tree of life and all the other rewards offered in these seven epistles, can be enjoyed by the believers as a foretaste in this age. For example, we can partake of Christ as our nourishing tree of life and as our hidden manna in the intimacy of God's presence, to be transformed into a stone for God's building today. Actually, these are aspects of the normal Christian life. If we enjoy Christ in all these ways today, we will be rewarded with Him in full in the coming age. In addition, by enjoying Christ in these ways we are strengthened and enabled to overcome the degradation in the church. Thus, the means to obtain the reward in the next age is *by enjoying it in this age.*

The church in Thyatira had fallen to an enormous degree. Their degradation had reached the lowest point. Fornication and idol worship were common. Furthermore, not only was the satanic presence among them, but they even taught and practiced the deep things of Satan.* The Lord calls His people out of this vile decay by offering a marvelous incentive: to those who overcome the rottenness of the degradation in Thyatira, the Lord will give authority over the nations to shepherd them with a rod of iron.† Only the overcomers will partake of the kingdom reign with Christ during that time. Only they will be co-kings of Christ ruling over the cities and nations. The defeated Christians will not take part in the reign over the nations during the Millennium.

The Lord also offers those who overcome in Thyatira the morning star. The Lord will appear in His second coming as the bright sun to many believers. He will come as the shining dawn upon the whole earth, to bring mankind out from the satanic darkness into the shining light of His kingdom. However, here the Lord offers Himself not as the sun in the dawn, but rather as a morning star. The morning star appears some hours before the dawn. As the dawn nears, the morning star appears first. The morning star is a reference to the Lord's secret appearing to the overcoming believers for an early rapture before the great tribulation.‡

The Lord speaks a strong word of rebuke and warning to the church in Sardis. Though they have a name that they are living, they are actually dead; though they bear the name of Christ, in their daily life they do not express him. They are spiritually dead. A life without Christ as its substance, a life void of Christ as the true, spiritual life-element, is altogether dead, corrupted, and defiled in the Lord's eyes.

But, there are a few in Sardis who have not defiled their garments§ and are worthy. There are some to whom Christ is not

---

* This, as we have seen, is a reference to the condition of Catholicism. See *The Destruction of Religious Babylon* in Chapter 6 for more details.

† This is fulfilled, at least in part, by the overcomers who constitute the manchild (Rev. 12:5), who will reign over the earth during the Millennium.

‡ This is fulfilled in Revelation 12 and 14, where the overcomers are taken to the heavens before the last $3\frac{1}{2}$ years of this age.

§ The garments spoken of here do not refer to Christ as our objective righteousness to justify us before God (that garment could never be defiled), but to our daily living, including all our actions and deeds. It is possible for believers to defile this garment by acting immorally or unrighteously. Spiritual death in particular defiles our daily living.

merely an object of worship, but their very life and content for their practical daily life. To these overcoming believers the Lord offers the reward of being clothed in white garments. This is to experience Christ as our righteous, God-approved expression and covering in our everyday behavior and conduct. This is to enjoy Christ, not merely as our objective justification for salvation, but as our practical expression through His subjective operation from within us. To have such a Christ seen in every facet of our living is indeed a great reward.

The Lord will also reward those who overcome by keeping their names in the book of life, and by confessing them before the Father and His angels. For our name to be in the Lamb's book of life and confessed before the Father and His angels is for us to participate in all the riches of the divine life to the fullest during the Millennium. It is also to enjoy the Father's precious, gracious, and eternal acceptance during that thousand years. Only the believers who overcome will enter into the Father's presence with joy during the millennial kingdom.

The defeated Christians will suffer a loss during that time. They will not walk in white; their names will be blotted out from the book of life; they will not be confessed before the Father. In other words, during the thousand-year reign of Christ the defeated Christians will not enjoy Him as their subjective righteousness lived out from within them. Although their names will be in the book of life in eternity future, for that thousand years their names will be erased. To them there will be no enjoyment of Christ as life. Finally, they will be denied before the Father, disapproved and put away from the presence of God, Christ, and the holy angels. They will experience Christ's rejection in outer darkness.

To those who overcome in the church in Philadelphia, the Lord offers perhaps the greatest reward. He first encourages them with the reward of an early rapture. He promises to keep them from the hour of trial coming upon the whole earth—that is, from the great tribulation. More importantly, the Lord promises to make them pillars in the temple of His God and to write upon them His new name, the name of His God, and the name of the city of His God, the New Jerusalem. These promises are too great! To have Christ's new name and the name of Christ's God written on our foreheads is to be wholly possessed, owned, filled, and saturated with God in Christ. It is to have our whole being occupied with God alone. What a wonderful reward to the overcoming believers. During the Millennium their every thought, feeling, and choice, their character, disposition, and whole person will be nothing but Christ! What can compare with this reward?

Furthermore, these will be pillars in the temple of God, which is the New Jerusalem, and will go out no more. Their dwelling for eternity will be the New Jerusalem, which they will enjoy as a reward during the whole of the Millennium. They will enjoy this union of God and man as a mutual dwelling place for the thousand-year kingdom. They will be the pillars, the ones who uphold God's testimony. They will be the supports of God's dwelling. How wonderful, how excellent this reward is!

The Lord will not give an early rapture to the defeated ones. They are left behind to pass through the tribulation. They are not kept from the hour of trial. In addition, the defeated ones will not be made pillars in the temple of their God. In fact, they will be put out from the enjoyment of the New Jerusalem for the whole Millennium. The defeated Christians will not enjoy Christ's new name, the name of His God, and the name of the New Jerusalem being written upon them. They will be apart from Christ. This is the Lord's strong warning to all the believers in these epistles.

In the last of the seven epistles in Revelation 2-3, the Lord gives the most severe rebuke. To those who think they are spiritually wealthy, having no spiritual needs, the Lord speaks frankly in love. He says that these do not know that they are wretched, miserable, poor, blind, and naked. They are actually without Christ practically: Christ is outside, knocking on the door of the church to enter in. They are counseled to buy gold refined by fire, garments that they might be clothed and their nakedness not manifested, and eyesalve that they may really see. They need to gain Christ in their experience—as the divine nature (signified by gold), as their practical righteousness (signified by garments), and as the healing, anointing, illuminating Spirit (signified by eyesalve). This is the Triune God in three aspects, that the believers may be delivered from their most pitiful condition.

The Lord then gives a final word of encouragement to empower the believers to overcome their lukewarmness in degradation. He offers them to sit with Him on His throne and reign with Him over the nations and the earth during the kingdom. This is the end of God's salvation: reigning with Christ through grace, having been brought from a wretched sinner, dead in sins! Yet, this reward also clearly implies a warning: those who do not overcome will suffer the loss of the kingdom reign with Christ. Many dear believers who have been misled to believe that there could never be a problem between them and the Lord, and consequently, have lived a defeated Christian life by condoning and taking part in the degradation of the church, will lose that kingdom reward at the Lord's return. This is the Lord's unambiguous word to all the believers.

By all the warnings, rebukes, and exhortations in these seven epistles, we must be sobered to realize the seriousness of our daily life with the Lord, and the responsibility we bear in our relationship with Him. If we will not turn our heart to seek Him first above all other things and gain Him for our spiritual maturity in this age, then we will suffer a great loss in the next age, being disciplined, reproved, rebuked, and rejected by the Lord at His judgment seat. If we would not exercise before the Lord to be a faithful, prudent, and good servant to dispense Christ as food to God's children, then at the judgment seat He will put us into outer darkness, and perhaps even punish us with lashes. He may even purify us through fire. The daily Christian life is not a small matter. It is of the utmost importance. We will give account to the Lord for *all* our actions since believing into Him.

Reward and Punishment

These are but some of the verses in the New Testament that relate to the matters of reward and punishment. There are many others, such as in Matthew 5-7, 1 Jn 2:28, and First and Second Peter. We must see that the reward and punishment apportioned by the Lord at His judgment seat is a crucial matter. Whenever it is mentioned in the New Testament it is with the utmost seriousness. According to the New Testament, all the believers will stand before the judgment seat of Christ and give account for everything done in their Christian life from the time they were first regenerated. According to what we have done and according to the motive, intent, and source of our deeds, we will receive from the Lord a reward or a punishment. This will determine our state during the millennial kingdom. Some, perhaps even most, of the believers will be ashamed before the Lord at that time.

During the Millennium the believers will receive varying degrees of reward or punishment. Some will rule over ten cities, others over five. Some will be punished by being put into outer darkness where there will be weeping and gnashing of teeth. Others will be lashed—some a few times, others many times. Some will even be touched by the second death. These are very serious words for our most thoughtful and prayerful consideration. We all must pray much over the matter of reward and punishment. We must realize that all believers will enjoy the blessing of the New Jerusalem after the Millennium for eternity. Once a man has been saved he is always saved. His eternal state is secured. But, he may still suffer loss at the Lord's judgment seat and be punished, disciplined, and chastised by the Lord for the thousand years of the kingdom age. May these words sober us during this current age. May we all find mercy from the Lord at His judgment seat and not be put away from the glory of His presence.

References

[1] 2 Cor 5:10
[2] Rom. 5:10
[3] 1 Cor. 1:30; Gal. 3:27
[4] 1 Pet. 3:18
[5] Rom. 8:10; Col. 1:28
[6] Col. 3:4
[7] Jn. 1:12-13
[8] Jn. 10:10; 2 Pet. 1:4; Col. 1:27
[9] 1 Cor. 1:30
[10] Jn. 3:15-16
[11] Heb. 13:5
[12] Eph. 1:4-5
[13] 1 Jn. 4:10; Jn. 3:16; Jer. 31:3; Jn. 13:1; Rom. 8:35-38; Eph. 2:4-5
[14] Jn. 3:16
[15] Rom. 8:39
[16] Jn. 1:12-13
[17] Rom. 1:16-17; 3:25-26
[18] Heb. 1:8
[19] 2 Cor. 5:21
[20] 1 Pet. 2:24

[21] 2 Cor. 5:21
[22] 1 Cor. 15:17
[23] Rom. 3:26
[24] Jn. 6:37, 40
[25] Tit. 1:2; Heb. 6:18
[26] Mal. 3:6; Heb. 13:8
[27] 1 Cor. 1:9
[28] Jn. 10:28-29
[29] Matt. 28:18
[30] Rom. 8:38-39
[31] Heb. 12:6
[32] Heb. 12:10
[33] 1 Cor. 5:5
[34] 1 Cor. 11:29-30
[35] 1 Tim. 1:20
[36] 2 Tim. 1:15
[37] Act. 15:39; 2 Tim. 4:10
[38] Matt. 25:9-10
[39] Phil. 3:7-9
[40] Matt. 16:24
[41] 1 Jn. 2:15
[42] Rev. 12:6
[43] Jn. 5:29
[44] Rev. 20:4
[45] Rev. 11:7-12
[46] Heb. 4:16; Rom. 14:10; 2 Cor. 5:10
[47] 2 Tim. 4:8
[48] Rev. 20:11
[49] Matt. 25:20-23
[50] Matt. 25:24-30
[51] 1 Cor. 1:30
[52] Gal. 3:27
[53] Jn. 11:11; 1 Cor. 11:30; 1 Cor. 15:51
[54] Rev. 20:12
[55] Gen. 2:7
[56] 1 Thes. 5:23
[57] Heb. 4:12
[58] 1 Cor. 6:17
[59] Rom. 9:23-24
[60] Jn. 3:5-6; 7:39; 20:22
[61] Eph. 4:23
[62] 2 Cor. 3:18
[63] Phil. 1:19
[64] Phil. 3:7-8
[65] Heb. 12:6
[66] 2 Cor. 3:18
[67] Col. 3:6
[68] Matt. 20:28

[69] Heb. 6:1

[70] cf. Act. 19:14-16

[71] Jn. 21:15-17

[72] Matt. 25:1-30; Luk. 12:45-48; 19:12-26; etc.

[73] Jn. 15:5

[74] Jn. 15:8

[75] Mk. 3:11-12; Lk. 4:41

[76] Matt. 8:4; 9:30; Mk. 7:36; Lk. 8:56

[77] Jn. 6:15

[78] Act. 1:15

[79] 2 Cor. 4:8-11

[80] 2 Cor. 5:15

[81] 1 Cor. 1:12-13

[82] Gal. 2:20

[83] 2 Cor. 11:2

[84] 1 Cor. 3:2

[85] 2 Tim. 4:8

[86] Matt. 1:1; 2:2; 21:5; 25:34; 27:11

[87] Luk. 1:3

[88] Rev. 1:5-6; 1 Pet. 2:9-10

[89] Jn. 21:15, 17

[90] Eph. 4:7, 16

[91] Eph. 3:8

[92] Eph. 4:16

[93] 1 Jn. 5:19

[94] Heb. 10:19; 3:1

[95] Act. 2:41; 4:4

[96] Act. 2:45; Heb. 10:34

[97] Eph. 2:14-16

[98] 2 Cor. 5:21

[99] Jn. 1:12

[100] Rom. 8:23

[101] Matt. 16:24; Gal. 6:14; 5:24

[102] Eph. 1:5, 13-14

[103] Rom. 8:17

[104] Heb. 2:10

[105] Heb. 4:11

[106] 1 Cor. 3:15

[107] 1 Jn. 2:13-14; 4:4

[108] Rev. 1:4

[109] Rev. 1:11

[110] Rev. 2:4

[111] Matt. 25:11-13

[112] Rev. 2:10-11; 20:14

[113] 1 Cor. 3:15

[114] Heb. 12:29

[115] Heb. 9:4

CHAPTER 9

A Wedding and a War

At His judgment seat, Christ will clear up all things regarding the believers. Everything that is hidden today, whether negative or positive, will be brought to light at that time. All the intents of the heart will be manifested. The genuine nature of every work will be revealed. The real condition of every Christian will be made known. The true behavior of all the Lord's children will be brought out into the open. According to these, according to the maturity in the divine life and faithfulness in service to the Lord, every Christian will be judged. Some among the Christians will receive a reward, others a dispensational punishment that will last for one thousand years. Those receiving a reward will enter into the Lord's joy and glory in His kingdom to feast and reign with Him for the Millennium. Those receiving a punishment will be put into some kind of darkness away from the glory of the Lord in His kingdom and outside of the joy of the Lord's presence. In addition, they may suffer some further punishment to help mature them for the New Jerusalem.

The Marriage of the Lamb

Let us rejoice and be exceeding glad, and let us give the glory unto him: for the marriage of the Lamb is come, and his wife hath made herself ready. And it was given unto her that she should array herself in fine linen, bright and pure: for the fine linen is the righteous acts of the saints. And he saith unto me, Write, Blessed are they that are bidden to the marriage supper of the Lamb. And he saith unto me, These are true words of God. (Revelation 19:7-9)

Then shall the kingdom of heaven be likened unto ten virgins, who took their lamps, and went forth to meet the bridegroom. And five of them were foolish, and five were wise. For the foolish, when they took their lamps, took no oil with them: but the wise took oil in their vessels with their lamps. Now while the bridegroom tarried, they all slumbered and slept. But at midnight there is a cry, Behold, the bridegroom! Come ye forth to meet him. Then all those virgins arose, and trimmed their lamps. And the foolish said unto the wise, Give us of your oil; for our lamps are going out. But the wise answered, saying, Peradventure there will not be enough for us and you: go ye rather to them that sell, and buy for yourselves. And while they went away to buy, the bridegroom came; and they that were ready went in with him to the marriage feast: and the door was shut. (Matthew 25:1-10)

He that hath the bride is the bridegroom... (John 3:29)

And I saw the holy city, new Jerusalem, coming down out of heaven of God, made ready as a bride adorned for her husband. (Revelation 21:2)

... but in the days of the voice of the seventh angel, when he is about to sound, then is finished the mystery of God, according to the good tidings which he declared to his servants the prophets. (Revelation 10:7)

Immediately after the Lord has determined who will receive a reward there will be a wonderful wedding. By that time the bride of Christ will have prepared herself. She will be clothed with the righteousnesses of the saints. This is the wedding garment spoken of in Matthew 22.[1] It is Christ, not as a garment for justification, but rather as our life lived out in our daily living. This Christ, as the righteous One living in, through, and out of us, produces a righteous living with many righteous aspects and deeds. This is Christ as the second garment, the wedding garment, which is needed to participate in the marriage of the Lamb. This is Christ lived out to be the righteousnesses of the saints, according to which the Lord can approve us at His judgment seat and join to us in His marriage. It is the fully matured and perfected believers who will be the constituents of the bride of Christ at that wedding. The defeated Christians, those suffering a discipline during the Millennium, will miss this marriage and the wedding feast due to their immaturity and slothfulness in service in this age. However, after the Millennium they will be members of the New Jerusalem as the wife of the Lamb for eternity.

This marriage will be the consummate eternal union of God with man, of the Lamb with His bride. The proper human marriage today is but a picture of this joining of God with man. This union of Christ with the matured believers will be the completion, dispensationally, of God's eternal mystery. It will be a glorious display of God's operation throughout the ages to produce His eternal purpose.

It is impossible to adequately describe the experience of this heavenly couple in that day, for today we enjoy it only as a small foretaste. In that day there will be no more veil, fallen flesh, self, world, natural being, spot, blemish, wrinkle, or obstacle of any kind between us and Christ. Our union with our dear Lord will be complete and full. This enjoyment will be unspeakable!

The Constitution of Christ's Armies

And I saw the heaven opened; and behold, a white horse, and he that sat thereon called Faithful and True; and in righteousness he doth judge and make war. ... And the armies which are in heaven followed him upon white horses, clothed in fine linen, white and pure. (Revelation 19:11, 14)

These shall war against the Lamb, and the Lamb shall overcome them, for he is Lord of lords, and King of kings; and they also shall overcome that are with him, called and chosen and faithful (Revelation 17:14)

And to these also Enoch, the seventh from Adam, prophesied, saying, Behold, the Lord came with ten thousands of his holy ones... (Jude 1:14-15)

Haste ye, and come, all ye nations round about, and gather yourselves together: thither cause thy mighty ones to come down, O Jehovah. (Joel 3:11)

For the Son of man shall come in the glory of his Father with his angels... (Matthew 16:27)

The constituents of the bride are also some of the constituents of the heavenly armies. Christ's bride is actually a warrior-bride.* The very ones who are the bride of Christ in love are heavenly armies to destroy His enemies. The warrior-bride will be composed of all the perfected believers—that is, those who are called, *chosen*, and faithful. It is not enough to be called by the Lord. Rather, to be a member of Christ's army requires that we be chosen by the Lord at His judgment seat. The Lord will select those who have been faithful in their daily lives to be the members of His warrior-bride. Many children of God will miss this portion of God's full salvation because they have been unfaithful to Him in the present age.

The overcoming saints are called the holy ones and the mighty ones. They are holy by virtue of God's own divine and holy nature saturating their being.[2] They are mighty by being empowered by the might of Christ's strength to overcome God's enemy day by day.[3]

The holy angels will also take part in this battle since it will be fought not only against Christ's human opposers, but also against the evil spirits—Satan, the fallen angels, and the demons. All the overcoming saints and the angels will be with Christ in the air, waiting—waiting for the Lord's appearing to the whole earth in glory with great power, waiting for His descent to battle. The stage will be set: Christ's armies will be prepared; all will await the order from the Commander-in-Chief, Christ Himself, to descend for battle and destroy God's enemies.

The Desperate Situation in Israel

And it shall come to pass, that in all the land, saith Jehovah, two parts therein shall be cut off and die; but the third shall be left therein. And I will bring the third part into the fire, and will refine them as silver is refined, and will try them as gold is tried. (Zechariah 13:8-9)

For I will gather all nations against Jerusalem to battle; and the city shall be taken, and the houses rifled, and the women

---

* This corresponds with Ephesians 5-6 where the church is first seen as a bride and then as a warrior to defeat God's enemy.

ravished; and half of the city shall go forth into captivity, and the residue of the people shall not be cut off from the city. (Zechariah 14:2)

And thou shalt ascend, thou shalt come like a storm, thou shalt be like a cloud to cover the land, thou, and all thy hordes, and many peoples with thee. ... And thou shalt come from thy place out of the uttermost parts of the north, thou, and many peoples with thee, all of them riding upon horses, a great company and a mighty army; and thou shalt come up against my people Israel, as a cloud to cover the land: it shall come to pass in the latter days, that I will bring thee against my land, that the nations may know me, when I shall be sanctified in thee, O Gog, before their eyes. (Ezekiel 38:9, 15-16)

But immediately after the tribulation of those days the sun shall be darkened, and the moon shall not give her light, and the stars shall fall from heaven, and the powers of the heavens shall be shaken... (Matthew 24:29)

And it shall come to pass in that day, that there shall not be light; the bright ones shall withdraw themselves: but it shall be one day which is known unto Jehovah; not day, and not night; but it shall come to pass, that at evening time there shall be light. (Zechariah 14:6-7)

For, behold, darkness shall cover the earth, and gross darkness the peoples... (Isaiah 60:2)

As the judgment upon the believers, the marriage of the Lamb, and the assembling of Christ's armies is taking place in the air, on the earth the situation in Israel will become dire. It will appear as if Israel has ceased to exist. Two-thirds of the Jews will have died; a good portion of the remaining Jews will have been carried away and scattered throughout the earth. Half of Jerusalem will be brought into captivity. The armies of the Antichrist, Gog and Magog, and the kings of the east will be pouring into Israel, flooding it with worldly forces numbering perhaps in the hundreds of millions.

For all intents and purposes Israel will not be. It will seem as if there is absolutely no hope left, that there is no possibility for Israel to pass through this crisis. Yet, all this is arranged by the

Lord to bring the Jews to an end, that they would turn to Him in repentance. This all will be ordered by the Lord to end the hardness, rebelliousness, and self-dependency of those Jews who remain on the earth.

At that time the great tribulation upon the Jews will come to an end. The Antichrist will be occupied with the upcoming battle against Gog and Magog and the horsemen from the east. The persecution of the Jews will be put aside as the preparation for war takes place. There will be a short lull in the violence taking place in Israel, but it will be the lull before the storm. Then there will be great signs in the heavens, and great darkness will envelop the earth. Both the moon and the sun will not give their light, and gross darkness will cover all the peoples.

Israel's Salvation

... and then shall appear the sign of the Son of man in heaven: and then shall all the tribes of the earth mourn, and they shall see the Son of man coming on the clouds of heaven with power and great glory. (Matthew 24:30)

Behold, he cometh with the clouds; and every eye shall see him, and they that pierced him; and all the tribes of the earth shall mourn over him. Even so, Amen. (Revelation 1:7)

And I will bring the third part into the fire, and will refine them as silver is refined, and will try them as gold is tried. They shall call on my name, and I will hear them: I will say, It is my people; and they shall say, Jehovah is my God. (Zechariah 13:9)

Oh that thou wouldest rend the heavens, that thou wouldest come down, that the mountains might quake at thy presence, as when fire kindleth the brushwood, and the fire causeth the waters to boil; to make thy name known to thine adversaries, that the nations may tremble at thy presence! When thou didst terrible things which we looked not for, thou camest down, the mountains quaked at thy presence. For from of old men have not heard, nor perceived by the ear, neither hath the eye seen a God besides thee, who worketh for him that waiteth for him. Thou meetest him that rejoiceth and worketh righteousness, those that remember thee in thy ways: behold, thou wast wroth, and we sinned: in them have we been of long time; and shall we be saved? For we are all become as one that is unclean, and all our righteousnesses are as a polluted garment: and we all do fade as a leaf; and our iniquities, like the wind, take us away. And there is none that calleth upon thy name, that stirreth up himself to take hold of thee; for thou hast hid thy face from us, and hast consumed us by means of our iniquities. (Isaiah 64:1-7)

The armies in the heavens will be ready; Israel will be in great desperation; the heavens will show forth great signs. At this juncture the Lord Jesus will intervene to bring all Israel to salvation. He will give them some particular sign in the heavens. What this will be we cannot say for sure—perhaps it will be some sort of cross. Whatever it is, it will certainly be supernatural. This sign will cause the remaining Jews on the earth to recognize that Jesus is the Messiah, the Christ. It will cause the Jews to repent from their unbelief. The Jews will mourn and wail in repentance for their rejection of Jesus, their King, their Messiah, their Savior, and their God. Every Jew remaining alive will turn to the Lord, calling on His name.[4] Thus, all of Israel will be saved.[5] At that time Isaiah 64 will be fulfilled: the Jews will long for the Lord to rend the heavens and come down to save them from their desperate plight.

The Lord's Appearing

And it shall come to pass in that day, that Jehovah will punish the host of the high ones on high, and the kings of the earth upon the earth. And they shall be gathered together, as prisoners are gathered in the pit, and shall be shut up in the prison; and after many days shall they be visited. Then the moon shall be confounded, and the sun ashamed; for Jehovah of hosts will reign in mount Zion, and in Jerusalem; and before his elders shall be glory. (Isaiah 24:21-23)

And I saw the heaven opened; and behold, a white horse, and he that sat thereon called Faithful and True; and in righteous he doth judge and make war. And his eyes are a flame of fire, and upon his head are many diadems; and he hath a name written which no one knoweth but he himself. And he is arrayed in a garment sprinkled with blood: and his name is called The Word of God. And the armies which are in heaven followed him upon white horses, clothed in fine linen, white and pure. And out of his mouth proceedeth a sharp sword, that with it he should smite the nations: and he shall rule them with a rod of iron: and he treadeth the winepress of the fierceness of the wrath of God, the Almighty. And he hath on his garment and on his thigh a name written, KINGS OF KINGS, AND LORD OF LORDS. (Revelation 19:11-16)

For as the lightning cometh forth from the east, and is seen even unto the west; so shall be the coming of the Son of man. ... and they shall see the Son of man coming on the clouds of heaven with power and great glory. (Matthew 24:27, 30)

Thou sawest till that a stone was cut out without hands, which smote the image upon its feet that were of iron and clay, and brake them in pieces. Then was the iron, the clay, the brass, the silver, and the gold, broken in pieces together, and became like the chaff of the summer threshing-floors; and the wind carried them away, so that no place was found for them: and the stone that smote the image became a great mountain, and filled the whole earth. ... And in the days of those kings shall the God of heaven set up a kingdom which shall never be destroyed, nor shall the sovereignty thereof be left to another people; but it shall break in pieces and consume all these kingdoms, and it shall stand for ever. (Daniel 2:34-35, 44)

Wheresoever the carcase is, there will the eagles be gathered together. (Matthew 24:28)

This time will be the darkest moment in earth's history. Israel will be all but destroyed. The Antichrist, Gog and Magog, and the two hundred million[*] from the far east will be preparing for battle with each other to determine who will rule the earth. The whole world will be covered with great darkness. The sun and the moon will give no light. Evil will reign throughout the earth. Then, at that very instant, the Lord Jesus will suddenly appear.

---

[*] That is, however many are left of the two hundred million after rampaging across Asia.

His appearing will be a great salvation to Israel and a stunning shock to the Antichrist and the armies gathered in Israel for battle. It will also be a great wonder to all the peoples upon the face of the earth.

The Lord's appearing will come as lightning.* He will shine from the east to the west. The glory of His appearing will illuminate the whole earth, penetrating even to Hades itself.† The Lord in His glorious coming will be accompanied by the brightly shining overcoming saints. He will descend in glory from the clouds with the saints and the angels, to do battle with all His opposers.

Christ will come as the smiting stone, to grind the Antichrist to dust and all the earthly armies to powder. He will tread the winepress of God's fury. He and the overcoming saints will be like vultures circling over the Antichrist and his armies. They will encompass these "rotting corpses," swooping down upon them to destroy them.‡

The Great Battle

And except those days had been shortened, no flesh would have been saved: but for the elect's sake those days shall be shortened. (Matthew 24:22)

... for they are spirits of demons, working signs; which go forth unto the kings of the whole world, to gather them together unto

---

* The Lord's coming for the believers is hidden and secret, like a thief in the night coming to steal precious jewels. However, His coming to the unbelievers is open, like lightning illuminating the whole sky.

† Those who pierced Him—that is, His crucifiers—will see the Lord's appearing in glory and be aware of His coming.

‡ The Lord's coming in this way, to destroy all the armies of the world, was foreshadowed by Gideon in his battle with the Midianites (Judg. 7:1-25, Is. 9:4-5). There, Gideon with 300 Israelites fell into the camp of the Midianites in the dark of night. This threw the Midianite armies into a great confusion, in which they fought against one another and eventually destroyed themselves. This will also happen when the Lord returns. His coming will throw all the armies of the earth into a great confusion, during which they will destroy one another. Some of them may even dream of the coming destruction at Christ's hands, just as those in Gideon's day did, and spend the time immediately before Christ's appearing trembling in foreboding and dread.

the war of the great day of God, the Almighty. ... And they gathered them together into the place which is called in Hebrew Har-magedon. (Revelation 16:14, 16)

Then shall Jehovah go forth, and fight against those nations, as when he fought in the day of battle. (Zechariah 14:3)

And it shall come to pass in that day, that I will make Jerusalem a burdensome stone for all the peoples; all that burden themselves with it shall be sore wounded; and all the nations of the earth shall be gathered together against it. ... And it shall come to pass in that day, that I will seek to destroy all the nations that come against Jerusalem. (Zechariah 12:3, 9)

For Jehovah hath indignation against all the nations, and wrath against all their host: he hath utterly destroyed them, he hath delivered them to the slaughter. Their slain also shall be cast out, and the stench of their dead bodies shall come up; and the mountains shall be melted with their blood. ... For my sword hath drunk its fill in heaven: behold, it shall come down upon Edom, and upon the people of my curse, to judgment. The sword of Jehovah is filled with blood, it is made fat with fatness, with the blood of lambs and goats, with the fat of the kidneys of rams; for Jehovah hath a sacrifice in Bozrah, and a great slaughter in the land of Edom. (Isaiah 34:2-3, 5-6)

Who is this that cometh from Edom, with dyed garments from Bozrah? this that is glorious in his apparel, marching in the greatness of his strength? I that speak in righteousness, mighty to save. (Isaiah 63:1)

And the chieftains of Judah shall say in their heart, The inhabitants of Jerusalem are my strength in Jehovah of hosts their God. In that day will I make the chieftains of Judah like a pan of fire among wood, and like a flaming torch among sheaves; and they shall devour all the peoples round about, on the right hand and on the left; and they of Jerusalem shall yet again dwell in their own place, even in Jerusalem. Jehovah also shall save the tents of Judah first, that the glory of the house of David and the glory of the inhabitants of Jerusalem be not magnified above Judah. In that day shall Jehovah defend the inhabitants of Jerusalem: and he that is feeble among them at that day shall be as David; and the house of David shall be as God, as the angel of Jehovah before them. (Zechariah 12:5-8)

... he shall also stand up against the prince of princes; but he shall be broken without hand. (Daniel 8:25)

And I saw the beast, and the kings of the earth, and their armies, gathered together to make war against him that sat upon the horse, and against his army. (Revelation 19:19)

In that day, saith Jehovah, I will smite every horse with terror, and his rider with madness; and I will open mine eyes upon the house of Judah, and will smite every horse of the peoples with blindness. (Zechariah 12:4)

And it shall come to pass in that day, that a great tumult from Jehovah shall be among them; and they shall lay hold every one on the hand of his neighbor, and his hand shall rise up against the hand of his neighbor. (Zechariah 14:13)

And I will call for a sword against him unto all my mountains, saith the Lord Jehovah: every man's sword shall be against his brother. (Ezekiel 38:21)

And this shall be the plague wherewith Jehovah will smite all the peoples that have warred against Jerusalem: their flesh shall consume away while they stand upon their feet, and their eyes shall consume away in their sockets, and their tongue shall consume away in their mouth. ... And so shall be the plague of the horse, of the mule, of the camel, and of the ass, and of all the beasts that shall be in those camps, as that plague. (Zechariah 14:12, 15)

And then shall be revealed the lawless one, whom the Lord Jesus shall slay with the breath of his mouth, and bring to nought by the manifestation of his coming... (2 Thessalonians 2:8)

At this time the Lord will intervene in order to save Jerusalem and Israel. Were He to allow the tribulation of those days to continue, no flesh would survive; mankind would be utterly destroyed. But, in order to save His elect—the chosen Jews of Israel—the Lord will cut short those days by His physical appearing. He will begin the destruction of His opposers from

Bozrah, which is in Jordan south of the Dead Sea. He will continue to battle northward, annihilating His opposers as He goes. He will save Judah first, that those dwelling in Jerusalem might not be proud. He will then empower the remaining Jews to fight against all the armies invading them. He will energize them by His appearing and by His Spirit, which will rest upon them for battle. The Jews will fight like David and like God, destroying hundreds of thousands of those surrounding them.

The Antichrist and all the earthly armies will fight back against Christ and the saints with him. They will attack with all the weapons at their disposal, including whatever bombs, artillery, missiles, and perhaps even nuclear weapons they may have. However, everything they do will be of no avail against the spiritual armies attacking them. Christ and the saints will destroy all those who have overrun Israel in opposition to God. Christ will smite all the armies of the earth with madness, and their horses with terror and blindness. The earthly armies will fight against each other, destroying one another in a panic of chaotic madness. The Lord will also smite the earthly armies with a horrific plague. Their flesh and their eyes will melt away. The brightness of the Lord's appearing will consume them. The slaughter will be unbelievable and unimaginable.

The Seventh Bowl

And the seventh poured out his bowl upon the air; and there came forth a great voice out of the temple, from the throne, saying, It is done: and there were lightnings, and voices, and thunders; and there was a great earthquake, such as was not since there were men upon the earth, so great an earthquake, so mighty. And the great city was divided into three parts, and the cities of the nations fell: and Babylon the great was remembered in the sight of God, to give unto her the cup of the wine of the fierceness of his wrath. And every island fled away, and the mountains were not found. And great hail, every stone about the weight of a talent, cometh down out of heaven upon men: and men blasphemed God because of the plague of the hail; for the plague thereof is exceeding great. (Revelation 16:17-21)

And the seventh angel sounded; and there followed great voices in heaven, and they said, The kingdom of the world is become the kingdom of our Lord, and of his Christ: and he shall reign for ever and ever. ... And there was opened the temple of God that is in heaven; and there was seen in his temple the ark of his covenant; and there followed lightnings, and voices, and thunders, and an earthquake, and great hail. (Revelation 11:15, 19)

And it shall come to pass in that day, when Gog shall come against the land of Israel, saith the Lord Jehovah, that my wrath shall come up into my nostrils. For in my jealousy and in the fire of my wrath have I spoken, Surely in that day there shall be a great shaking in the land of Israel; so that the fishes of the sea, and the birds of the heavens, and the beasts of the field, and all creeping things that creep upon the earth, and all the men that are upon the face of the earth, shall shake at my presence, and the mountains shall be thrown down, and the steep places shall fall, and every wall shall fall to the ground. ... And with pestilence and with blood will I enter into judgment with him; and I will rain upon him, and upon his hordes, and upon the many peoples that are with him, an overflowing shower, and great hailstones, fire, and brimstone. And I will magnify myself, and sanctify myself, and I will make myself known in the eyes of many nations; and they shall know that I am Jehovah. (Ezekiel 38:18-20, 22-23)

And his feet shall stand in that day upon the mount of Olives, which is before Jerusalem on the east; and the mount of Olives shall be cleft in the midst thereof toward the east and toward the west, and there shall be a very great valley; and half of the mountain shall remove toward the north, and half of it toward the south. And ye shall flee by the valley of my mountains; for the valley of the mountains shall reach unto Azel; yea, ye shall flee, like as ye fled from before the earthquake in the days of Uzziah king of Judah; and Jehovah my God shall come, and all the holy ones with thee. And it shall come to pass in that day, that there shall not be light; the bright ones shall withdraw themselves... And it shall come to pass in that day, that living waters shall go out from Jerusalem; half of them toward the eastern sea, and half of them toward the western sea... All the land shall be made like the Arabah, from Geba to Rimmon south of Jerusalem; and she shall be lifted up... (Zechariah 14:4-6, 8, 10)

And when he had said these things, as they were looking, he was taken up; and a cloud received him out of their sight. And while they were looking stedfastly into heaven as he went, behold, two men stood by them in white apparel; who also said, Ye men of Galilee, why stand ye looking into heaven? this Jesus, who was received up from you into heaven shall so come in like manner as ye beheld him going into heaven. (Acts 1:9-11)

And a strong angel took up a stone as it were a great millstone and cast it into the sea, saying, Thus with a mighty fall shall Babylon, the great city, be cast down, and shall be found no more at all. (Revelation 18:21)

Thou shalt fall upon the mountains of Israel, thou, and all thy hordes, and the peoples that are with thee: I will give thee unto the ravenous birds of every sort, and to the beasts of the field to be devoured. Thou shalt fall upon the open field; for I have spoken it, saith the Lord Jehovah. (Ezekiel 39:4-5)

At about this time the seventh bowl will be poured out. As the battle of Armageddon is raging, probably as it reaches its climax, the seventh and final plague will smite mankind. With this the fury of God will be finished. God's wrath will be consummated with this last and greatest of plagues. When this strikes, an enormous earthquake, one beyond measure, will rock the earth. This will be the crowning blow to smite the earth, Christ's coup de grâce. This earthquake will be greater than any that have struck the earth since man was created. It will be far greater than the one of the sixth seal. It will be greater than the other tremendous quakes during the tribulation. During the sixth seal the earthquake merely moved the mountains and islands out of their place. During the earthquake of the seventh bowl all the mountains upon the earth will be leveled; all the islands will be found no more; all the cities of the nations will crumble. Babylon the Great, the city of Rome, will come into remembrance before God. She will be destroyed utterly and cast into the sea forever. Rome will fall into the Mediterranean, never to be found again. Jerusalem, the "great city," will be split into three parts. Probably as this quake is rending the earth, the Lord Himself will descend to the earth to the Mount of Olives. That mount will split in two, half toward the north and half toward the south. The Jews in Jerusalem will flee into the cleft of this great rock and thus be saved from the plague of consumption that will strike the earthly armies.* The earth will reel from the violence of this quake. The Mediterranean area, in particular, will suffer great upheaval. Israel itself will go through an enormous topological change. As the mountains surrounding her are leveled, Zion itself will be uplifted.†

This intense shaking will be accompanied by immense hailstones, weighing a hundred pounds apiece. These will fall upon the earthly armies that have invaded Israel, crushing all of God's opposers. Gog and Magog will be massacred. The Antichrist and the armies of the east will be decimated. The Lord will make a quick end of those who oppose Him.

The Slaughter of Christ's Opposers

Another angel came out from the temple which is in heaven, he also having a sharp sickle. And another angel came out from the altar, he that hath power over fire; and he called with a great voice to him that had the sharp sickle, saying, Send forth thy sharp sickle, and gather the clusters of the vine of the earth; for her grapes are fully ripe. And the angel cast his sickle into the earth, and gathered the vintage of the earth, and cast it into the winepress, the great winepress, of the wrath of God. And the winepress are trodden without the city, and there came out blood from the winepress, even unto the bridles of the horses, as far as a thousand and six hundred furlongs. (Revelation 14:17-20)

---

* The salvation of the Jews in Jerusalem by fleeing into the cleft of the rent Mount of Olives will serve as an eternal reminder to them that they were saved by being put into the cleft of the real Rock, Christ, that they were saved by being put into Christ in His death.

† Through this enormous topological alteration, waters will burst forth from the hills in Israel. Water will flow out from the temple in Jerusalem toward the east and the west to give life to the once-parched land of Israel (Ez. 47:1, 9).

And I saw an angel standing in the sun; and he cried with a loud voice, saying to all the birds that fly in mid heaven, Come and be gathered together unto the great supper of God; that ye may eat the flesh of kings, and the flesh of captains, and the flesh of mighty men, and the flesh of horses and of them that sit thereon, and the flesh of all men, both free and bond, and small and great. ... and the rest were killed with the sword of him that sat upon the horse, even the sword which came forth out of his mouth: and all the birds were filled with their flesh. (Revelation 19:17-18, 21)

The sword of Jehovah is filled with blood, it is made fat with fatness, with the blood of lambs and goats, with the fat of the kidneys of rams; for Jehovah hath a sacrifice in Bozrah, and a great slaughter in the land of Edom. And the wild-oxen shall come down with them, and the bullocks with the bulls: and their land shall be drunken with blood, and their dust made fat with fatness. (Isaiah 34:6-7)

Who is this that cometh from Edom, with dyed garments from Bozrah? this that is glorious in his apparel, marching in the greatness of his strength? I that speak in righteousness, mighty to save. Wherefore art thou red in thine apparel, and thy garments like him that treadeth in the winevat? I have trodden the winepress alone; and of the peoples there was no man with me: yea, I trod them in mine anger, and trampled them in my wrath; and their lifeblood is sprinkled upon my garments, and I have stained all my raiment. For the day of vengeance was in my heart, and the year of my redeemed is come. And I looked, and there was none to help; and I wondered that there was none to uphold: therefore mine own arm brought salvation unto me; and my wrath, it upheld me. And I trod down the peoples in mine anger, and made them drunk in my wrath, and I poured out their lifeblood on the earth. (Isaiah 63:1-6)

Thou shalt fall upon the mountains of Israel, thou, and all thy hordes, and the peoples that are with thee: I will give thee unto the ravenous birds of every sort, and to the beasts of the field to be devoured. ... And they that dwell in the cities of Israel shall go forth, and shall make fires of the weapons and burn them, both the shields and the bucklers, the bows and the arrows, and the handstaves, and the spears, and they shall make fires of them seven years; so that they shall take no wood out of the field, neither cut down any out of the forests; for they shall make fires of the weapons; and they shall plunder those that plundered them, and rob those that robbed them, saith the Lord Jehovah. And it shall come to pass in that day, that I will give unto Gog a place for burial in Israel, the valley of them that pass through on the east of the sea; and it shall stop them that pass through: and there shall they bury Gog and all his multitude; and they shall call it The valley of Hamon-gog. And seven months shall the house of Israel be burying them, that they may cleanse the land. Yea, all the people of the land shall bury them; and it shall be to them a renown in the day that I shall be glorified, saith the Lord Jehovah. And they shall set apart men of continual employment, that shall pass through the land, and, with them that pass through, those that bury them that remain upon the face of the land, to cleanse it: after the end of seven months shall they search. And they that pass through the land shall pass through; and when any seeth a man's bone, then shall he set up a sign by it, till the buriers have buried it in the valley of Hamon-gog. And Hamonah shall also be the name of a city. Thus shall they cleanse the land. And thou, son of man, thus saith the Lord Jehovah: Speak unto the birds of every sort, and to every beast of the field, Assemble yourselves, and come; gather yourselves on every side to my sacrifice that I do sacrifice for you, even a great sacrifice upon the mountains of Israel, that ye may eat flesh and drink blood. Ye shall eat the flesh of the mighty, and drink the blood of the princes of the earth, of rams, of lambs, and of goats, of bullocks, all of them fatlings of Bashan. And ye shall eat fat till ye be full, and drink blood till ye be drunken, of my sacrifice which I have sacrificed for you. And ye shall be filled at my table with horses and chariots, with mighty men, and with all men of war, saith the Lord Jehovah. (Ezekiel 39:4, 9-20)

Thou hast multiplied the nation, thou hast increased their joy: they joy before thee according to the joy in harvest, as men rejoice when they divide the spoil. For the yoke of his burden, and the staff of his shoulder, the rod of his oppressor, thou hast broken as in the day of Midian. For all the armor of the armed man in the tumult, and the garments rolled in blood, shall be for burning, for fuel of fire. (Isaiah 9:3-5)

Christ, in His appearing to destroy the nations, will first come to Bozrah. He will work His way north to Armageddon and Jerusalem. As He proceeds, He will destroy all those who oppose Him. The blood from all the massacred earthly armies will reach up to the bridles of the horses for a distance of 1,600 stadia, or about 184 miles. This is the distance from Bozrah to Armageddon. The Lord's garments will be splattered with the blood. This is the "wine" from the winepress of God's fury, which winepress the Lord will tread. At Jerusalem the Lord will make a final end of all the opposers; none will be left. This will mark the finish of the battle at Armageddon.

A great feast for the birds and the beasts will be spread by God throughout Israel. Birds from all directions will gather to sup on the flesh of the slaughtered armies. The birds and the beasts will pick clean many of the bodies of the armies that lay dead in the fields and mountains. The bodies from this battle will be gathered up by dedicated workers who will be sent out to cleanse the land of Israel from all that remains of the battle of Armageddon. It will take seven months to finally rid Israel of all the bodies of the slaughtered earthly armies.

The enormity of this battle can be seen by the arms left behind by the forces that will invade Israel. The weapons of these earthly armies will be used to make fires in Israel to warm the Jews when it is cold. It will take seven years to burn all the weapons remaining after the slaughter at Armageddon.

The Fate of the Antichrist

And then shall be revealed the lawless one, whom the Lord Jesus shall slay with the breath of his mouth, and bring to nought by the manifestation of his coming... (2 Thessalonians 2:8)

And the beast was taken, and with him the false prophet that wrought the signs in his sight, wherewith he deceived them that had received the mark of the beast and them that worshipped his image: they two were cast alive into the lake of fire that burneth with brimstone... (Revelation 19:20)

I beheld till thrones were placed, and one that was ancient of days did sit: his raiment was white as snow, and the hair of his head like pure wool; his throne was fiery flames, and the wheels thereof burning fire. A fiery stream issued and came forth from before him: thousands of thousands ministered unto him, and ten thousand times ten thousand stood before him: the judgment was set, and the books were opened. I beheld at that time because of the voice of the great words which the horn spake; I beheld even till the beast was slain, and its body destroyed, and it was given to be burned with fire. (Daniel 7:9-11)

And he shall plant the tents of his palace between the sea and the glorious holy mountain; yet he shall come to his end, and none shall help him. (Daniel 11:45)

Of all the armies invading Israel, only two men will remain alive at the end of this great battle—the Antichrist and the false prophet. All the remaining millions will be slain by the sword proceeding out from the mouth of the Lord Jesus, by the Lord's word of power. However, the Antichrist with the false prophet will be taken and thrown alive into the lake of fire. These two should be the first ones to taste perdition. Their bodies will be destroyed and given up to the flames. They will be destroyed by the brightness of the Lord's appearing and slain by the word out of the Lord's mouth. All these are different aspects of the destruction of the Antichrist and false prophet. From the Lord's mouth will come forth the word commanding them into the lake of fire. That word will sweep them in fire, according to the brightness of the Lord's appearing, into the lake of fire, where they will be consumed and destroyed unto eternity. Their torment will go up forever and ever. There will be no end to their suffering. Their destruction is not an annihilation, but a perpetual, continual destroying of their spirit, soul, and body by the fire of the lake of fire, as it consumes all three parts of their beings forever.

The Consequences of the Lord's Appearing

But the saints of the Most High shall receive the kingdom, and possess the kingdom for ever, even for ever and ever. ... But the judgment shall be set, and they shall take away his dominion, to consume and to destroy it unto the end. And the kingdom and the dominion, and the greatness of the kingdoms under the whole heaven, shall be given to the people of the saints of the Most High: his kingdom is an everlasting kingdom, and all dominions shall serve and obey him. (Daniel 7:18, 26-27)

Blessed are the meek: for they shall inherit the earth. (Matthew 5:5)

The result of the Lord's physical appearing will be fourfold. First, in a very short time, perhaps no more than an hour or two, all the armies of the earth—those from Russia, from Europe, and from the East—will be destroyed. The Antichrist and the false prophet will be thrown into the lake of fire. This will put an end to warfare for the thousand years of the kingdom.

Second, by the Lord's appearing, Israel will be saved from destruction. In addition, all the Jews within Israel will repent, turning their heart to the Lord for salvation. Every Jew living upon the earth will become one of the Lord's believers, and the nation of Israel will become a nation of believers.

Third, all the nations on the face of the earth will be broken to pieces.[6] There will be no more earthly governments to resist Christ's reign in righteousness and His rule through the saints. The rebellion of man against the divine authority and administration will be fully subdued. All the nations will be smitten by the Lord's coming.

Finally, the time will come for the saints to possess the kingdom. The meek will at last inherit the earth. All the kingdoms of the earth will become the kingdom of God and of His Christ.[7] Christ will share His kingdom with His overcoming saints, who will reign with Him over the nations during the Millennium.[8]

In a very short time, the Lord Jesus will clean up the whole situation of rebellion on the earth, dealing with His earthly opposers, saving Israel, and establishing His divine administration through His believers. Praise Him!

References

[1] Matt. 22:12
[2] 2 Pet. 1:3-4
[3] Eph. 3:16; 6:10
[4] Rom. 10:13-14
[5] Rom. 11:26
[6] Rev 2:27
[7] Rev. 11:15
[8] Rev. 20:4

CHAPTER 10

Ushering in the Millennium

The kingdom will be a time of joy and exultation to all those who partake of it—to the overcoming saints, to the remnant of Israel, and to the remaining nations. All will be blessed with Christ's presence in splendor during that one thousand years. God will be satisfied and man will be satisfied. There will be no lack; every need will be met. The earth will flourish under the righteous, life-giving reign of Christ and the saints.

The Initiation of the Kingdom

I saw in the night-visions, and, behold, there came with the clouds of heaven one like unto a son of man, and he came even to the ancient of days, and they brought him near before him. And there was given him dominion, and glory, and a kingdom, that all the peoples, nations, and languages should serve him: his dominion is an everlasting dominion, which shall not pass away, and his kingdom that which shall not be destroyed. ... I beheld, and the same horn made war with the saints, and prevailed against them; until the ancient of days came, and judgment was given to the saints of the Most High, and the time came that the saints possessed the kingdom. ... And the kingdom and the dominion, and the greatness of the kingdoms under the whole heaven, shall be given to the people of the saints of the Most High: his kingdom is an everlasting kingdom, and all dominions shall serve and obey him. (Daniel 7:13-14, 21-22, 27)

And I saw thrones, and they sat upon them, and judgment was given unto them: and I saw the souls of them that had been beheaded for the testimony of Jesus, and for the word of God, and such as worshipped not the beast, neither his image, and received not the mark upon their forehead and upon their hand; and they lived, and reigned with Christ a thousand years. ... Blessed and holy is he that hath part in the first resurrection: over these the second death hath no power; but they shall be priests of God and of Christ, and shall reign with him a thousand years. (Revelation 20:4, 6)

Or know ye not that the saints shall judge the world? ... Know ye not that we shall judge angels? how much more, things that pertain to this life? (1 Corinthians 6:2-3)

Then shall the righteous shine forth as the sun in the kingdom of their Father. ... (Matthew 13:43)

And Jesus said unto them, Verily I say unto you, that ye who have followed me, in the regeneration when the Son of man shall sit on the throne of his glory, ye also shall sit upon twelve thrones, judging the twelve tribes of Israel. (Matthew 19:28)

... so there may come seasons of refreshing from the presence of the Lord; and that he may send the Christ who hath been appointed for you, even Jesus: whom the heaven must receive until the times of restoration of all things, whereof God spake by the mouth of His holy prophets that have been from of old. (Acts 3:19-21)

He shall build a house for my name, and I will establish the throne of his kingdom for ever. (2 Samuel 7:13)

At His ascension, Christ as the Son of Man came to the Ancient of Days to receive the kingdom. He, in turn, will share this kingdom with the overcoming saints in the coming age. Together they will reign over the nations during the Millennium.

The kingdom Christ receives will be of two parts, one heavenly, the other earthly. The heavenly section will be for the overcoming saints. It is called the kingdom of the Father, and is the manifestation of the kingdom of the heavens.[1] It will consist of a thousand-year wedding feast in which Christ will enjoy His glorious bride and the overcoming saints will partake of the peak and most extraordinary enjoyment of Christ. Together, as God's many sons, they will satisfy the Father's eternal heart's desire. Christ and the saints will reign over the whole earth, judging the nations, the tribes of Israel, and even the angels. In their reign, mankind and the earth will be restored back to their original condition, as they were before the fall. This time is therefore called the "restoration of all things."

The kingdom of the heavens will be enjoyed by the overcoming saints from both the Old and New Testaments. It will include Abraham, Isaac, Jacob, and many other saints from Old Testament times.[2] It will also include all the New Testament overcoming believers, such as those revealed in Revelation 2-3. All the righteous saints will shine forth like the sun. The glory of God will permeate their entire being and break forth in splendor to the whole creation. Even now the whole creation earnestly expects this manifestation of the sons of God.[3]

The second section of the millennial kingdom is the earthly part. This section is for the restored nation of Israel, consisting of the believing Jewish remnant. During the Millennium, the Jews will be priests to the nations to bring unregenerated mankind back to a proper relationship between the Creator and the creature.[4] The children of Israel will teach the nations how to worship God properly.

The millennial kingdom will have as its purpose the restoration of all things. It will be a time to restore Israel, the nations, and the earth. By that time, Israel will have been fully destroyed, the Jews will have been scattered, Jerusalem will have been devastated, and the temple defiled. The nations will be in chaos. They will have been broken to pieces by the events of the tribulation and the Lord's second coming. They will be in great suffering from what they have endured during the last 3½ years of this age. Many will be wounded, maimed, diseased, or afflicted by some other kind of malady. Mankind will need to be healed physically, psychologically, and spiritually. In addition, God's judgments during the tribulation, along with the enormous destruction caused by man,[5] will leave the earth barren and devastated. Thus, the creation will be in great need of healing to bring it into a fruitful, pleasant condition.

The Divine Administration

Thou sawest till that a stone was cut out without hands, which smote the image upon its feet that were of iron and clay, and brake them in pieces. Then was the iron, the clay, the brass, the silver, and the gold, broken in pieces together, and became like the chaff of the summer threshing-floors; and the wind carried them away, so that no place was found for them: and the stone that smote the image became a great mountain, and filled the whole earth. ... And in the days of those kings shall the God of heaven set up a kingdom which shall never be destroyed, nor shall the sovereignty thereof be left to another people; but it shall break in pieces and consume all these kingdoms, and it shall stand for ever. (Daniel 2:34-35, 44)

For unto us a child is born, unto us a son is given; and the government shall be upon his shoulder: and his name shall be called Wonderful, Counsellor, Mighty God, Everlasting Father, Prince of Peace. Of the increase of his government and of peace there shall be no end, upon the throne of David, and upon his kingdom, to establish it, and to uphold it with justice and with righteousness from henceforth even for ever. The zeal of Jehovah of hosts will perform this. (Isaiah 9:6-7)

And the first came before him, saying, Lord, thy pound hath made ten pounds more. And he said unto him, Well done, thou good servant: because thou wast found faithful in a very little, have thou authority over ten cities. And the second came, saying, Thy pound, Lord, hath made five pounds. And he said unto him also, Be thou also over five cities. (Luke 19:16-19)

When Christ comes, He will come as the smiting stone to crush the nations. Then He will become a great mountain to fill the earth. This mountain depicts Christ in His increase, filling the earth in His divine administration. There will be no end to the increase of His government. His administration will reach every part of the earth and extend throughout the universe. In His government peace will reign.

Christ as the smiting stone will become a mountain to fill the earth. This increase of Christ from a stone to a mountain refers to the saints. The bride of Christ is His increase.[6] It is Him spreading, growing, and increasing in humanity. The saints are simply more of Christ. They are partakers of His divine life and nature, conformed to His image, and members of His Body.[7] In every way they are the same as He (except that Christ alone is part of the Godhead with the Father and the Spirit).[8] It is through the saints that Christ will reign over the earth. They, with Christ, will rule the peoples that remain after the tribulation.[9] They will judge between the peoples and shepherd them with a rod of iron.[10] This will bring the peoples back to a righteous living before God and man.

Christ and the overcoming saints will heal the peoples as well. Even today, before the tribulation, all the nations are in great need of healing. They are spiritually sick, psychologically damaged, and physically diseased. There is an enormous need for the healing of the peoples. Through Christ and the saints, the peoples will be restored to health and brought into a proper standing before God.

Finally, Christ and the overcoming saints will rule over the peoples to prepare them for the coming final purification of mankind. This preparation will be to inoculate and guard them against the Satan-instigated last rebellion of mankind under Gog and Magog.[11] It will also prepare the peoples for the judgment of the great white throne and for their entrance into the new heaven and the new earth with the New Jerusalem.[12] A good number of the peoples during the Millennium will be properly prepared to enter that time. Not every one of the peoples will rebel with Gog and Magog, nor will they all be thrown into the lake of fire at the great white throne. Some will pass into eternity, to be the peoples in the new heaven and the new earth.[13]

The Binding of Satan

And I saw an angel coming down out of heaven, having the key of the abyss and a great chain in his hand. And he laid hold on the dragon, the old serpent, which is the Devil and Satan, and bound him for a thousand years, and cast him into the abyss, and shut it, and sealed it over him, that he should deceive the nations no more, until the thousand years should be finished: after this he must be loosed for a little time. (Revelation 20:1-3)

At the end of the battle of Armageddon, the Antichrist and the false prophet will be thrown into the lake of fire. However, one very important matter will still remain unresolved. Though the Antichrist and the false prophet will be dealt with, the source of all problems will remain: Satan, with all of his angels, will still be at large. Before anything else takes place, the universal source of evil and rebellion will be bound. An angel with a chain will bind Satan, cast him into the abyss, and seal him there for the one thousand years of the kingdom. The evil angels who have followed Satan in his rebellion will probably be bound in the abyss with him. This will fully clear up the spiritual realm for the kingdom age. There will no longer be any evil and deceiving spirits during the thousand years of Christ's reign in righteousness.

The Gathering of the Jews

And he shall send forth his angels with a great sound of a trumpet, and they shall gather together his elect from the four winds, from one end of heaven to the other. (Matthew 24:31)

And it shall come to pass in that day, that the Lord will set his hand again the second time to recover the remnant of his people, that shall remain, from Assyria, and from Egypt, and from Pathros, and from Cush, and from Elam, and from Shinar, and from Hamath, and from the islands of the sea. (Isaiah 11:11)

Fear not; for I am with thee: I will bring thy seed from the east, and gather thee from the west; I will say to the north, Give up; and to the south, Keep not back; bring my sons from far, and my daughters from the end of the earth; every one that is called by my name, and whom I have created for my glory, whom I have formed, yea, whom I have made. (Isaiah 43:5-7)

And a highway shall be there, and a way, and it shall be called The way of holiness; the unclean shall not pass over it; but it shall be for the redeemed: the wayfaring men, yea fools, shall not err therein. No lion shall be there, nor shall any ravenous beast go up thereon; they shall not be found there; but the redeemed shall walk there: and the ransomed of Jehovah shall return, and come with singing unto Zion; and everlasting joy shall be upon their heads: they shall obtain gladness and joy, and sorrow and sighing shall flee away. (Isaiah 35:8-10)

Lift up thine eyes round about, and see: they all gather themselves together, they come to thee; thy sons shall come from far, and thy daughters shall be carried in the arms. Then thou shalt see and be radiant, and thy heart shall thrill and be enlarged... (Isaiah 60:4-5)

And they shall bring all your brethren out of all the nations for an oblation unto Jehovah, upon horses, and in chariots, and in litters, and upon mules, and upon dromedaries, to my holy mountain Jerusalem, saith Jehovah, as the children of Israel bring their oblation in a clean vessel into the house of Jehovah. (Isaiah 66:20)

Immediately after the end of the tribulation, the Lord will gather the Jews from throughout the earth, from all the places to which they will be scattered. He will sound the trumpet and send forth His angels to gather His elect. The Old Testament feast of the blowing of trumpets foreshadowed this event.[14] This gathering will occur on the first day of the seventh month of the Jewish year, exactly as specified in Leviticus. It will also occur immediately after the battle of Armageddon.

The Lord will gather the Jews from every part of the earth. On their way to Israel they will find a highway set apart for them, where they cannot lose their way. They will come with singing and rejoicing as God brings them to Zion. The Jews who remain in Israel will exult when they see all those returning. The Lord will use all the peoples who remain to bring His elect back to Zion. They will carry the Jews in chariots and litters. They will bring them upon horses, mules, and camels. By every available means the people of the earth will bring the Jews back to Israel, to present them to the Lord as an offering.

The Deeper Repentance of Israel

... and I will bring you out from the peoples, and will gather you out of the countries wherein ye are scattered, with a mighty hand, and with an outstretched arm, and with wrath poured out; and I will bring you into the wilderness of the peoples, and there will I enter into judgment with you face to face. Like as I entered into judgment with your fathers in the wilderness of the land of Egypt, so will I enter into judgment with you, saith the Lord Jehovah. And I will cause you to pass under the rod, and I will bring you into the bond of the covenant; and I will purge out from among

you the rebels, and them that transgress against me; I will bring them forth out of the land where they sojourn, but they shall not enter into the land of Israel: and ye shall know that I am Jehovah. (Ezekiel 20:34-38)

... when the Lord shall have washed away the filth of the daughters of Zion, and shall have purged the blood of Jerusalem from the midst thereof, by the spirit of justice, and by the spirit of burning. (Isaiah 4:4)

And I will pour upon the house of David, and upon the inhabitants of Jerusalem, the spirit of grace and of supplication; and they shall look unto me whom they have pierced; and they shall mourn for him, as one mourneth for his only son, and shall be in bitterness for him, as one that is in bitterness for his first-born. In that day shall there be a great mourning in Jerusalem, as the mourning of Hadadrimmon in the valley of Megiddon. And the land shall mourn, every family apart; the family of the house of David apart, and their wives apart; the family of the house of Nathan apart, and their wives apart; the family of the house of Levi apart, and their wives apart; the family of the Shimeites apart, and their wives apart; all the families that remain, every family apart, and their wives apart. In that day there shall be a fountain opened to the house of David and to the inhabitants of Jerusalem, for sin and for uncleanness. And it shall come to pass in that day, saith Jehovah of hosts, that I will cut off the names of the idols out of the land, and they shall no more be remembered; and also I will cause the prophets and the unclean spirit to pass out of the land. (Zechariah 12:10-14; 13:1-2)

But this is the covenant that I will make with the house of Israel after those days, saith Jehovah: I will put my law in their inward parts, and in their heart will I write it; and I will be their God, and they shall be my people: and they shall teach no more every man his neighbor, and every man his brother, saying, Know Jehovah; for they shall all know me, from the least of them unto the greatest of them, saith Jehovah: for I will forgive their iniquity, and their sin will I remember no more. (Jeremiah 31:33-34)

Over the next ten days the Jews will return to Zion. From the first day of the seventh month to the tenth day, the scattered of Israel will be brought back by the nations. On the tenth day of the seventh month, all of the Jews will have returned to Israel to celebrate the day of atonement. This will be the fulfillment of the Old Testament feast of Propitiation.[15] It also will occur exactly as set forth in Leviticus.

At that time the Jews will be judged by Christ. He will deal with them face to face. He will touch the depths of the hearts of the saved Jewish remnant. He will expose their real inward condition in their prior rejection of Him, dealing with them by the judging and burning Spirit in righteousness.

The result of Christ's dealing with Israel will be much wailing throughout the whole land. They will mourn over Christ and over their rejection of Him. They will be in much bitterness and anguish for their actions and motives. All the families will mourn apart from one another. All the wives will also be set apart from the families. This weeping of the nation of Israel will last for five days.

By this judgment of the people of Israel, the Lord will bring them into the blessing of His millennial kingdom. There, they will serve Christ as priests on the earth and usher the nations into the knowledge and presence of Christ.

Judging the Nations

For, behold, in those days, and in that time, when I shall bring back the captivity of Judah and Jerusalem, I will gather all nations, and will bring them down into the valley of Jehoshaphat; and I will execute judgment upon them there for my people and for my heritage Israel, whom they have scattered among the nations... Let the nations bestir themselves, and come up to the valley of Jehoshaphat; for there will I sit to judge all the nations round about. (Joel 3:1-2, 12)

Again, the kingdom of heaven is like unto a net, that was cast into the sea, and gathered of every kind: which, when it was filled, they drew up on the beach; and they sat down, and gathered the good into vessels, but the bad they cast away. So shall it be in the end of the world: the angels shall come forth, and sever the wicked from among the righteous, and shall cast them into the furnace of fire: there shall be the weeping and the gnashing of teeth. (Matthew 13:47-50)

But when the Son of man shall come in his glory, and all the angels with him, then shall he sit on the throne of his glory: and before him shall be gathered all the nations: and he shall separate them one from another, as the shepherd separateth the sheep from the goats; and he shall set the sheep on his right hand, but the goats on the left. Then shall the King say unto them on his right hand, Come, ye blessed of my Father, inherit the kingdom prepared for you from the foundation of the world: for I was hungry, and ye gave me to eat; I was thirsty, and ye gave me drink; I was a stranger, and ye took me in; naked, and ye clothed me; I was sick, and ye visited me; I was in prison, and ye came unto me. Then shall the righteous answer him, saying, Lord, when saw we thee hungry, and fed thee? or athirst, and gave thee drink? And when saw we thee a stranger, and took thee in? or naked, and clothed thee? And when saw we thee sick, or in prison, and came unto thee? And the King shall answer and say unto them, Verily I say unto you, Inasmuch as ye did it unto one of these my brethren, even these least, ye did it unto me. Then shall he say also unto them on the left hand, Depart from me, ye cursed, into the eternal fire which is prepared for the devil and his angels: for I was hungry, and ye did not give me to eat; I was thirsty, and ye gave me no drink; I was a stranger, and ye took me not in; naked, and ye clothed me not; sick, and in prison, and ye visited me not. Then shall they also answer, saying, Lord, when saw we thee hungry, or athirst, or a stranger, or naked, or sick, or in prison, and did not minister unto thee? Then shall he answer them, saying, Verily I say unto you, Inasmuch as ye did it not unto one of these least, ye did it not unto me. And these shall go away into eternal punishment: but the righteous into eternal life. (Matthew 25:31-46)

And he charged us to preach unto the people, and to testify that this is he who is ordained of God to be the Judge of the living and the dead. (Acts 10:42)

...Christ Jesus, who shall judge the living and the dead... (2 Timothy 4:1)

Let both grow together until the harvest: and in the time of the harvest I will say to the reapers, Gather up first the tares, and bind them in bundles to burn them; but gather the wheat into my barn... And he answered and said, He that soweth the good seed is the Son of man; and the field is the world; and the good seed, these are the sons of the kingdom; and the tares are the sons of the evil one; and the enemy that sowed them is the devil: and the harvest is the end of the world; and the reapers are angels. As therefore the tares are gathered up and burned with fire; so shall it be in the end of the world. The Son of man shall send forth his angels, and they shall gather out of his kingdom all things that cause stumbling, and them that do iniquity, and shall cast them into the furnace of fire: there shall be the weeping and the gnashing of teeth. (Matthew 13:30, 37-42)

While the Lord is gathering the Jews back to Israel at the beginning of the Millennium, He will also gather all the nations. He will assemble all the people who remain from the nations in Israel that He might judge them. Everyone upon the face of the earth will be brought to Israel into the valley of Jehoshaphat. There the Lord will pronounce judgment on all who remain of the nations. This is the judgment of the living spoken of in Acts 10 and 2 Timothy 4. The Lord will separate the nations into two groups. In His eyes they will be as good fish, and bad or rotten fish, all caught in His net. The good will be separated from the rotten and kept. The bad will be cast into the lake of fire.

The nations will also be as sheep and goats. At the beginning of the tribulation, the eternal gospel was preached to all the unbelievers throughout the earth.* During the tribulation many will heed that eternal gospel. They will fear God and, consequently, treat the believers and the Jews with kindness and compassion during that time of suffering. These will be counted as sheep by the Lord. They will be rewarded by entering into the millennial kingdom on the earth. They will partake of the blessing of life. This will not make them sons of God; it is not that eternal life enters into them, but rather that they enter into the realm of life. This will keep them from perdition in the lake of fire. Thus,

---

* See *The Eternal Gospel* in Chapter 4.

they will enjoy the blessing of the Lord's presence as the nations on the earth.

At the same time, the Lord will also pronounce judgment upon the evil among the nations. He will consider them goats. During the tribulation they will not heed the eternal gospel and will mistreat the believers and the Jews. They will not feed, clothe, or visit them in prison. Rather, these unbelievers will only increase the suffering of the Lord's brothers. Therefore, at the judgment of the nations, the Lord Jesus will cast these evil ones alive into the lake of fire for eternity.

As depicted in Matthew 13, all the false believers, those who claim to be of Christ but are not, will be gathered and bound into bundles. These "tares," or false wheat, will be thrown into the lake of fire. The Jehovah's Witnesses, the Mormons, and any other false believers in the Catholic Church and the other denominations should be included among them. This judgment upon the false believers may also occur at the same time that the nations are judged.

By this, the Lord will rid the earth of every offensive thing. All offensive people will be thrown into the lake of fire, including the tares and those of the nations who do not fear God. The Lord will also remove every other offensive thing that might still exist on the earth. Everything will be thrown into the lake of fire. Through this, the Lord will purify the earth for His reign during the Millennium.

Israel's Enjoyment of the Kingdom Feast

And it shall come to pass, that every one that is left of all the nations that came against Jerusalem shall go up from year to year to worship the King, Jehovah of hosts, and to keep the feast of tabernacles. And it shall be, that whoso of all the families of the earth goeth not up unto Jerusalem to worship the King, Jehovah of hosts, upon them there shall be no rain. And if the family of Egypt go not up, and come not, neither shall it be upon them; there shall be the plague wherewith Jehovah will smite the nations that go not up to keep the feast of tabernacles. This shall be the punishment of Egypt, and the punishment of all the nations that go not up to keep the feast of tabernacles. (Zechariah 14:16-19)

After the day of atonement will come the feast of tabernacles. This feast will be according to its Old Testament depiction in Leviticus and Deuteronomy.[16] It will occur on the fifteenth day of the seventh month after the days of mourning and weeping in deeper repentance. After all the matters between Israel and Christ are cleared away, the Jews will enter into a feast of enjoyment with Christ, which will last the entire Millennium as signified by the seven days[*] of the feast of tabernacles. This will be a time of rest, enjoyment, and rejoicing in the riches of Christ.[†] At that time the Jews will dwell in booths. That is, they will testify that their dwelling on the earth is temporary.[‡] They will be awaiting the New Jerusalem in the new heaven and the new earth.

Cleansing the Temple

And from the time that the continual burnt-offering shall be taken away, and the abomination that maketh desolate set up, there shall be a thousand and two hundred and ninety days. (Daniel 12:11)

And the glory of Jehovah came into the house by the way of the gate whose prospect is toward the east. And the Spirit took me up, and brought me into the inner court; and, behold, the glory of Jehovah filled the house. And I heard one speaking unto me out of the house; and a man stood by me. And he said unto me, Son of man, this is the place of my throne, and the place of the soles of my feet, where I will dwell in the midst of the children of Israel for ever. And the house of Israel shall no more defile my holy name, neither they, nor their kings, by their whoredom, and

---

[*] Seven days signifies a complete course of time and refers to the entire period of the Millennium.

[†] This is signified by all the green trees of the feast of tabernacles (Lev. 23:40). All the trees denote different aspects of Christ's rich and flourishing humanity, which will bless Israel during the Millennium.

[‡] In addition, the Israel and the whole earth will be in such a shambles that they will need to construct small dwellings in order to house themselves.

by the dead bodies of their kings in their high places... (Ezekiel 43:4-7)

At the beginning of the tribulation, the Antichrist will defile the temple. Before Christ could dwell in it this defilement must be cleansed away. This will take about thirty days from the end of the tribulation. It will be accomplished on the 1290th day after the defilement by the Antichrist. This cleansing will be to restore the temple from its devastated, defiled condition. It will cleanse God's dwelling from the presence of the Antichrist, the false prophet, and also from the abomination of desolation.

After this, God in Christ will dwell in the temple. The temple is not for a physical ark as in the Old Testament, but for a person—Christ, the embodiment of God. Christ is the real ark of testimony in whom and with whom God dwells. He is the One bearing God's person, presence, and glory. Once the temple is cleansed, Christ will enter it to dwell with the people of Israel forever.

Ordering the People

Blessed is he that waiteth, and cometh to the thousand three hundred and five and thirty days. (Daniel 12:12)

And they shall bring all your brethren out of all the nations for an oblation unto Jehovah, upon horses, and in chariots, and in litters, and upon mules, and upon dromedaries, to my holy mountain Jerusalem, saith Jehovah, as the children of Israel bring their oblation in a clean vessel into the house of Jehovah. And of them also will I take for priests and for Levites, saith Jehovah. (Isaiah 66:20-21)

But ye shall be named the priests of Jehovah; men shall call you the ministers of our God: ye shall eat the wealth of the nations, and in their glory shall ye boast yourselves. (Isaiah 61:6)

And it shall come to pass in that day, that Jehovah will beat off his fruit from the flood of the River unto the brook of Egypt; and ye shall be gathered one by one, O ye children of Israel. (Isaiah 27:12)

Thus saith the Lord Jehovah: This shall be the border, whereby ye shall divide the land for inheritance according to the twelve tribes of Israel... (Ezekiel 47:13)

They therefore, when they were come together, asked him, saying, Lord, dost thou at this time restore the kingdom to Israel? And he said unto them, It is not for you to know times or seasons, which the Father hath set within His own authority. (Acts 1:6-7)

The Lord will also set up the priesthood in Israel at the beginning of the Millennium. This will occur up to the 1335th day after the Antichrist defiles the temple. That is, it will take another 45 days after the cleansing of the temple for the priesthood to be set up. The priesthood will be eradicated by the Antichrist and the false prophet. Therefore, after the cleansing of the temple the Lord will restore both the priestly and Levitical services.

The Lord will also divide the Good Land among the remnant of Israel. At that time Israel will extend from the River Euphrates to the brook of Egypt. It will include a large portion of what is now Iraq. All the tribes will be allotted a portion of the good land for their enjoyment during the Millennium. The double portion will go to Joseph.[17] A particular portion, special in position, will be given to the priests and Levites.[18] They will be the ones closest to Christ, and thus have the highest enjoyment of Christ's earthly reign.

At the beginning of the Millennium the Lord will restore the earthly kingdom to Israel, as it was in the days of David and Solomon. At that time God lifted Israel above all the nations, making it the center of the earth. During the Millennium, Christ will reign as the real David and the real Solomon. He will be enthroned in Jerusalem and reign over the whole earth as King. Through the reigning Christ Israel will be exalted over all the nations. The nations will flow into Israel to Christ, the King.[19]

References

[1] Matt. 13:43
[2] Matt. 8:11
[3] Rom. 8:19

[4] Is. 66:21; Zech. 8:23-24
[5] Rev. 11:17
[6] Jn. 3:29-30
[7] Jn. 10:28; 2 Pet. 1:4; Rom. 8:29; 1 Cor. 12:27
[8] 1 Jn. 3:2
[9] Rev. 20:4
[10] Rev. 2:26-27
[11] Rev. 20:7-8
[12] Rev. 20:11-15
[13] Rev. 21:3-4, 24
[14] Lev. 23:23
[15] Lev. 23:27-29
[16] Lev. 23:33-36, 42-43; Deut. 16:13
[17] Ez. 47:13
[18] Ez. 48:8-14
[19] 1 Ki. 10:1-10

CHAPTER 11

The Beauty of the Kingdom

During the millennial kingdom, as Christ reigns in His glory, nearly everything will be excellent. Christ will be beautiful in every aspect. The overcoming saints, who reign with Him, will also be beautiful in their manifestation of God's glory in Christ. Israel will be a treasure to God, the gem of the earth. The nations, subdued in their rebellion toward God and brought back to the proper worship of the Creator, will be excellent. The earth itself will flourish in beauty under Christ's blessing. Even the heavens will manifest God's glory in splendor.

The Beauty of Christ

Verily I say unto you, there are some of them that stand here, who shall in no wise taste of death, till they see the Son of man coming in his kingdom. ... and he was transfigured before them; and his face did shine as the sun, and his garments became white as the light. (Matthew 16:28; 17:2)

And as he was praying, the fashion of his countenance was altered, and his raiment became white and dazzling. (Luke 9:29)

And the Word became flesh, and dwelt among us (and we beheld his glory, glory as of the only begotten from the Father), full of grace and truth. (John 1:14)

For we did not follow cunningly devised fables, when we made known unto you the power and coming of our Lord Jesus Christ, but we were eyewitnesses of his majesty. For he received from God the Father honor and glory, when there was borne such a voice to him by the Majestic Glory, This is my beloved Son, in whom I am well pleased... (2 Peter 1:16-17)

...at midday, O king, I saw on the way a light from heaven, above the brightness of the sun, shining round about me and them that journeyed with me. (Acts 26:13)

*But we behold ... Jesus ... crowned with glory and honor...
(Hebrews 2:9)*

*Father, I desire that they also whom thou hast given me be with
me where I am, that they may behold my glory, which thou hast
given me: for thou lovedst me before the foundation of the world.
(John 17:24)*

*But unto you that fear my name shall the sun of righteousness
arise with healing in its wings; and ye shall go forth, and gambol
as calves of the stall. (Malachi 4:2)*

*Arise, shine; for thy light is come, and the glory of Jehovah is
risen upon thee. (Isaiah 60:1)*

*In those days, and at that time, will I cause a Branch of righteous-
ness to grow up unto David; and he shall execute justice and
righteousness in the land. In those days shall Judah be saved, and
Jerusalem shall dwell safely; and this is the name whereby she
shall be called: Jehovah our righteousness. For thus saith Jehovah: David shall never want a man to sit upon the throne of the
house of Israel... (Jeremiah 33:15-17)*

*In that day shall the branch of Jehovah be beautiful and glorious,
and the fruit of the land shall be excellent and comely for them
that are escaped of Israel. (Isaiah 4:2)*

*For unto us a child is born, unto us a son is given; and the govern-
ment shall be upon his shoulder: and his name shall be called
Wonderful, Counsellor, Mighty God, Everlasting Father, Prince
of Peace. (Isaiah 9:6)*

*And it shall come to pass in that day, that the root of Jesse, that
standeth for an ensign of the peoples, unto him shall the nations
seek; and his resting-place shall be glorious. (Isaiah 11:10)*

*Cry aloud and shout, thou inhabitant of Zion; for great in the
midst of thee is the Holy One of Israel. (Isaiah 12:6)*

During the Millennium, Christ will shine as the most beautiful, most attractive person in the whole universe. The overcoming
saints will enjoy Him as the heavenly One while they feast with
Him for a thousand years.[1] The beauty of Christ will be manifested in full to all the transfigured saints.[2] They will behold the

Lord Jesus in all His glory and honor with unveiled eyes and unveiled hearts.[3] Christ will manifest in full all His divine attributes in the divine glory through all of His perfect, resurrected human virtues for all His members to behold, appreciate, and enjoy. He will irradiate the saints with His shining. He will be unsurpassed in beauty and splendor, and attractive beyond measure. To the overcoming saints He will be the most pleasant and most intimate One. There are no human words to convey the preciousness of the heavenly Christ whom the overcoming saints will enjoy during the Millennium.

On earth Christ's beauty will be seen in Israel. He will reign in Jerusalem as the King over all the earth. He will be the sun of righteousness, shining to illuminate the children of Israel and bring them out of darkness. He will be the risen Glory, delivering them from the nighttime of this age. He will be recognized as the branching out of God into humanity, as the very God incarnate. He will be the Wonderful Counselor, the Mighty God, the Everlasting Father, and the Prince of Peace. He will be the source of God's people, Israel—the root of Jesse.

To the nations He will be an ensign to whom all mankind will seek. He will be the Holy One of Israel, sanctifying not only the nation of Israel, but all mankind. These are but a few of the aspects of the beauty of Christ on the earth during the Millennium. The facets of His glory in His expression of God are too many to enumerate.

All that Christ will be in those days He is to us today in spirit. He can be experienced and enjoyed *today* by the believers, in all of His many attributes and virtues, as a foretaste of that time.[4] By partaking of this beautiful, glorious, and splendid Christ in His divinity and humanity, the believers are prepared, equipped, and qualified for the coming age. It is our portion to enjoy this unsearchably rich Christ today as a foretaste of the coming Millennium.

The Beauty of the Overcoming Saints

... and that he might make known the riches of his glory upon vessels of mercy, which he afore prepared unto glory... (Romans 9:23)

Then shall the righteous shine forth as the sun in the kingdom of their Father. ... and he was transfigured before them; and his face did shine as the sun, and his garments became white as the light. (Matthew 13:43; 17:2)

... even the mystery which hath been hid for ages and generations: but now hath it been manifested to his saints, to whom God was pleased to make known what is the riches of the glory of this mystery among the Gentiles, which is Christ in you, the hope of glory... When Christ, who is our life, shall be manifested, then shall ye also with him be manifested in glory. (Colossians 1:26-27; 3:4)

...who shall fashion anew the body of our humiliation, that it may be conformed to the body of his glory, according to the working whereby he is able even to subject all things unto himself. (Philippians 3:21)

Beloved, now are we children of God, and it is not yet made manifest what we shall be. We know that, if he shall be manifested, we shall be like him; for we shall see him even as he is. (1 John 3:2)

For it became him, for whom are all things, and through whom are all things, in bringing many sons unto glory, to make the author of their salvation perfect through sufferings. (Hebrews 2:10)

During the Millennium the overcoming believers will shine with Christ's glory in beauty. They will be made like Him in every way. All spots, blemishes, and wrinkles will be washed completely away in His life. They will be Christ's brothers in every respect. They will share in full His divine life, His divine nature, and His divine glory. In spirit, soul, and body they will be the same as He is today. They will be conformed to His image and made like Him totally.[5]

These believers are those who enjoy and experience Christ in their daily life. The Christ who is the Spirit was first deposited within their spirit as the divine life.[6] Day by day these overcoming saints partake of and enjoy this divine life, allowing it to spread throughout their soul that they might be sanctified, renewed, and transformed.[7] They thus become identical to Christ in spirit and soul. Finally, even the body of their humiliation will be transfigured into a body like His own, a body of glory. Consequently, these overcoming saints become Christ's "twins" in spirit, soul, and body. They will shine as the sun with God in Christ as the light.

To God the Father, the overcoming saints will be His many sons, Christ's many brothers.[8] All issues and troubling factors will be totally eliminated, that they might be holy and without blemish before Him in love.[9] They will be led by Christ in praise to the Father.[10] In every way God will be their Father. They will partake fully of the divine nature in the divine life.[11] They will be human, yet divine. They will be divine, yet still human. They will express the divine glory. To God the Father they will be the completion of His mystery.[12] They will be a satisfaction and sweetness to God, the dispensational consummation of His work throughout all ages, the fulfillment of His purpose.

To Christ, the perfected saints will be His glorious bride in love.[13] They will share with Him the most intimate love and oneness. They will be cleansed entirely, to be without spot, wrinkle, or any such thing, but be wholly glorious.[14]

The overcoming ones will also be Christ's Body to express Him. They will express Him in perfect oneness: oneness with the Triune God and oneness with each other. All taints of division and dissension of any kind will be done away with. They will express the very oneness of the Triune God, the oneness of the Trinity within the Godhead. This is the oneness of the Spirit. This oneness will be fulfilled in them, even as the Lord prayed in John 17, "… that they may all be one; even as thou, Father, art in me, and I in thee, that they also may be in us …"[15]

As Christ's Body, these overcoming saints will be Christ's fullness, constituted of His unsearchable riches.[16] They will tell forth Christ's excellence in His many virtues, thus manifesting the many divine attributes of God.[17] By partaking of the divine nature, they too will manifest the divine attributes in their resurrected and uplifted human virtues.

Through the Body of Christ, God will head up all things in Christ. This begins with the heading up of the members of the Body of Christ. When this is consummated, God in Christ through the Body will head up the whole earth and the whole universe. This heading up is seen during the Millennium in Christ's administration in His kingdom. It is the members of Christ who form His administration, to rule over the earth in the coming age.

During the Millennium, the overcoming saints will reign in glory as kings over all the peoples of the earth.[18] They will shepherd mankind, healing them from all damage.[19] They will also be as precious jewels to the rest of the creation. They will irradiate the creation with God's splendor. By this illumination they will free all the creation from its subjection to vanity and from the bondage of corruption in which it is bound, into the glory of the sons of God.[20] It is this glory, this manifestation of God, for which the whole creation groans today.

The Beauty of Israel

And he brought me back unto the door of the house; and, behold, waters issued out from under the threshold of the house eastward; (for the forefront of the house was toward the east;) and the waters came down from under, from the right side of the house, on the south of the altar. ... And it shall come to pass, that every living creature which swarmeth, in every place whither the rivers come, shall live... (Ezekiel 47:1, 9)

In that day shall the branch of Jehovah be beautiful and glorious, and the fruit of the land shall be excellent and comely for them that are escaped of Israel. (Isaiah 4:2)

The sun shall be no more thy light by day; neither for brightness shall the moon give light unto thee: but Jehovah will be unto thee an everlasting light, and thy God thy glory. Thy sun shall no more go down, neither shall thy moon withdraw itself; for Jehovah will be thine everlasting light, and the days of thy mourning shall be ended. (Isaiah 60:19-20)

In that day will Jehovah of hosts become a crown of glory, and a diadem of beauty, unto the residue of his people... (Isaiah 28:5)

And Jehovah will create over the whole habitation of mount Zion, and over her assemblies, a cloud and smoke by day, and the shining of a flaming fire by night; for over all the glory shall be spread a covering. And there shall be a pavilion for a shade in the day-time from the heat, and for a refuge and for a covert from storm and from rain. (Isaiah 4:5-6)

And, behold, the glory of the God of Israel came from the way of the east: and his voice was like the sound of many waters; and the earth shined with his glory. ... And the glory of Jehovah came into the house by the way of the gate whose prospect is toward the east. And the Spirit took me up, and brought me into the inner court; and, behold, the glory of Jehovah filled the house. And I heard one speaking unto me out of the house; and a man stood by me. And he said unto me, Son of man, this is the place of my throne, and the place of the soles of my feet, where I will dwell in the midst of the children of Israel for ever. ... (Ezekiel 43:2, 4-7)

The glory of Lebanon shall come unto thee, the fir-tree, the pine, and the box-tree together, to beautify the place of my sanctuary; and I will make the place of my feet glorious. (Isaiah 60:13)

And it shall come to pass in the latter days, that the mountain of Jehovah's house shall be established on the top of the mountains, and shall be exalted above the hills; and all nations shall flow unto it. And many peoples shall go and say, Come ye, and let us go up to the mountain of Jehovah, to the house of the God of Jacob; and he will teach us of his ways, and we will walk in his paths: for out of Zion shall go forth the law, and the word of Jehovah from Jerusalem. (Isaiah 2:2-3)

After the Lord's return to the earth, He will heal both the land and people of Israel. Out of His throne in the temple life-giving waters will issue forth.[21] They will flow toward the east and the west. Wherever they flow they will heal the damage, destruction, and death. The land of Israel will be flooded with the life-giving waters to become the paradise of the earth. The mountains and hills will flow down wine and milk.[22] The arid, parched land of Israel will become a land filled with brooks and streams.[23] It will become full of life and exceedingly fruitful in vegetation. It will extend from the River Euphrates, in what is now present day Iraq, all the way to the brook of Egypt in the Negev.[24] What is now wilderness and desert will shine, like an emerald, with life.

The life-giving waters issuing from the throne of the Lord in Jerusalem will be a physical picture of the spiritual reality. He, as the Spirit, will flow throughout His people to guard them, keep them, heal them, and enliven them. Wherever His Spirit flows, life will come forth. The people of Israel will be healed from every negative thing.

God will dwell in the nation of Israel as light, illuminating her with His glory and filling her with His righteousness. She will become a crown of beauty and a royal diadem to the Lord, the choicest among all the peoples.[25] She will be filled with joy, songs, and praise.[26] There will be no more violence in Israel. This land, which has been repeatedly devastated and will be nearly completely destroyed in the future, will be filled with peace. Those within her will dwell in safety and quietness.[27] Israel will be built up with houses and full of cities.[28] Throughout her there will be fruitful vineyards, orchards, and rich produce of every kind.[29]

Today the Jews are a despised people. Throughout history they have been the target of hate, violence, and genocide. In the coming kingdom the Jews will no longer suffer any kind of reproach.[30] They will all be crowned and beautified by Christ. Everyone among them will be holy, righteous, and fruitful.[31] All of the Jews will bear many children as a blessing from the Lord. The land will be filled with playing children.[32] Each of the Jews will be rich in years.[33] None of them will die young. They will be planted forever in Israel and none will be able to uproot them.[34] Israel will be a nation of priests to all the peoples of the earth. Through Israel, the whole earth will be blessed in worship to God.

In the midst of Israel Jerusalem will shine. It will be Christ's resting place and a glory to God.[35] It will be called the city of Jehovah, the holy mountain, the city of righteousness, and the city of truth.[36] Over all the city, Christ will be a covering. He will be a cloud of smoke by day and a pillar of fire by night, even as He was to the children of Israel in the wilderness during the days of Moses.[37] He will be the glory over all: a canopy for shade in the daytime from the hot sun, and a refuge and a covert from storms. He will become Jerusalem's guard and protection, and her glory and treasure.

In the midst of Jerusalem, the temple will shine as the peak attraction of all the earth. The temple will be the place of the soles of Christ's feet. There Christ will dwell among the children of Israel forever. It will be the house of His glory.[38] There He will shine over Israel and all the earth. There will be no greater attraction in the physical universe than Christ in His dwelling place.

Throughout the earth the nations will flow into Israel, coming to Zion, the highest peak on the earth, with the house of the Lord as its center.[39] All the peoples of the earth will be attracted by the glory and majesty of Christ in Zion. The nations will come to Zion with wealth of all kinds to enrich Israel. They will learn to worship God from the Jews. They will also come to the Lord for His judgment between the nations. The Israelites will act as priests to the peoples of the earth. Those of the nations will grab the skirt of a Jew and ask to be brought to the Lord. What a beautiful picture the Scriptures set before us concerning Israel during the Millennium.

The Beauty of the Nations

... the leaves of the tree were for the healing of the nations. (Revelation 22:2)

Then the eyes of the blind shall be opened, and the ears of the deaf shall be unstopped. Then shall the lame man leap as a hart, and the tongue of the dumb shall sing; for in the wilderness shall waters break out, and streams in the desert. (Isaiah 35:5-6)

And he will judge between the nations, and will decide concerning many peoples; and they shall beat their swords into plowshares, and their spears into pruning-hooks; nation shall not lift up sword against nation, neither shall they learn war any more. (Isaiah 2:4)

And in this mountain will Jehovah of hosts make unto all peoples a feast of fat things, a feast of wines on the lees, of fat things full of marrow, of wines on the lees well refined. And he will destroy in this mountain the face of the covering that covereth all peoples, and the veil that is spread over all nations. (Isaiah 25:6-7)

At the start of the Millennium the nations will have great need of healing. Many, perhaps most, among them will have been wounded, maimed, or damaged during the tribulation. There will be much sickness and ill health. The events of the tribulation will truly break the nations into pieces. However, during the Millennium the healing power of the Lord through His Body, the overcoming saints, will be amplified to the extreme.* By the intensified healing power of the Spirit, all the nations will be healed physically, psychologically, and spiritually, and brought back to well-being in the restored earth.

Furthermore, the covering that keeps them from God will be taken away. The veil over their heart that prevents them from knowing God will be removed. By feasting in the presence of the Lord, the shroud that darkens their mind will be eliminated. They will enjoy enlightening and revelation from the glory of the Lord's appearing.

All the nations will be brought into harmony. Wars will be over; all arms will be beaten into farming tools; every kind of strife will be subdued by the Lord's presence. Every kind of problem will be resolved by the kings ruling over the earth—Christ and the saints.

Year by year the nations will go up to Jerusalem to worship God to keep the feast of tabernacles.[40] They will be attracted there by Christ's glory, and will learn from the Jews how to worship and serve the Lord. Eventually, all the nations will become a beauty to Christ during the Millennium.

The Beauty of the Earth

For the anxious watching of the creation eagerly awaits the revelation of the sons of God. For the creation was made subject to vanity, not of its own will, but because of Him who subjected it, In hope that the creation itself will also be freed from the slavery of corruption into the freedom of the glory of the children

---

* Today many Christians seek gifts such as healing or speaking in tongues. Very few realize that this age is not the age for the exercise of these gifts. The gifts in this age are mostly for a sign to the unbelievers (1 Cor. 14:22). According to Hebrews it is the next age, the kingdom age, during which the gifts will be freely exercised for the benefit of the nations (Heb. 6:4-5).

of God. For we know that the whole creation groans together and travails in pain together until now. (Romans 8:19-22)

The wolf and the lamb shall feed together, and the lion shall eat straw like the ox; and dust shall be the serpent's food. They shall not hurt nor destroy in all my holy mountain, saith Jehovah. (Isaiah 65:25)

... until the Spirit be poured upon us from on high, and the wilderness become a fruitful field, and the fruitful field be esteemed as a forest. Then justice shall dwell in the wilderness; and righteousness shall abide in the fruitful field. And the work of righteousness shall be peace; and the effect of righteousness, quietness and confidence for ever. (Isaiah 32:15-17)

The wilderness and the dry land shall be glad; and the desert shall rejoice, and blossom as the rose. It shall blossom abundantly, and rejoice even with joy and singing; the glory of Lebanon shall be given unto it, the excellency of Carmel and Sharon: they shall see the glory of Jehovah, the excellency of our God. ... Then shall the lame man leap as a hart, and the tongue of the dumb shall sing; for in the wilderness shall waters break out, and streams in the desert. And the glowing sand shall become a pool, and the thirsty ground springs of water: in the habitation of jackals, where they lay, shall be grass with reeds and rushes. (Isaiah 35:1-2, 6-7)

And the wolf shall dwell with the lamb, and the leopard shall lie down with the kid; and the calf and the young lion and the fatling together; and a little child shall lead them. And the cow and the bear shall feed; their young ones shall lie down together; and the lion shall eat straw like the ox. And the sucking child shall play on the hole of the asp, and the weaned child shall put his hand on the adder's den. They shall not hurt nor destroy in all my holy mountain; for the earth shall be full of the knowledge of Jehovah, as the waters cover the sea. (Isaiah 11:6-9)

Today the whole creation has been subjected to vanity. It is under the bondage of corruption. Furthermore, it is being damaged by mankind. Pollution, overpopulation, and numerous other factors are destroying the earth. The coming great tribulation will damage the earth to the utmost. The Antichrist and his followers, along with the other warring nations, will cause much devastation, and God's judgments upon the creation will greatly damage the earth and the life on it. The creation is now and will be even the more in great need of Christ.

At the beginning of the Millennium, the whole creation will be freed into the glory of God by the shining of the sons of God. The curse in Genesis 3 will be removed.[41] All the damage from all ages will be undone: pollution will be eliminated, any kind of devastation will be swallowed up, all kinds of disease will be eradicated. The earth will be turned into a garden. It will bring forth bountifully, even amazingly. The earth's foliage will be extraordinary. There will be no lack of food or water again.[*] The earth will truly become a worldwide "Eden," bearing fruit, flowers, foliage, and water abundantly.

The animals will also be healed. The enmity between man and the animals which has existed since Genesis 3 will be removed. During the kingdom age the wolf will lie down with the lamb and the leopard with the kid; the calf, lion, and fatling will lie down together; the lion will eat straw rather than meat; the cow and the bear will feed together. The suckling child will play on the hole of an asp, and the weaned child in the den of an adder. There will be no enmity between man and the animals. There will be no more hurt or destruction. The glory of the Lord will fill the whole earth, doing away with every kind of evil, violence, and damage.

The Beauty of the Heavens

Moreover the light of the moon shall be as the light of the sun, and the light of the sun shall be sevenfold, as the light of seven days, in the day that Jehovah bindeth up the hurt of his people, and healeth the stroke of their wound. (Isaiah 30:26)

Even the heavens themselves will be beautiful. Today they suffer in disorder from God's prior judgments due to Satan's

---

[*] Except as a judgment for rebellion (Zech. 14:17-19).

rebellion.* In addition, they will be greatly damaged during the tribulation. However, during the Millennium the heavens will be healed. Everything in the whole creation will be brought into peaceful harmony under Christ's reigning in glory. During the kingdom the sun will shine seven times brighter than today, and the moon will shine like the sun. The whole creation will be filled with intense light, which will swallow up every kind of darkness.

The whole universe will be filled with beauty during the kingdom: Christ, the overcoming saints, Israel, the nations, the earth, and the heavens will all proclaim the glory of God. It will be a time of splendor and joy. In every direction and in every way the beauty of God will be manifested. All of this will come from the presence of God in Christ through the man Jesus and the overcoming saints. How wonderful to be those who partake of the glory of that time!

The Final Purification

And when the thousand years are finished, Satan shall be loosed out of his prison, and shall come forth to deceive the nations which are in the four corners of the earth, Gog and Magog, to gather them together to the war: the number of whom is as the sand of the sea. And they went up over the breadth of the earth, and compassed the camp of the saints about, and the beloved city: and fire came down out of heaven, and devoured them. And the devil that deceived them was cast into the lake of fire and brimstone, where are also the beast and the false prophet; and they shall be tormented day and night for ever and ever. And I saw a great white throne, and him that sat upon it, from whose

---

* One such judgment occurred in the age immediately prior to the creation of man. At that time, the earth was judged and the heavens put into darkness (Gen. 1:2a). God came in to restore the earth (Genesis 1:2b-31) that He might have the proper environment in which to create man. Nevertheless, the earth and the heavens were left in a somewhat disordered state. For example, Satan with his evil host still remain in the air above the earth (Gen. 1:6-8; Eph. 2:2; 6:12). Similarly, the great upheaval in Noah's time brought a flood that also changed the earth (Gen. 7:10-12, 17-24). Furthermore, the very presence of Satan as the chaotic, rebellious element who attempts to overthrow God to bring the creation into a devilish anarchy (2 Thes. 2:7) greatly contributes to the current disorder in the universe.

face the earth and the heaven fled away; and there was found no place for them. And I saw the dead, the great and the small, standing before the throne; and books were opened: and another book was opened, which is the book of life: and the dead were judged out of the things which were written in the books, according to their works. And the sea gave up the dead that were in it; and death and Hades gave up the dead that were in them: and they were judged every man according to their works. And death and Hades were cast into the lake of fire. This is the second death, even the lake of fire. And if any was not found written in the book of life, he was cast into the lake of fire. (Revelation 20:7-15)

There shall be no more thence an infant of days, nor an old man that hath not filled his days; for the child shall die a hundred years old, and the sinner being a hundred years old shall be accursed. (Isaiah 65:20)

And it shall be, that whoso of all the families of the earth goeth not up unto Jerusalem to worship the King, Jehovah of hosts, upon them there shall be no rain. And if the family of Egypt go not up, and come not, neither shall it be upon them; there shall be the plague wherewith Jehovah will smite the nations that go not up to keep the feast of tabernacles. (Zechariah 14:17-18)

... but the heavens that now are, and the earth, by the same word have been stored up for fire, being reserved against the day of judgment and destruction of ungodly men. ... But the day of the Lord will come as a thief; in the which the heavens shall pass away with a great noise, and the elements shall be dissolved with fervent heat, and the earth and the works that are therein shall be burned up. Seeing that these things are thus all to be dissolved, what manner of persons ought ye to be in all holy living and godliness, looking for and earnestly desiring the coming of the day of God, by reason of which the heavens being on fire shall be dissolved, and the elements shall melt with fervent heat? But, according to his promise, we look for new heavens and a new earth, wherein dwelleth righteousness. (2 Peter 3:7, 10-13)

And I saw a new heaven and a new earth: for the first heaven and the first earth are passed away; and the sea is no more. (Revelation 21:1)

And all the host of heaven shall be dissolved, and the heavens shall be rolled together as a scroll; and all their host shall fade away, as the leaf fadeth from off the vine, and as a fading leaf from the fig-tree. (Isaiah 34:4)

Although the Millennium will be extraordinarily beautiful and wonderful, there will still be problems remaining. There will still be uncompleted matters with respect to God's eternal economy. Both sin and death will still be present during the kingdom age. There will still be sinners on the earth, and men will still die. In addition, there will still be some element of rebellion among the nations.* Furthermore, the whole creation, though healed and restored, will still be the *old* creation. It must be renewed to become the *new* creation. Finally, there will still be the remaining problems of Satan and his angels (who will be sealed in the abyss), the dead unbelievers (who will be in Hades), and the demons. All these matters must be cleared up before eternity future can be brought in.

At the end of the Millennium, the Lord will quickly dispose of all remaining problems in the creation. He will start with the nations living on the earth. Satan will be released from the abyss. His angels will no doubt follow with him. Together they will stir up all the nations starting from Gog and Magog. This final rebellion against God will begin in what is now Russia. The Lord will use Satan to expose the evil and rebellious element still within mankind. All of the nations (but not every one of every nation) will take part in this rebellion. The number of those taking part in this revolt will be like the sand of the sea—virtually uncountable.

The rebellious ones among the nations will surround the beloved city, Jerusalem, and the camp of the saints. It will be their intent to destroy God's people. As they surround God's redeemed, fire will come down from heaven and devour them, sweeping them away into the lake of fire for eternity. This will purify the living nations of the remaining sinful element within them.

The Lord will next judge the angels. For his part in the final rebellion against God, Satan will be cast into the lake of fire. His

---

* It is recorded, for example, that Egypt and other nations will at some time refuse to go up to Jerusalem for the feast of tabernacles (Zech. 14:17-19).

evil host of followers will be cast into the lake of fire with him.* Satan and the evil angels will join the Antichrist and the false prophet, with the tares and the goats from among the nations,† in eternal perdition in the lake of fire.

Immediately after ridding the universe of the source of all evil, the Lord will set up His great white throne, at which He will judge all the remaining dead of mankind from all ages. All the dead unbelievers will be resurrected to judgment and judged according to their deeds. All those not found written in the book of life will be cast into the lake of fire. Included among them will be the cowardly, the unbelieving, the abominable,‡ the unclean, sorcerers, fornicators, murderers, idolaters, and liars.[42] They will be cast together into the lake of fire for eternity.

Some of mankind will pass through this judgment to become the nations in the new heaven and new earth. This should include many of those among the nations, such as the sheep§ who entered into the Lord's blessing of life at the beginning of the Millennium. It should also include those among the nations who did not rebel against God at the end of the Millennium.

At this time the Lord will also judge the demons. The demons are the disembodied spirits of a pre-adamic race. They are not the same as the angels.[43] These are the evil spirits of the race or races of beings who were on the earth before the creation of man and who joined Satan in his rebellion against God. They were judged at the time the earth became waste and empty, as shown in Genesis 1:2.** The demons will also be cast into the lake of fire.

---

* The judgment of the evil angels will occur either at this time with Satan, or perhaps at the great white throne that immediately follows the casting of Satan into the lake of fire.

† See *Judging the Nations* in Chapter 10.

‡ This should refer to those who continue in acts that are abominations, which according to the Bible are practices such as homosexuality (Lev. 18:22) and wizardry (Deut. 18:10-12), until they themselves become abominable in the sight of God.

§ See *Judging the Nations* in Chapter 10.

** As revealed in Matthew 8:28-32 and Luke 11:24, where the demons are shown seeking watery places in which to dwell, the demons' habitat is now the water. Thus, the dead which the sea gives up, mentioned in Revelation 20:13, do not

After Satan, the fallen angels, mankind, and the demons have been judged, the Lord will deal with the final enemy, death. Today, death is a great enemy of God. According to the Old Testament, it is more defiling in God's eyes to touch death than to be sinful. Death is an insult to God's very nature for God is a God of life. God gives life to all things. To His children He even *is* life. Thus, death is opposed to God's very nature. At the end of the Millennium the Lord will deal with this final troubling factor, death, by casting it too into the lake of fire.

Once the Lord has dealt with all the remaining problems in the universe—the angels, mankind, the demons, and death—there will no longer be any further use for Hades. Today Hades is the keeping place of the dead. Once the dead have been resurrected to judgment, and once death itself has been thrown into the lake of fire, Hades will no longer have any utility. The Lord will throw it into the lake of fire as well.

The Lord will use the lake of fire as a universal refuse bin into which He throws all the useless, irreparable, and corrupted things. Everything in the universe that will not pass into the new creation will be discarded into the lake of fire, to be consumed unto eternity.

Having dealt with all the negative factors within the whole universe, there will be nothing left but for the Lord to roll the universe up. At that time it will still be an *old* creation. God desires a *new* creation. Therefore, heaven and earth will flee away. They will be rolled up like a scroll as the universe is burned with the consuming, purifying fire of God, and all the elements within the universe dissolve with intense heat. What remains will be God's new creation—a new heaven and new earth, with the New Jerusalem as the center.

The Eternal State

And I saw a new heaven and a new earth: for the first heaven and the first earth are passed away; and the sea is no more. And I saw the holy city, new Jerusalem, coming down out of heaven of God, made ready as a bride adorned for her husband. ... Come hither,

---

refer to the dead of mankind (who are in Hades, not in the sea), but to the demons.

I will show thee the bride, the wife of the Lamb. And he carried me away in the Spirit to a mountain great and high, and showed me the holy city Jerusalem, coming down out of heaven from God, having the glory of God: her light was like unto a stone most precious, as it were a jasper stone, clear as crystal... (Revelation 21:1-2, 9-11)

And he showed me a river of water of life, bright as crystal, proceeding out of the throne of God and of the Lamb, in the midst of the street thereof. And on this side of the river and on that was the tree of life, bearing twelve manner of fruits, yielding its fruit every month: and the leaves of the tree were for the healing of the nations. And there shall be no curse any more: and the throne of God and of the Lamb shall be therein: and his servants shall serve him; and they shall see his face; and his name shall be on their foreheads. And there shall be night no more; and they need no light of lamp, neither light of sun; for the Lord God shall give them light: and they shall reign for ever and ever. (Revelation 22:1-5)

And the Spirit and the bride say, Come. And he that heareth, let him say, Come. And he that is athirst, let him come: he that will, let him take the water of life freely. (Revelation 22:17)

For, behold, I create new heavens and a new earth; and the former things shall not be remembered, nor come into mind. But be ye glad and rejoice for ever in that which I create; for, behold, I create Jerusalem a rejoicing, and her people a joy. (Isaiah 65:17-18)

At the end of the Millennium the Lord will create the new heaven and the new earth. God Himself in His person and presence will be the continual renewing factor within the new heaven and the new earth. All things will be new, recreated in newness by God. They will remain new for eternity. The striking quality throughout the whole creation will be newness.

At the center of this new creation will be the consummation of God's operation throughout all ages—the New Jerusalem. This is not a physical city. It is, after all, called the bride, the wife of the Lamb. A person does not marry a physical city. The New Jerusalem includes all the saints from all ages. All the overcomers, as well as the saints who will be perfected by being disciplined during the thousand years of the kingdom age, will be included in this wonderful city. They, with God, *are* this city. The New Jerusalem is the eternal completion of God's joining with man, which He accomplished throughout all preceding ages. This city is a great sign showing God's union with His redeemed people. It is a mutual abode: in this city God dwells in His redeemed people, and His redeemed people dwell in Him. They are His tabernacle, and He is their temple. The New Jerusalem is an eternal abode in which God and the redeemed of mankind coinhere. That is, they exist and live within each other.

This city depicts the eternal state of God with His redeemed, a state of marriage. The Spirit as the consummation of God through all of His processes, including incarnation, crucifixion, resurrection, and ascension, and His bride—the aggregate of God's chosen people from all ages, who have been fully matured and transfigured in the divine glory—will live together in the reality of a most intimate, personal, and affectionate union depicted here as a marriage.

In this wonderful city the saints from both the Old and New Testament are seen. The gates of the New Jerusalem have upon them the names of the twelve tribes of Israel, showing that the Old Testament seekers of God are present in this city.* The New

---

* The place of Israel in God's plan for the accomplishment of His purpose is significant. In the Old Testament the law was given to Israel. The law is a picture of God showing that He is a God of life, light, love, holiness, and righteousness. It is the standard by which mankind is measured and judged. In order for mankind to meet with God, commune with Him, and dwell in His presence he must meet the standard of the law. This standard was given to Israel to expose their true condition, and thus lead them to Christ, the fulfillment of this standard. It was therefore through Israel that Christ came, ushering in the New Testament age of grace with all the New Testament believers. Israel was the means through which God brought in the very heart, center, and focus of His eternal purpose: Christ with the church.

In the coming kingdom age, Israel will once again occupy a special place in the fulfillment of God's eternal purpose. At that time all the nations will flow into Israel. It is there that they will learn how to worship God and serve God. Thus, it is through the Jews in the coming age that all of unregenerated man-kind will come to God.

Testament saints are also a part of this wonderful city. This is indicated by the names of the twelve apostles upon the twelve foundations of the wall of the city. The New Testament saints, as living stones, are the constituents of the wall. Thus, the redeemed, regenerated, sanctified, transformed, and transfigured believers are the main components* from among mankind of the New Jerusalem. They will shine as the sun, with God in Christ as the light, pervading and passing through them as the wall to illuminate not only the whole earth, but the whole universe!

This mysterious, yet wonderful dwelling place of God and His redeemed will be a blessing to everyone and everything for eternity. In this city God will enjoy His people forever. He will enjoy them as His many sons, as priests who serve Him, and as kings who rule for Him over the whole creation. In the New Jerusalem all the believers will enjoy God in Christ. We will enjoy Him as the light of life illuminating us, shining from within

------

In the New Jerusalem, both of these aspects of Israel are seen. On the one hand, Israel was the doorway—the "gates" mentioned below—through which all the New testament believers entered into Christ: salvation came through Christ, who was born of Israel and who satisfied all the righteous requirements of God's law, that God's chosen people from among the nations could be redeemed, regenerated, and transformed to be the very constituents of His eternal city.

On the other hand, Israel will act as the doorway into the New Jerusalem for the nations in eternity. Israel will continue to exist as a nation forever (Ez. 43:7; 2 Sam. 7:24). It is to Israel that the nations will continue to flow (Rev. 21:24-26), even as they will in the kingdom age. There, the nations will be brought to the dwelling place of God with His redeemed, including all the Old and New Testament saints.

Thus, the New Jerusalem is shown having twelve gates with the names of the children of Israel upon them. These gates signify not only the Old Testament saints, but also the eternal nation of Israel as a doorway for mankind to come to God in His dwelling place forever.

* It is the New Testament believers—those who overcome the satanic darkness by Christ in them as the light—who, as the stones of the wall of the New Jerusalem, will separate all that is of God from everything common. All the filthy and unclean things will be outside of the New Jerusalem in the lake of fire (Rev. 21:8, 27 ; 22:15). Even the more, these believers, as this wall, will keep out every disturbing factor to eternally maintain the great peace of the New Jerusalem.

us to fill our being with God as light. We will enjoy Him as the water of life flowing out from Himself on the throne, to water us and satisfy all our inward longings by filling us with Himself as the Spirit. We will enjoy Him as the tree of life, the flourishing and rich Christ growing out from the river of water of life and bearing new fruits each month. He will nourish us, feed us, and be our supply unto the ages of the ages. Forever, all of God's redeemed will enjoy Him as their rich supply in every way.

Praise our dear Lord for all that He is, for all that He has accomplished, and for all that He will accomplish. No matter what our condition is today, and no matter what might happen in the future, our God could never be kept from the accomplishment of His purpose. All of God's redeemed will be brought into the glory of that coming city, the New Jerusalem. It is for this that we must pray, it is for this that we must labor, and it is this for which we, even as Abraham, wait in hope! It is our portion to enjoy God as our dwelling place today as a foretaste. In the future we, as the New Jerusalem, will enjoy our God in Christ to the full, even as He will enjoy us as well. Glory to our God and to His Christ unto all the ages of the ages. Amen!

References

1 Matt. 22:8-10
2 1 Jn. 3:2
3 Jn. 17:24; Heb. 2:9
4 Eph. 1:13-14
5 Rom. 8:29; Phil. 3:21
6 Jn. 7:39; Rom. 8:2
7 Heb. 2:11; Eph. 4:23; Rom. 12:2; 2 Cor. 3:18
8 Rom. 8:29
9 Eph. 1:4
10 Rev. 14:1-5
11 2 Pet. 1:4
12 Rev. 10:7
13 Rev. 19:6-8; Eph. 5:25
14 Eph. 5:27
15 Jn. 17:21
16 Eph. 3:16-19
17 1 Pet. 2:9
18 Luk. 19:17; Rev 20:4
19 Heb. 6:5
20 Rom. 8:19-22
21 Ez. 47:1, 8-10, 12
22 Amos 9:13
23 Is. 35:6
24 Is. 27:12
25 Is. 62:2-3
26 Is. 24:14-16; 12:3-6
27 Is. 32:18; 60:18; 65:25; Amos 9:15
28 Is. 65:21; Amos 9:14
29 Is. 65:21; Amos 9:13-14; Zech. 8:12
30 Is. 25:8
31 Is. 4:3; 60:21-22; 27:6; Hos. 14:5-7; Jer. 33:22
32 Zech. 8:5
33 Is. 65:20, 22; Zech. 8:4
34 Is. 60:21
35 Jer. 33:9
36 Is. 60:14; 1:26; Zech. 8:3
37 Ex. 13:21
38 Is. 60:7
39 Is. 11:10; 60:5-7, 10-11, 13-14, 16; 66:12; Zech. 8:20-23
40 Zech. 14:16
41 Zech. 14:11
42 Rev. 21:8
43 Acts 23:9

APPENDIX A

Events at the Start of the Tribulation

The events at the beginning of the great tribulation, namely the sixth and seventh seals and the first five trumpets, have remained mysterious since the time the book of Revelation was given to the Apostle John nearly two thousand years ago. However, in these last days, the Lord, through recent scientific discoveries and observations, has begun to unveil these events as never before. As the day of His coming nears and the events that begin the tribulation approach, the Lord has opened His Word in a fresh way. He desires that all believers grow to maturity to be spared the suffering of the great tribulation. He also desires that all mankind would repent. Thus, He has given new light in His Word, that both believers and unbelievers might be warned concerning the events that are about to occur on the earth.

The Extinction of the Dinosaurs

In order to bring the beginning of the tribulation into focus it is useful to examine some current scientific theories and observations. A 1996 article[*] in the magazine, *Astronomy*, discusses the extinction of the dinosaurs 65 million years ago. Two planetary scientists, Owen Toon and Kevin Zahnle, detail the probable sequence of events that took place at that time.

It is now a known fact that an asteroid or comet, perhaps as large as five miles across, struck the Yucatan Peninsula in a place called Chicxulub at the time of this extinction.[†] A timeline of the

---

[*] Cowen 1996. "The Day the Dinosaurs Died." *Astronomy* April, 34-41

[†] Scientists have also discovered a number of other craters that seem to date to that same time. It may be that the extinction of the dinosaurs was caused by a string of asteroid strikes similar to what occurred on Jupiter when comet Shoemaker-Levy struck it (see *The Collision of Comet Shoemaker-Levy 9 with Jupiter* below).

events surrounding this impact is helpful to our study of the endtime. When this object struck the earth it "generated a shock wave that blew a hole in the air."[*] In the first few seconds after impact the massive body passed through more than half a mile of ocean to burrow into the earth's crust. The destructive force of that collision generated quakes "at every exposed fault line over the next few hours."[†] The whole earth shuddered as quakes convulsed and rocked the planet. "Minutes after the impact, billions of tons of debris blasted into space, three to four times the mass"[‡] of the object that struck earth. The hail of debris reentered the atmosphere over a large area of the earth, much of it far from the location of impact. Upon reentry it heated and became red-hot.

"For 30 minutes to an hour after the impact the entire sky was like a big glowing sheet of rock."[§] The hail of debris, like thousands of shooting stars, struck the earth's atmosphere and burned up from atmospheric friction, ablating at perhaps 40 miles above the earth's surface. "The sky would turn from its normal transparent blue to a brilliant red sheet of glowing lava."[**]

Though this superheated debris did not, in general, strike the ground, the heat of its reentry bathed the earth with an enormous amount of radiation. The temperature in the upper atmosphere reached many thousands of degrees. At the earth's surface this intense shower of radiation was "hot enough to set paper on fire."[††] Wherever this storm overshadowed the earth enormous

---

In addition, scientists have discovered what appears to be a chain of craters in the country of Chad, which could have been caused by the impact of a fragmented asteroid or comet. The scientists estimate that the craters were formed about 360 million years ago. This was about the same time the earth was suffering another episode of mass extinction similar to the extinction of the dinosaurs. It is possible that these impacts were in some way related to the cataclysm that destroyed life on the earth at that time.

[*] Ibid., 37

[†] Ibid.

[‡] Ibid.

[§] Ibid.

[**] Ibid.

[††] Ibid.

fires raged. In the case of the impactor that struck earth 65 million years ago it is thought that these fires were global. "The bigger animals would have been broiled in their tracks."[*] Only those smaller animals who were underwater or underground would have survived the intense radiation and the rampaging fires of the cataclysm.

Within an hour of the impact, huge waves about 100 feet high devastated all the nearby coastal plains. The shock from the impact killed most of the sea life within the immediate area.

After an hour or so the glowing "red sky would cool and blacken. By the end of the first day, soot from the charred debris would block out the Sun, plunging the world into darkness."[†] In the case of the extinction of the dinosaurs, it is estimated that this blackout lasted for up to a year. This killed much of the oceanic plankton that depended upon sunlight for its existence. In turn, the entire food chain within much of the oceans' waters was disrupted and destroyed.

The scientists note that the debris ejected into the atmosphere could have enhanced this blackout by changing the composition of the air. The sulfur spewed into the atmosphere slowly changed into "sulfuric acid, a highly efficient Sun blocker."[‡] This would only compound the long-term effects of the asteroid/comet collision with the earth. Due to this blackout the temperatures on earth plummeted after the impact, causing further destruction of life on the earth.

The scientists also mention that the huge amounts of sulfuric acid, which could have been created in the air due to this collision, would have fallen to the earth and the oceans, lakes, and rivers as acid rain. Much of the vegetation and sea life on earth probably died from this poisoning.

The Collision of Comet Shoemaker-Levy 9 with Jupiter

Another recent event has shed more light upon the effects of a planetary collision. In 1994 the comet Shoemaker-Levy 9,

---

[*] Ibid.

[†] Ibid.

[‡] Ibid.

which had previously been broken into 21 pieces, slammed into the planet Jupiter. These impacts were like enormous bombs shelling the giant planet. As Jupiter rotated beneath the incoming bombardment, the cometary fragments plunged one after another into the Jovian atmosphere. Each struck Jupiter at approximately the same distance from the Jovian equator. Eventually, a string of enormous fireballs* lit Jupiter about its southern pole like a string of blazing pearls.

It is worth noting some of the specifics of this collision. All the pieces struck Jupiter at nearly the same latitude, or distance from its equator. The time between impacts ranged from less than 30 minutes to nearly 15 hours. The largest of the pieces, estimated to have been about two miles in diameter, struck Jupiter with an estimated energy of 6 *million* megatons of TNT, about 600 times the explosive force of the world's entire nuclear arsenal. The plume of debris produced by some of these pieces spread out over a surface area more than twice the size of earth. Temperatures reached many thousands of degrees as debris reentered the Jovian atmosphere.† The observations of the impact between Shoemaker-Levy and Jupiter have vividly confirmed scientists' theories concerning the events that took place during the extinction of the dinosaurs 65 million years ago.

One research scientist, Clark R. Chapman, spoke about the effects that might occur on the earth if a comet or asteroid similar to Shoemaker-Levy 9 were to strike the earth. He said (italics have been added for emphasis), "Surely, if an impact is ever predicted, it would be good to be indoors, *preferably underground,*

---

* These fireballs were mostly visible in the infrared region of the electromagnetic spectrum, which is the region that indicates the presence of heat. The visible spectrum showed giant areas of blackened atmosphere surrounding the points of impact.

† The temperature of the fireball, created as the largest fragment of Shoemaker-Levy 9 entered Jupiter's atmosphere, reached about 14,000° Fahrenheit, hotter than the surface of the sun. The plume of debris created a far brighter and more energetic display as it reentered Jupiter's atmosphere after being ejected by the collision.

during the hours following impact—*even if the point of impact is another continent.*" *

The Warnings to Mankind

It is no accident that the discoveries concerning the extinction of the dinosaurs (as well as other mass extinctions) are coming to light now. It is also no accident that a fragmented comet has impacted Jupiter at the same time, in an amazing display of destruction. These are well-timed warnings from God, messengers of impending destruction. The discoveries in the Yucatan and elsewhere show that the earth has been struck and judged before. The impacts on Jupiter are a graphic illustration that these collisions cause enormous destruction. These show mankind what could happen in but a short time, as foretold more than nineteen hundred years ago in the book of Revelation. For, in the events from the sixth seal through the fifth trumpet, all of the scientific observations of planetary collision and its results are depicted.

It is indisputable that at least two large masses will strike the earth as the tribulation starts. These impacts are recorded in the second and third trumpets (Rev. 8:8-11). In one case, a great burning mountain falls into the sea. In the second, a burning star falls upon the rivers and springs of the waters. Because these two masses strike the earth at nearly the same time, it is not unlikely that they are but the larger pieces of a fragmented comet or asteroid, similar to the comet Shoemaker-Levy 9.

It is also a fact that the collision of a large asteroid with a planet such as the earth causes a huge amount of debris to be ejected out from the atmosphere. The reentry of this debris produces an immense display of shooting stars. Furthermore, upon reentering the air, the debris is greatly heated by atmospheric friction resulting in an enormous amount of radiation, which bathes the planet's surface below. This would, in turn, ignite great fires. This type of phenomenon was observed when the comet Shoemaker-Levy struck Jupiter.

---

* Spencer and Mitton, *The Great Comet Crash* (Cambridge: Cambridge University Press, 1995), 108

Furthermore, it is a fact that the impact of such a massive asteroid with water would produce enormous waves. These would destroy the coastal regions of the earth. The concussive force of such a collision would certainly destroy the sea life in the proximity of the impact.

Finally, the burning of the debris as it reenters the atmosphere, as mentioned above, would produce huge amounts of ash to darken the sky. All these matters are not in dispute.

It is also known that through the judgments of the first through fourth trumpets, the third part of the earth will be burned, the third part of the creatures in the sea and the third part of the ships in the sea will be destroyed, the third part of the earth's waters will be poisoned, and the third part of the earth's atmosphere will be darkened so that the sun and moon will not appear over the third part of the earth. These are scriptural facts.

One final important piece of information is that a string of cometary fragments striking the earth would follow a straight line stretched out upon the earth. This behavior was observed in the collisions of the comet Shoemaker-Levy 9 with Jupiter. The pieces of a fractured comet or asteroid do not impact in a random fashion. If the bodies that strike the earth at the beginning of the tribulation are fragments of the same asteroid or comet (as seems likely from the description of those events), then the collisions of these fragments with the earth should occur along a straight line, and possibly at a similar latitude (as was the case when Shoemaker-Levy 9 struck Jupiter).

With these pieces of information as a base, and with other scriptural inferences which are detailed below, I now present one possible scenario of the events surrounding the beginning of the great tribulation. Without a clear scriptural word we cannot write with absolute certainty concerning the details of these events. It may be that many of the details presented here will need to be adjusted. As the Lord's return draws nearer I believe He will more finely focus our sight on the endtime events, eventually giving us a view that is crystal clear and without ambiguity. Nevertheless, I believe what I present here will bear a close resemblance to what will actually happen. I have provided explanations of my reasonings and conclusions in the footnotes where appropriate. These should help the reader understand the bases for this depiction.

The Beginning of the Tribulation

Revelation 6:12-7:3; 8:1-12   And I saw when he opened the sixth seal, and there was a great earthquake; and the sun became black as sackcloth of hair, and the whole moon became as blood; and the stars of the heaven fell unto the earth, as a fig tree casteth her unripe figs when she is shaken of a great wind. And the heaven was removed as a scroll when it is rolled up; and every mountain and island were moved out of their places. And the kings of the earth, and the princes, and the chief captains, and the rich, and the strong, and every bondman and freeman, hid themselves in the caves and in the rocks of the mountains; and they say to the mountains and to the rocks, Fall on us, and hide us from the face of him that sitteth on the throne, and from the wrath of the Lamb: for the great day of their wrath is come; and who is able to stand? After his I saw four angels standing at the four corners of the earth, holding the four winds of the earth, that no wind should blow on the earth, or on the sea, or upon any tree. And I saw another angel ascend from the sunrising, having the seal of the living God: and he cried with a great voice to the four angels to whom it was given to hurt the earth and the sea, saying, Hurt not the earth, neither the sea, nor the trees, till we shall have sealed the servants of our God on their foreheads. ... And when he opened the seventh seal, there followed a silence in heaven about the space of half an hour. And I saw the seven angels that stand before God; and there were given unto them seven trumpets. And another angel came and stood over the altar, having a golden censer; and there was given unto him much incense, that he should add it unto the prayers of all the saints upon the golden altar which was before the throne. And the smoke of the incense, with the prayers of the saints, went up before God out of the angel's hand. And the angel taketh the censer; and he filled it with the fire of the altar, and cast it upon the earth: and there followed thunders, and voices, and lightnings, and an earthquake. And the seven angels that had the seven trumpets prepared themselves to sound. And the first sounded, and there followed hail and fire, mingled with blood, and they were cast upon the earth: and the third part of the earth was burnt up, and the third part of the trees was burnt up, and all green grass was burnt up. And the second angel sounded, and as it were a great mountain burning with fire was cast into the sea: and the third part of the sea became blood; and there died the third part of the creatures which were in the sea, even they that had life; and the third part of the ships was destroyed. And the third angel sounded, and there fell from heaven a great star, burning as a torch, and it fell upon the third part of the rivers, and upon the fountains of the waters; and the name of the star is called Wormwood: and the third part of the waters became wormwood; and many men died of the waters, because they were made bitter. And the fourth angel sounded, and the third part of the sun was smitten, and the third part of the moon, and the third part of the stars; that the third part of them should be darkened, and the day should not shine for the third part of it, and the night in like manner.

It is two (or perhaps three) days before the beginning of the Passover in Israel.* We do not know the year or the exact day of

---

* It is not difficult to determine the approximate time of year when the tribulation will start. At the very end of the tribulation the Lord will send out His angels with a loud trumpet call to gather all the scattered Jews from the four corners of the earth (Matt. 24:29-31). This ingathering of the Jews corresponds to the Old Testament feast of the blowing of trumpets (Lev. 23:24). As the feasts of Passover, firstfruits, and Pentecost were all fulfilled on the exact day of their celebration, so will the feast of blowing of trumpets be fulfilled on the first day of the seventh month of the Jewish year, the day on which the Jews celebrate this feast by God's ordination. (It is clear that God ordained that the Jewish feasts be celebrated on the days of the year when the events depicted by the celebrations would actually occur.) Since we know that the tribulation will last 1,260 days, we can simply subtract this number of days from the first day of the seventh month for any year, to see when the tribulation would have started if it were to end in that year. In general, the computed date is two to five days (depending on the years involved) before the Passover, three and a half years before the fulfillment of the feast of the blowing of trumpets. (This could be shifted a month in either direction depending on the number of intervening intercalary months. Such a shift is a somewhat infrequent occurrence however.) Furthermore, the full moon always occurs on the Passover. Since the sixth seal is opened about the time of the full moon (see Rev. 6:12) this means the events of the sixth seal should happen very close to the Passover. Five days before the

the year. This will be the first Passover to be celebrated in the newly completed temple in Jerusalem, and the first time the Passover lamb will be sacrificed since the destruction of Herod's temple in AD 70. The sky is clear.[*] It is late in the afternoon somewhere between four and six o'clock.[†] The sun is shining in the west and the nearly full moon has risen in the east.[‡] It has indeed been a day of strange happenings. The great leader of the European union, the one who had brought peace and prosperity to Israel, and the one in whom so many of the Jews had placed their hope for the future, has been assassinated. The assassin, in an attempt to save Israel from what he thought would be certain destruction at the hands of this leader, has slain him with a

---

Passover would put the moon at less than three quarters full. Therefore, the sixth seal should be opened two or perhaps three days before the Passover in some as yet unknown year.

This view is also supported by the sealing of the 144,000 in Israel, which takes place as the signs of the sixth seal are happening. There must be some extraordinary event in Israel to gather so many Jews from across the nation, perhaps from around the world, at the same time. The feast of the Passover in Jerusalem after the rebuilding of the temple could be just such an event. It may be that this will be the first Passover to be celebrated with the animal sacrifices at the newly rebuilt temple. God in His righteous anger will put an end to those vain sacrifices, sacrifices that were fulfilled by Christ's death on the cross and of which He is the reality.

[*] When the sixth seal is opened, many signs appear in the heavens: the sun is blackened, the moon turns to blood, the sky is filled with falling stars, there are great pillars of smoke, and the sky is rolled up. For these to be seen the sky must be clear.

[†] According to Joel 2:30-31 a number of signs will be seen in Israel just before the tribulation starts. Two of these are the sun being blackened and the moon turning to blood. Since both these signs are seen in Israel at the same time, both the sun and moon must be in the sky at the same time. In addition, according to Revelation 6:12 the moon will be about full when these signs occur. Over Israel the sun and the nearly full moon are seen in the sky at the same time for the few days before the moon is actually full, when it rises two to three hours before the sun sets in the late afternoon.

The same window of visibility does not occur as the full moon is waning. It and the rising sun are visible together only for a very short time in the early morning for the few days after the full moon.

[‡] Since it will be late afternoon, the sun will be in the west. Furthermore, the nearly full moon will be opposite the sun rising in the east, just as it always is as it nears fullness.

sword.* Furthermore, worldwide reports have begun to surface of a fairly large number of disappearances that occurred some days ago.† While the number of missing persons is nowhere near what some religious people had been prophesying, numbering only in the tens of thousands, the disappearance of any number around this time is both striking and peculiar.‡ Finally, there have also been reports that thousands of Israelis have experienced strange dreams and visions. This has been happening for days and appears to be intensifying.§ Some of these report seeing great disaster and destruction striking the earth; others talk of the appearing of the Messiah from the heavens. These are, indeed, strange times for the nation of Israel and for the whole earth as well.

In the sky above, unknown to the scientists, politicians, and others on earth, a string of asteroid** fragments hurtles toward earth like bombs falling from the bay of a B-52. These are set in a row, predestined to strike the earth at exact times and in precise places. Though Christian books have predicted this, many have scoffed at the idea and politicians in general have ignored this possibility. The massive asteroids about to strike the earth have

---

* Revelation 13:3, 14 tell us clearly that the Antichrist will be killed by a stroke of the sword.

† The firstfruits will be taken sometime prior to the calamity of the sixth seal. This is prophesied by the Lord in Luke 17:26-30. This event will fulfill numerous prophecies.

‡ Most Christians mistakenly think that *all* believers will be taken from the earth before the tribulation. This error has led a great number among them to predict that many millions of people will disappear from the earth before any of the calamities of the endtime strike. Such false predictions will be fully exposed at the time of the great tribulation. At that time a much smaller number of Christians will be raptured to the heavens. Nevertheless, the disappearance of these saints will still be a great shock to the earth.

§ These dreams and visions are foretold in Joel 2:28. It should be by these dreams and visions that the Lord will prepare the 144,000 among the Jews to receive salvation as predicted in Joel 2:29. These dreams and visions should relate to the endtime and the Lord's second coming.

** These could be the fragments of a comet. However, comets are much easier to see in the heavens, especially as they near the sun. Since these particular heavenly bodies will escape detection, they will probably be fragments of an asteroid as opposed to a comet.

escaped their observation.* Most of the fragments are too small to be discerned in the darkness of space. The three larger masses among them have evaded detection. Mankind does not know what is about to occur.

Unseen to human eyes, in the heavens, a great battle is taking place. Satan, with his angels, is fighting to maintain his position. Michael and his angels are fighting to expel him. There is no longer any room found for the evil one. He, with all his rebellious followers, is cast from the heavens to the earth.†

Suddenly, unexpectedly, the sky over Israel lights up.‡ A huge meteor§ arcs across the sky toward the west. It is followed shortly by a second and then others.** The earth is engulfed by a huge meteor storm. On the dark side of the earth meteoroids fall in every direction, as if a fig tree were casting its unripe figs from a heavy wind.†† The large masses, so bright as to be seen in the Israeli sky during the daytime, strike to the west of Israel, perhaps in northern Africa.‡‡ These are but the first few smaller fragments

---

* The collision of the first few fragments with the earth will certainly be altogether unexpected and a great shock to the world, in spite of the predictions of Christians that just such an event would occur. The Lord's description of this event and the days preceding it in Matthew 24 and Luke 17 indicates that mankind will not know that the judgment is about to strike.

† This would fulfill Revelation 12:7-9.

‡ Since the signs of the sixth seal are seen in Israel, including the blood, fire, and multiple pillars of smoke recorded in Joel 2:29-30, this event must occur near Israel. The signs of this seal may help bring the 144,000 of Israel to repentance. Thus, it is reasonable to expect that these first fragments will be seen in Israel.

§ As Satan falls from heaven, so will also the first piece of the asteroid. The latter is a sign of the former. As is often the case, the physical realm mirrors the spiritual.

** Joel 2:30 mentions multiple pillars of smoke. A single fragment of an asteroid would cause at most one pillar of smoke. Thus, there must be multiple fragments all striking the earth near Israel at about the same time.

†† This would fulfill Revelation 6:13.

‡‡ Since the sun over Israel is blotted out, but not the moon, this must mean that only part of the sky over Israel is darkened during the sixth seal. As we have

of a fractured asteroid.* However, the combined concussive force of these impacts sets off an enormous worldwide earthquake. Fault after fault throughout the earth gives way. For the next two to three hours the whole earth trembles—every fault line is shaken, every mountain and every island is moved. There has been no other earthquake so great in recorded history.

From the impact sites debris erupts heavenward. Huge pillars† of smoke billow forth from the craters. The debris super-heats as it reenters the upper atmosphere. The sky fills with fire, turning blood-red from the heat of the burning debris. As the sky cools, the ash and soot in the air from the ablating debris and columns of smoke darken the sky. The heavens over Israel are "rolled up" as the cloud of ash spreads. The western sky where the sun once shone is totally darkened, blotting the sun out entirely. However, the spreading ash does not reach fully from horizon to horizon. Rather, only a small percentage of it reaches to the eastern horizon. The recently risen moon, nearly full, turns

---

seen above, the sun will probably be in the west at that time. This—the pillars of smoke with their billowing soot and ejected debris—should occur to the west of Israel. Furthermore, in Revelation 9:1-2 Satan is seen having fallen to the earth. He opens the pit of the abyss to free the Antichrist and the demons. Smoke comes forth from the pit. This should be one of the pillars of smoke mentioned in Joel 2. However, Revelation 12:18-13:1 shows Satan standing on the sand of the Mediterranean Sea and the Antichrist arising from the Sea. Thus, this indicates that the pit of the abyss should be somewhere around the Mediter-ranean, and that the fragments of the asteroid should fall in that area, to the west of Israel.

* There are a number of indications that these fragments must be very small compared to the "great mountain burning with fire" of the second trumpet as mentioned in Revelation 8:8. First, the sixth seal is but a warning to mankind that the tribulation is about to begin. Thus, it should be merely a foretaste of what will happen. Second, it is clear that these fragments will strike near the Mediterranean area. But Rome and the Antichrist's European empire evidently do not experience overwhelming damage from this event. Rome remains luxurious and wealthy until the end of the tribulation (Rev. 18). Finally, Revelation 7:3 says clearly that the earth, the sea, and the trees will not be hurt until after the 144,000 are sealed from Israel. Since the sixth seal occurs before this time, it must not inflict great damage. Therefore, these fragments must be small in size, and merely harbingers of the beginning of the tribulation.

† Again, the multiple pillars of smoke mentioned in Joel 2:30 indicate multiple impacts from a number of asteroid fragments, causing multiple craters.

blood-red from this ash.* The impacts of these smaller fragments, however, do not cause widespread damage. The major destruction is yet to come. These shocks are but a sign and a warning of what is about to happen.

In Israel, an hour or two after the initial impact, the upheaval begins to subside. The ones who had previously received visions and dreams have seen them fulfilled. The signs in Joel 2 have come to pass before their eyes. At this time the Spirit of God intervenes. He outpours Himself upon many in Israel. In some as yet unknown way, He gathers them together, perhaps to Moses and Elijah, who have been kept by God for this very moment and for the last 3½ years of this age. The speaking from these ancient leaders of Israel convicts them and turns them to call upon the name of the Lord. In all, 144,000 of the children of Israel repent and believe in the Lord Jesus. Moses and Elijah encourage and exhort them to pray much upon their return home. There will be no feast of the Passover this year. Rather, the 144,000 are to spend much time beseeching the Lord—praying for His care and safeguard during the upheaval which is about to occur, praying that they would be enabled to flee from the tribulation about to befall Israel, praying that their flight from that tribulation would not occur on a Sabbath day† or during winter.‡ They are told to be prepared to flee at any time. They are expressly told not to turn back for any goods, clothing, or food when the time to flee comes. To do so may cost them their lives and their portion of the work to which they have been called. In the very near future the

---

* By all these events the signs prophesied in Joel 2:28-31 will be fulfilled. These signs are to accompany the outpouring of the Spirit upon many in Israel *before* the Day of the Lord, for the salvation of the 144,000 mentioned in Revelation 7. The Spirit will also be outpoured upon all the Jews at the *end* of the tribulation, for the salvation of all Israel (Zech. 12:10; Rom. 11:26).

† On the Sabbath day the distance a Jew is allowed to walk, under the law, is not sufficient to flee from the tribulation that will occur in Judah. Therefore, they are to pray that their flight be not on a Sabbath.

‡ The Passover that year will occur near the changing of seasons from winter to spring. With the huge amount of ash in the atmosphere and the resultant damping of the sun's warming rays, it will be unknown what the future weather conditions will be. Furthermore, it will not be known when the abomination of desolation will be set up in the temple. Therefore, these young believers must pray that their flight be not in winter.

Antichrist, resuscitated after his assassination, will gather his armies to surround Jerusalem. An idol, the abomination of desolation, will be set up in the temple. Whoever is in Judah at that time will experience tribulation as has never been since man was on the earth. Thus, when they see Jerusalem surrounded by armies and the abomination of desolation set up in the temple, they must immediately flee out of Judah northward into the mountains of Galilee and into an area of the Golan Heights (see *The Desolation of the Temple* in Chapter 6 for more detail concerning this). There they will be nurtured, nourished, and strengthened for the five months of the fifth trumpet until the immediate tribulation in Israel has subsided. After that they will come forth to preach the gospel to every Jew in Israel.

As the 144,000 of Israel are being sealed, Satan is standing on the shore of the Mediterranean Sea. When the fragments of the asteroid impacted the earth near the Mediterranean, Satan, having been cast from heaven to earth, takes the opportunity to open the shaft of the abyss in which the spirits of the dead dwell. As he stands upon the shore of the Mediterranean, the spirit of Caesar Nero as well as the spirits of numerous demons stream forth from the abyss, out from the pillar of smoke arising from the site of the impacts.* As it approaches morning in Israel, the spirit of Nero enters into the dead body of the great European leader to resuscitate him. In addition, the numerous demons who came forth from the abyss with the spirit of Nero enter into the European armies of the Antichrist, many of whom are stationed in Israel to secure a peace pact between Europe, Israel, and her Arab neighbors. The resuscitated Antichrist will present himself in the dawn of the morning as resurrected, the one whom all the world, including Israel, should worship as God. He will shortly seat himself in the temple declaring that he is God. He, with the help of his Israeli co-conspirator, the false prophet, will set up an idol of himself in the temple to be worshipped instead of God. He will begin his reign of terror by gathering his demon-possessed forces toward Jerusalem, intending to devastate the city and

---

* This would fulfill Revelation 9:1-3 as the background for the five months of woe of the fifth trumpet.

torment the Jews, forcing them, if possible, to worship him and his image.

A few hours after the time of impact, as the convulsions shaking the earth begin to diminish, scientists begin to analyze trajectory data for the objects that have just struck the earth. A gut-wrenching and terrifying discovery is made. What has struck the earth are but the first few smaller pieces of a fractured asteroid, the rest of which is heading toward earth. The larger pieces are yet to strike. Scientists compute that the next major pieces of the asteroid will strike the Asian mainland approximately 20 hours[*] after the initial impacts near Israel. This will be followed by the most massive fragment, which will strike the earth in the Pacific Ocean. A few hours[†] after that, a third large mass will fall into the Himalayan Mountains. There is less than a day in which the world can attempt to minimize in some way the enormous destruction about to take place. The first few fragments that fell in the Mediterranean were but a warning of the impending divine judgment. They were only a foretaste of what is about to strike the earth. There is very little mankind can do at this point. It is

---

[*] When the Lord opens the seventh seal, He will cast fire to the earth (Rev. 8:5). This is followed by the first four trumpets. The first trumpet damages the third of the earth, while the second trumpet damages the third of the sea. Of all the land masses on the earth, only Asia and the islands of Oceania account for a third of the earth's land mass. North and South America together have less than a third. Africa and Europe together also have less than a third of the earth's land mass. Furthermore, it is also evident that the area around the Mediterranean is relatively unscathed by the first four trumpets (Rev. 9:4). Thus, only the searing of Asia can fulfill the prophecy of the first trumpet. Similarly, only the Pacific Ocean accounts for more than a third of the earth's oceans. All the other oceans are too small. Thus, the first two trumpets should affect Asia and the Pacific. The fire cast by the Lord to the earth at the opening of the seventh seal may include one or more large asteroid fragments striking the Asian mainland. This would result in what is depicted when the first trumpet is blown. Now, the time difference between the Middle East and the Asian mainland (traveling westward, according to the earth's rotation) is about 20 hours. Thus, 20 hours after the initial impacts near the Mediterranean Sea, the earth will have rotated to where incoming pieces of a string of asteroid fragments would strike Asia.

[†] The falling star of the third trumpet falls on the rivers and springs of waters. This should refer to the Himalayas, from which flow all the waters that feed the Asian continent. It will take but a few hours from the time the burning mountain falls into the Pacific for the earth to rotate to where the next falling fragment would strike these mountains.

too late to try to divert the incoming asteroid. It is too late to withdraw ships from the vicinity of the impact in the Pacific Ocean. It is too late to evacuate all the coastal areas in the Pacific basin. It is too late even to contact all the people on earth to warn them of the impending firestorm.

All governments throughout the earth are notified of the incoming projectiles. A worldwide alert is issued. Wherever possible, people are warned to take shelter. The best place to be at the time of impact is underground. Caves and other underground burrows will provide the best protection against the intense radiation that will be generated by the blasts and firestorms, against the incredible earthquakes which will undoubtedly rock the earth yet again, and against the immense winds that will accompany the asteroid strikes. Wherever possible, people flee underground into caves, dens, cellars, evacuation shelters, bomb shelters—anywhere that might provide some refuge from what is sure to come to pass. Mankind is gripped in enormous terror. Men and women, young and old, great and small, rich and poor, presidents, premiers, kings, generals, politicians, scientists, men from every walk of life hide themselves wherever they can as the world prepares for the onslaught. As predicted by the faithful believers, the time of God's judgment is at hand. The wrath of God and of the Lamb has come. Men begin to call on the mountains and hills to fall on them and hide them from what is about to happen.[*]

At this time an angel appears in the sky above the earth.[†] He warns mankind that the hour of God's judgment has come and that all men should fear God and give Him glory. They must worship the One who created the heaven, earth, sea, and springs of water, for He as the Creator is about to judge His creation. This eternal gospel is a warning to all mankind to turn away from any

---

[*] This would fulfill Revelation 6:12-17.

[†] By this time mankind is aware that judgment is about to happen. Thus, God in His mercy sends an angel to bring man back to the proper relationship between the Creator and the creatures. This is the preaching of the *eternal* gospel by an angel, for the proper worship of the Creator by the creatures. It should not be confused with the preaching of the gospel of *grace* today, by redeemed mankind to produce sons of God.

This event would fulfill Revelation 14:6-7.

kind of idol (including the Antichrist) and back to the true God, the Creator.

The earth slowly turns under the targeting eye of the incoming bombardment. Numerous smaller fragments begin to strike the earth during this time. There is little more than half a day of respite as mankind awaits judgment. Men, women, and children hunker down in whatever shelter they can find, all gripped in unspeakable panic and terror. Many begin to pray in repentance crying out for mercy. Others curse God.

Scientists have calculated that the largest piece of the asteroid will strike the Pacific Ocean just south of Japan off the coast of China, at about 30° north latitude.[*] This projectile is estimated to be about four miles in diameter, the size of a great mountain.[†] For the ships in the Pacific Ocean—for all the navies and the many merchant ships in the area of the impact—there is no escape; it is too late to flee anywhere. Those ships that are able seek some shelter behind islands, in the hope that the islands may in some way protect them. For many others throughout the Pacific there is simply no place to hide. There is nothing to do but wait for the coming destruction. Death is imminent. Some seamen go below deck to pray; others weep in panic and grief; the extremely rebellious shake their fists at God. The judgment draws nearer. The world simply waits.

It is now morning in Israel, the morrow after the initial impacts by the smaller fragments of the asteroid. The great European leader is rising from the dead, resuscitated by the spirit of Nero. The sealed of Israel have returned to their homes, praying and looking to the Lord for the time at which they should flee. Christians throughout the earth, pressed by the impending judgment and their lack of spiritual maturity that has caused them to be left on earth for the tribulation, pray desperately for the Lord's mercy in His judgment.

---

[*] As mentioned at the beginning of this appendix, a string of asteroid or cometary fragments will strike a planet along a line. The first fragments will hit near Israel at about 30° N latitude. The remaining pieces will probably strike the earth about that same latitude. Asia, the Pacific coast of Asia, and the Himalayan Mountains are all about the same latitude as Israel.

[†] Revelation 8:8 predicts that such a great mountain will strike the earth.

In the heavens before the throne of God the seventh and final seal is opened. There is silence in heaven for about half an hour. It is an extremely solemn time. The age is changing. God's hand is about to be raised against mankind, the earth, and the heavens in judgment. The Lord Jesus takes fire from the altar and casts it to the earth. There are thunders, voices, lightnings, and an earthquake. [*]

On earth, the first large pieces of the asteroid strike Asia. An enormous cloud of fiery debris covers nearly the whole earth, but is most intense in Asia. Nearly all of Asia and the islands off its southeast coast are blanketed by a firestorm. The enormous heat ignites fires throughout Asia. An unparalleled conflagration breaks out. Wildfires swept by incredible winds consume all the vegetation upon the Asian mainland and the islands in the Pacific. Any exposed flesh, whether animal or human, is instantly broiled. The grass over the whole planet is blackened by the heat from the ablating debris. [†] Only the mercy of God in this judgment spares humanity from worse destruction. The few smaller fragments that impacted the day before have provided enough warning for many to seek shelter from the intense heat of the firestorm.

This is followed by the greatest and most massive piece of the asteroid impacting the earth in the middle of the Pacific Ocean. The earth convulses from the collision. Earthquakes spread throughout the world, far greater than those of the sixth seal. An immense mountain of earth, hundreds of cubic miles in volume, is cast upward out of the atmosphere. Within the first few minutes of impact this debris begins reentering the atmosphere. The sky is turned ablaze with fire. The temperature in the upper atmosphere reaches well over 5000° Fahrenheit.

The firestorm of debris turns the sky over the Pacific blood-red. The Pacific Ocean, reflecting the color of the sky above, also turns blood-red. This impact has the further effect of completely devastating the whole Pacific basin. The concussive force of the collision spreads in the air, upon the surface of the water through huge tsunamis, and under the ocean through great, radiating

---

[*] This would fulfill Revelation 7:1-5.

[†] This would fulfill Revelation 8:7.

shock waves. Any aircraft in the area are immediately disintegrated by the blast of the collision. The spreading shock wave destroys everything in the air throughout the region. The concussive force under the sea destroys the fish and other animal life within a large portion of the Pacific. All ships in most of the Pacific are obliterated. Very few, if any, are able to survive this incredible calamity. Giant tsunamis, perhaps miles high as they strike the coasts, also devastate the whole Pacific rim. The west coasts of South and North America, as well as the east coast of Asia with the islands of Oceania,* are obliterated. San Francisco is utterly destroyed; Los Angeles with Hollywood is washed away; the many great cities along the Pacific rim are inundated and leveled.[†]

A short while later the second large piece of the asteroid, smaller than the one striking the Pacific but still deadly, falls upon the Himalayas. Huge amounts of minerals are cast forth into the atmosphere. These settle upon the rivers and fountains of the Himalayas, which water the whole Asian continent. The springs coming forth in the Himalayan Mountains and the rivers spreading throughout Asia are poisoned by the minerals ejected in this impact and by the sulphuric acid formed in the air after the impact. Whoever drinks this bitter water dies.[‡]

The consequence of these impacts is an enormous volume of soot and ash in the atmosphere over Asia and the Pacific. This burned debris blocks out the sun, moon, and stars over this part of the earth for months. The third of the earth is thus darkened.[§]

The net result of these judgments will be a scorched Asia** (one-third of the earth), a devastated Pacific and obliterated

---

* The islands of the South, Central, and Western Pacific.

[†] This would fulfill Revelation 8:8-9.

[‡] This would fulfill Revelation 8:10-11.

[§] This would fulfill Revelation 8:12.

** Why would God choose Asia to be that particular third of the earth targeted by these four trumpets? Why would God view Asia as the most evil part of the earth, worthy of such a judgment? The gross idolatry in the worship of many of the Asian peoples may be part of the reason. More importantly, it may be that large persecutions will break out in Asia under the corrupt, evil governments

Pacific rim (one-third of the sea), poisoned waters throughout the Asian mainland (one-third of the rivers and springs), and a darkened sky over all Asia and most of the Pacific (one-third of the earth).

This depiction is one way in which the sixth seal, the first four trumpets, and the beginning of the fifth trumpet could be fulfilled. I believe that the actual events will be similar to what is written here. This is a very sobering and solemn word. This is a warning not only to unbelievers, but to believers as well. Many—perhaps most—Christians will be left on the earth to pass through this tumultuous time of upheaval. May we all find grace from the Lord to be counted worthy to escape that time.

---

there prior to the tribulation. The opening of the sixth seal and the judgments of the first four trumpets are a response to the cry of the martyred saints from under the earth as depicted in the opening of the fifth seal. As such, the judgment of the first four trumpets upon a particular third of the earth should be in response to some previous violent persecution of God's people.

APPENDIX B

Endtime Timelines

———————

The end of the age is a very complex time. God is dealing with at least four groups of people at the same time—the whole earth generally, Antichrist's kingdom specifically, the nation of Israel particularly, and the believers especially. It is very difficult to grasp all the events mentioned in the Bible that occur during the last seven years of this age. It is also difficult to separate the events occurring to one group of people from those happening to another. Readers, rightfully so, may wish for a visual timeline portraying the most important events of the last seven years of this age. However, a *single* timeline would be so complex as to possibly render it useless and risk further confusion. Therefore, the timeline of events has been simplified into four separate diagrams. Each of these depicts the happenings during the endtime (Daniel's 70th "week," or the last 2520 days of this age) from a particular vantage point: the first details God's judgments, the second shows the major events of the Church, the third depicts the happenings to Israel, and the fourth shows the major events of the Antichrist.

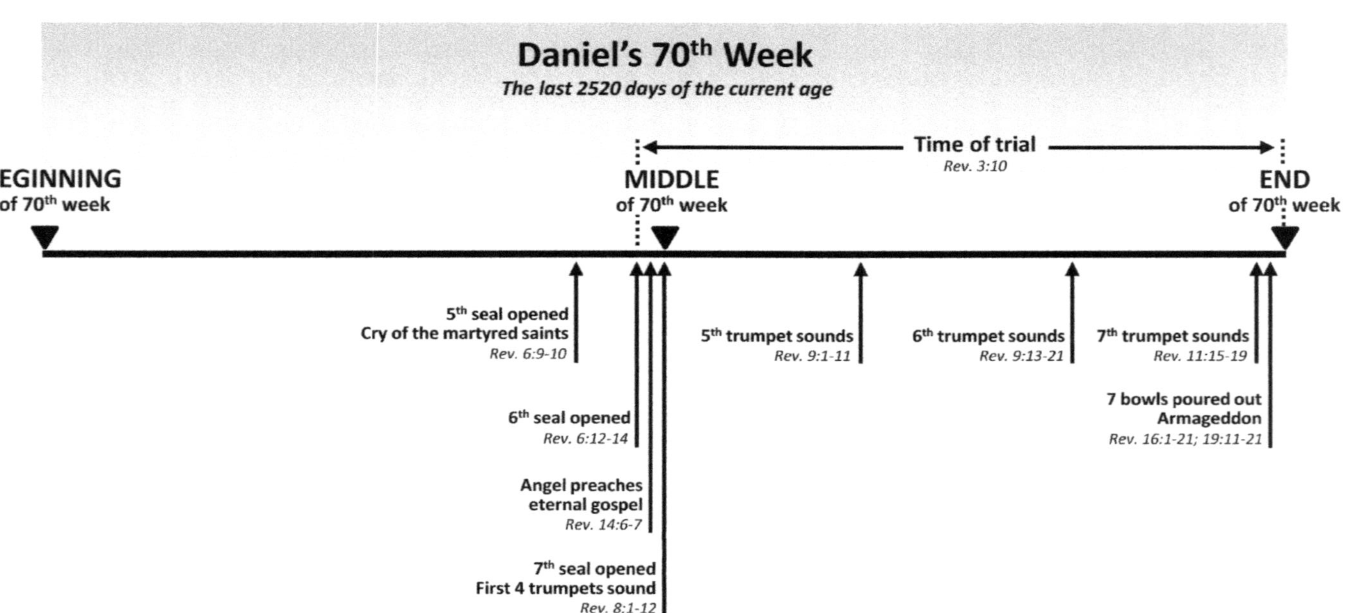

God's Judgments
During the Endtime
Daniel's 70th Week
The last 2520 days of the current age
BEGINNING
of 70th week
MIDDLE
of 70th week
Time of trial
Rev. 3:10
END
of 70th week
5th seal opened
Cry of the martyred saints
Rev. 6:9-10
6th seal opened
Rev. 6:12-14
Angel preaches
eternal gospel
Rev. 14:6-7
7th seal opened
First 4 trumpets sound
Rev. 8:1-12
5th trumpet sounds
Rev. 9:1-11
6th trumpet sounds
Rev. 9:13-21
7th trumpet sounds
Rev. 11:15-19
7 bowls poured out
Armageddon
Rev. 16:1-21; 19:11-21

The Church
During the Endtime

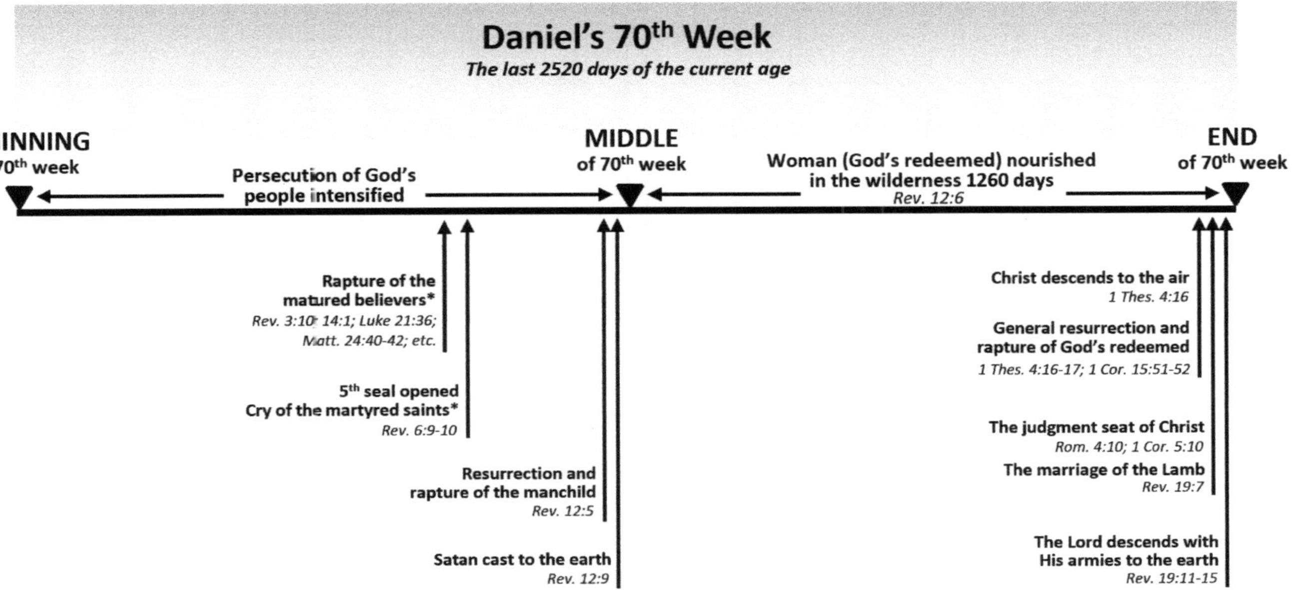

*The timing of both the rapture of the matured believers and the opening of the 5th seal is unknown, but both occur before the last 3 ½ years of this age.

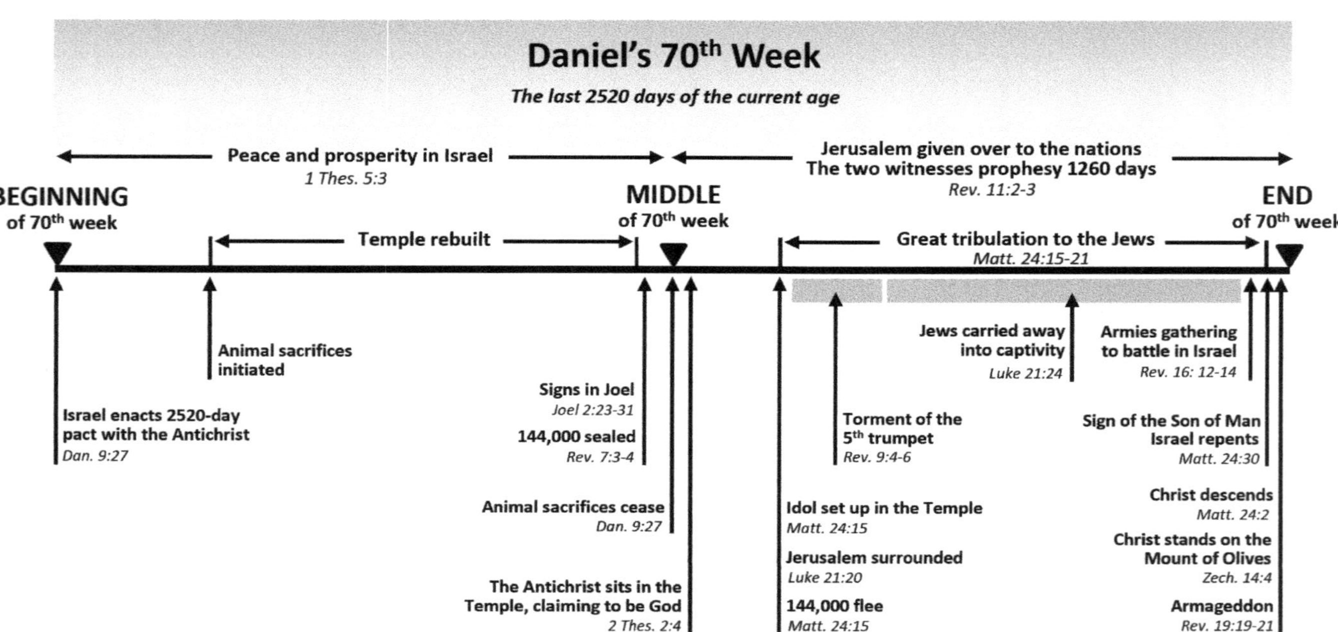
Israel
During the Endtime
Daniel's 70th Week
The last 2520 days of the current age
Peace and prosperity in Israel
1 Thes. 5:3
Jerusalem given over to the nations
The two witnesses prophesy 1260 days
Rev. 11:2-3
BEGINNING
of 70th week
MIDDLE
of 70th week
END
of 70th week
Temple rebuilt
Great tribulation to the Jews
Matt. 24:15-21
Animal sacrifices
initiated
Jews carried away
into captivity
Luke 21:24
Armies gathering
to battle in Israel
Rev. 16: 12-14
Israel enacts 2520-day
pact with the Antichrist
Dan. 9:27
Signs in Joel
Joel 2:23-31
144,000 sealed
Rev. 7:3-4
Torment of the
5th trumpet
Rev. 9:4-6
Sign of the Son of Man
Israel repents
Matt. 24:30
Animal sacrifices cease
Dan. 9:27
Idol set up in the Temple
Matt. 24:15
Christ descends
Matt. 24:2
Jerusalem surrounded
Luke 21:20
Christ stands on the
Mount of Olives
Zech. 14:4
The Antichrist sits in the
Temple, claiming to be God
2 Thes. 2:4
144,000 flee
Matt. 24:15
Armageddon
Rev. 19:19-21

The Antichrist
During the Endtime

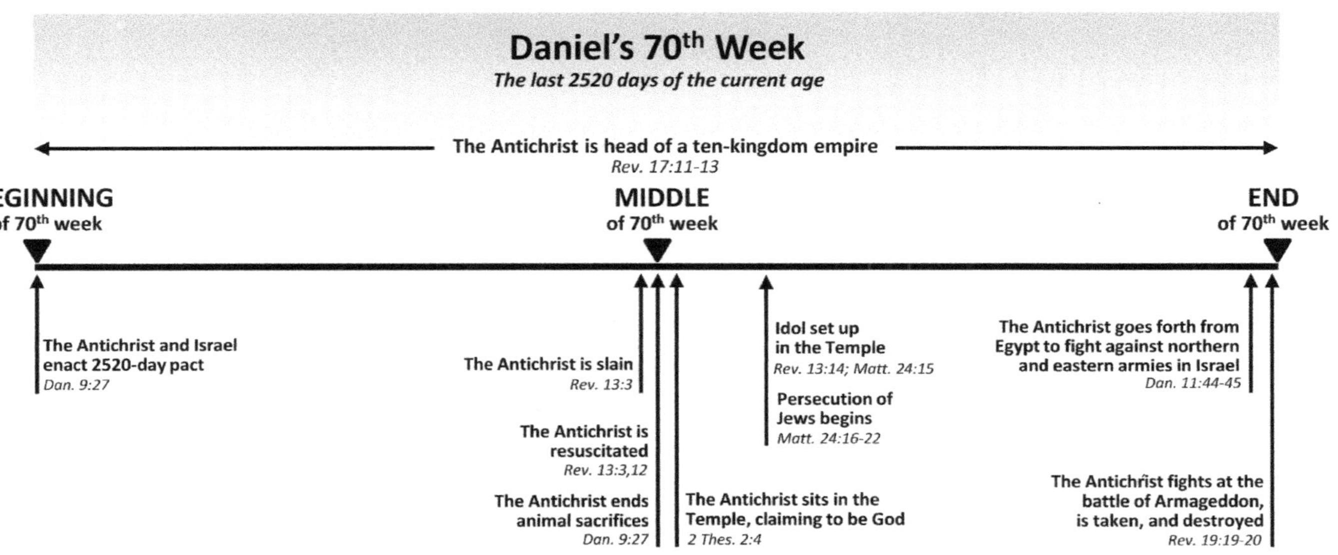

BIBLIOGRAPHY

Anderson, Sir Robert. *The Coming Prince.* Kregel Publications, 1972.

Cowen, Ron. "The Day the Dinosaurs Died." *Astronomy,* April 1996, pp. 34-41.

Cozza, Paul. *The Beast, His Image, and His Mark.* A Place in the Wilderness, 2018.

Foxe, John. *Foxe's Book of Martyrs.* Fleming H. Revell Company, 1976.

Hislop, Rev. Alexander. *The Two Babylons.* Loizeaux Brothers, 1959.

Spencer, John R., and Jacqueline Mitton. *The Great Comet Crash.* Cambridge University Press, 1995.

Vine, W.E. *Expository Dictionary of New Testament Words.* Fleming H. Revell Company, 1966.